Teaching Exceptional Children and Adolescents

A Canadian Casebook

Second Edition

Nancy L. Hutchinson
Faculty of Education
Queen's University

PEARSON

Prentice
Hall

Toronto

For Hugh, with love—
you inspire me and sustain me

National Library of Canada Cataloguing in Publication

Hutchinson, Nancy Lynn

   Teaching exceptional children and adolescents : a Canadian casebook / Nancy L. Hutchinson.
—2nd ed.

ISBN 0-13-121667-8

   1. Inclusive education—Canada—Case studies. I. Title.

LC1203.C3H87 2004   371.9'046'0971   C2003-901989-6

ISBN 0-13-121667-8

Vice President, Editorial Director: Michael J. Young
Acquisitions Editor: Christine Cozens
Marketing Manager: Ryan St. Peters
Associate Editor: Jennifer Murray
Production Editors: Charlotte Morrison-Reed, Martin Tooke
Copy Editor: John Firth
Proofreader: Julie Fletcher
Production Coordinator: Peggy Brown
Page Layout: Janet Zanette
Art Director: Julia Hall
Cover Design: Gillian Tsintziras
Cover Image: Digital Vision

12 13 14 15 16   08

Printed and bound in the USA.

Contents

Case 10: How Much Do I Have To Change For One Student?   89

A Grade 5 teacher who takes pride in his unique teaching style is challenged to change by the needs of a student with a hearing impairment who is frustrated in his class.

Case 11: I Simply Don't Know What To Do   97

A Grade 1 teacher agonizes about whether or not to report that she suspects one of her students is being physically abused.

Case 12: What Can I Do So I Can Teach Them?   108

A first-year teacher tries to use active learning approaches in an inner-city junior high school and feels that she is failing.

Case 13: Change Is So Hard!   118

A student in the final year of junior high prepares to make the transition to senior high school. The fact that he has Asperger syndrome seems to make everything so hard—for him and for the people around him.

Case 14: A Report To My Teachers   127

A Grade 11 student with a physical disability tries to advocate for herself in order to obtain adapted assessment in her classes.

Case 15: Sorry, I Got the Wrong Day, Again!   137

A resource teacher/counsellor conducts a range of pre-referral activities and provides support to teachers and to a Grade 10 student thought to have learning disabilities.

Case 16: Having Someone Explain Things To You Is Important   148

A history teacher confers with his department head and vice-principal about an enrichment program he has been offering to gifted Grade 11 students.

Case 20: Don't Push Me! I Can't Take It!   186

When a black student who is experiencing emotional and behavioural difficulties leaves the classroom, a Grade 9 science teacher questions what the school is doing.

Case 21: What a Puzzle!   194

A teacher describes the challenges of teaching a Grade 11 student whose attention deficit disorder influences his social interactions as much as his learning.

Case 22: She Doesn't Know Herself   204

A teacher seeks the support of a guidance counsellor in working with an Aboriginal student with traumatic brain injury who is in her Teacher Advisory Group.

How You Can Learn About Your Teaching Practice By Writing Cases   213

Matrix of Cases

Topics	Cases																					
	1	2	3	4	5	6	7	8	9	10	11	12	13	14	15	16	17	18	19	20	21	22
Elementary Education	✓	✓	✓	✓	✓	✓	✓	✓	✓	✓	✓	✓	✓									
Secondary Education												✓	✓	✓	✓	✓	✓	✓	✓	✓	✓	✓
Urban Schools												✓							✓	✓		
Rural Schools		✓		✓			✓											✓				
Reading		✓			✓				✓						✓				✓			
Math						✓								✓			✓					
Classroom Management				✓	✓						✓									✓		
Collaboration		✓	✓			✓		✓		✓			✓		✓		✓	✓		✓	✓	✓
Educational Assistants			✓		✓																✓	
Parent Communication		✓	✓				✓	✓		✓		✓	✓	✓				✓				
Adapting Teaching	✓			✓	✓	✓	✓		✓	✓		✓			✓	✓	✓		✓		✓	
Adapting Assessment							✓		✓			✓		✓							✓	
Behavioural Strategies					✓				✓			✓					✓			✓		
Cultural Diversity		✓		✓								✓							✓	✓		✓
Peer Relationships	✓		✓		✓			✓	✓									✓			✓	
Computers					✓											✓						
Action Research				✓															✓			
Setting Goals	✓		✓												✓	✓						✓
IEP	✓		✓		✓										✓	✓						
Collaborative Learning	✓		✓			✓		✓	✓		✓						✓					
School-Based Team		✓					✓					✓	✓	✓				✓		✓	✓	
Pre-Referral Actions							✓	✓							✓							
Self-Regulation			✓				✓	✓	✓						✓	✓	✓	✓			✓	✓
Self-Advocacy													✓	✓	✓							✓
Learning Strategies								✓							✓		✓					✓
Career Development																	✓					✓
Transitions													✓									✓
Learning Disabilities						✓			✓						✓		✓				✓	
Attention Deficit Disorders							✓														✓	
Developmental Disabilities			✓																			
Social and Emotional Difficulties					✓						✓		✓							✓		
Physical Disabilites		✓							✓					✓				✓				
Visually Impairments	✓																					
Hearing Impairments										✓												
Gifted Students				✓												✓						
At-Risk Students								✓			✓								✓	✓		
Fetal Alcohol Syndrome							✓															

Matrix of Cases (continued)

Topics	Cases																					
	1	2	3	4	5	6	7	8	9	10	11	12	13	14	15	16	17	18	19	20	21	22
Traumatic Brain Injury																						✓
Asperger Syndrome													✓									
Child Abuse											✓											

Preface

INTRODUCTION

Teaching Exceptional Children and Adolescents: A Canadian Casebook (second edition) brings to teacher education challenging dilemmas based on the experiences of beginning and experienced teachers in Canadian classrooms. These 22 cases focus on teaching exceptional learners in inclusive classrooms in elementary and secondary schools. In addition, issues of equity, cultural diversity, and child abuse arise in some cases.

Dilemma cases pose challenging, realistic situations without obvious right answers. Teacher candidates are stimulated to think like teachers. For candidates without practicum experience, case discussions serve as preparation to meet these challenges in a classroom. Candidates with practicum experience draw connections between what they are learning in their classes and what they have learned from experience. These cases are appropriate for, and have been used in, courses in Teaching Exceptional Learners, in The Psychology of Exceptional Children and Adolescents, and in Inclusive Education. *Teaching Exceptional Children and Adolescents* could be a course's primary text, with background information provided through lectures, readings available in the library, or instructor's handouts. It could also serve as a supplementary text to a traditional textbook on exceptional children or inclusive education. Used in either context, these cases should provoke discussion of some of the most important issues facing Canadian teachers.

KEY FEATURES

These dilemma cases are structured to stimulate discussion about specific aspects of teaching, including collaborating with other professionals and with parents, using Individual Education Plans (IEPs), setting goals for students, adapting teaching, adapting assessment, teaching strategies for independent learning, enhancing peer relations, using collaborative learning, and managing behaviour. The cases contain rich descriptions of classroom contexts, including descriptions of communities, families, schools, classrooms, peers, and curricula.

The cases contain three or more exhibits with supplementary information about the exceptionalities and the aspects of teaching under discussion, including characteristics of students with the exceptionality, checklists to assess the learning environment, teaching tips for adapting teaching for students with that exceptionality, Individual Education Plans, etc. These resources are drawn from Canadian sources such as provincial handbooks on exceptional learners, curriculum materials used in schools across the country, and research conducted in Canadian schools and around the world. A matrix shows the exceptionalities, teaching issues, and contextual details of each case.

A series of questions after each case focuses candidates on understanding the dilemmas in the case before rushing to premature solutions. These questions are designed to engage teacher candidates in critical reflection about the various perspectives that could be taken on the case (e.g., teacher, student, parent, society), about the positive and negative consequences that could follow from any decision taken, and about the taken-for-granted assumptions inherent in their analysis and discussion of the case. I have annotated a list of suggested readings and weblinks that may be used by teacher candidates in preparing for case discussions or as follow-up when seeking answers to questions raised during discussions of the cases.

The book opens with a brief introductory chapter on "How You Can Learn from Analyzing and Discussing Cases," written for teacher candidates. The closing chapter teaches teacher candidates "How You Can Learn about Your Teaching Practice by Writing Cases."

SUPPLEMENTS

Because I believe that the success of teaching with cases depends on both the quality of the cases and on the instructor's comfort and familiarity with this teaching approach, I have prepared a separate Facilitator's Guide. This manual includes a rationale for using dilemma cases, a summary of the research on teaching with dilemma cases, and general guidelines for teaching with cases.

For each case, the Facilitator's Guide provides a synopsis of the case, an analysis of the major issues, sample questions to use, and suggestions for leading discussions about that specific case. There are also suggested follow-up activities. Finally, the Facilitator's Guide includes rubrics for providing feedback to teacher candidates about written case analyses and about candidate-authored cases based on experience. Like the cases, many of the suggestions in the manual were field-tested in teacher education classrooms and revised prior to publication.

ACKNOWLEDGMENTS

I am indebted to my colleagues, friends, and family who have taught me, encouraged me, and kept me going in the writing of this book. Thanks to teachers and families who have shared their stories and to thousands of teacher candidates who have shown me the power of teaching with cases through their analyses, discussions, and the cases they have authored. Many have indulged me by providing feedback about individual cases. For this edition, graduate students Jenny Taylor and Karin Steiner Bell and teacher candidate Carrie Wise have been incredibly persistent in continuing the fine work that Shelley Gauthier-McMahon and Cinde Lock did on the first edition. Thank you! As always, I owe a huge thank you to Brenda Reed, an outstanding reference librarian. Andrea Martin has been my "critical friend" through many years of teaching with cases. Colleagues teaching the Critical Issues course at Queen's, especially Ruth Rees, and colleagues like Nancy Perry of the University of British Columbia have challenged my thinking about teaching with cases. My deans, first Rena Upitis and now Rosa Bruno-Jofré, have provided a stimulating community of teacher educators and researchers who care deeply and take time to debate issues like helping teacher candidates maintain their critical stance.

I would like to thank my reviewers John Boland of Malaspina University-College, Colin Lane of the University of Western Ontario, and Barbara Graves of the University of Ottawa for thoughtful critiques which improved this book of dilemma cases. Thanks to the team at Pearson Education for facilitating my efforts at every turn, especially Lori Will, Jennifer Murray, and Adrienne Shiffman. Finally, my family and my partner inspire me and sustain me. To Mom, Deb, Jim, Sandy, Jenny, and Hugh—thank you for your unending laughter and support.

Nancy L. Hutchinson
Queen's University

How You Can Learn from Analyzing and Discussing Cases

INTRODUCTION

For many of you, this book may be a new educational experience. It is a collection of case studies based on the experiences of Canadian elementary and secondary teachers. Case studies were first used as a teaching approach in business schools and have since come to be used in the education of professionals in medicine, nursing, pharmacy, education, engineering, and almost every area of endeavour that requires professional judgment. You may be wondering why the study of cases is so widely used in the education of professionals. After conducting research for almost 14 years with preservice teacher candidates learning from studying cases, I am convinced that case study really does help with the development of professional judgment.

Here are comments from one group of teacher candidates at Queen's University about learning from cases: "They give hands-on experience" and "I find this useful because it relates the information to the real-life situation rather than just getting the facts from a textbook." Almost half the comments of this group of 28 preservice teachers referred to the epistemology of studying cases; that is, the kind of knowledge they were developing. Learning from cases was valued because it was seen as "probably the best way to learn" to teach, "very real and practical." "Cases help you to internalize the thinking process required for problem solving."

Problem solving is at the heart of case study, and making decisions and solving problems are the essence of being a professional. How would you answer a teaching colleague who asked you the following questions?

- What should I do when students refuse to work together cooperatively?
- How can I enable a student with a physical disability to complete the same art project as everyone else, with the help of a teaching assistant, and still feel the satisfaction that comes from independent success?
- What do I do when a student challenges my authority in front of the class?
- How do I make enough time to meet one student's individual needs without ignoring the rest of the students in the class?

Would you ask for more detail about the student, the context, the classroom, and the teacher? Would you say, "It depends"? If so, you are ready to learn from cases.

RATIONALE FOR LEARNING FROM CASES: THINKING LIKE A TEACHER, EMBRACING DILEMMAS

Most of the questions teachers ask do not have "right answers." The answer that most often fits is "It depends." It depends on the age and abilities of the student. It depends on the philosophy and teaching strengths of the teacher. Other influences include the curriculum outcomes that are valued for all the students in the class and the individual goals that have been set for the exceptional student. It depends on the make-up of the classroom within which all of this occurs. Usually the policy of the school district figures in our decisions, as well. It is important to consider the perspectives of the student and the parents involved, and the consequences of any course of action. Decisions are made using the best information we have. They "depend" on the relevant contextual information, described above, and are informed by our beliefs and professional judgment as well as our knowledge of research and best practices.

In order to learn from what we have done, we must stop to think about it. When we reflect on our decisions and problem solving, we often find that we have taken things for granted that may not be the case. Let me give you an example. Suppose that a student in the class has a hearing loss, and this student needs to have the instructions repeated slowly and clearly. We may believe that stopping to repeat directions benefits only this child with a hearing impairment. However, it may turn out that this assumption is unfounded and that two or three students with identified or suspected learning disabilities thank us for repeating the directions. They may say, "I like it. Repeating the instructions really helps me know what I am supposed to do." At the same time, we should not assume that repeating the directions helps everyone. A gifted child in the class may also give us feedback: "Do you have to repeat so much? I know what to do and I get bored when you give the instructions again." You ask, "So, what should I do?" and we are back to "It depends." When you know the context, the students, and what is being learned, you can consider many solutions. Can the gifted child be encouraged to begin the activity after hearing the instructions for the first time, thus ignoring the repeated information? Perhaps the students with learning disabilities can give a semi-public "thumbs-down" sign when they need the directions repeated. Can the student with a hearing impairment check with an assigned buddy to ensure that the instructions were understood? These solutions focus on the characteristics of the students. You could also focus on the nature of the instructions given. Perhaps, when the instructions are complex, they should be both stated and written on the board. Maybe instructions should be repeated when there are many steps, say, more than three. Short, simple instructions can usually be handled through "thumbs-up" and buddy procedures. Although we began with a simple example, you can see that there are many strategies for solution, all depending on your perceiving, judging, and assessing situations, choosing courses of action, and being confronted with their consequences. These are the processes you will use in studying cases.

You would probably not want to read about every possible challenge that could arise in your classroom or listen to lectures on the rules for every possible form of decision making and problem solving. But you may want to get enough practice at making decisions and solving problems so that when you begin in your own first classroom, you know which details to pay attention to. You may also want to have enough practice reflecting on your decisions and problem solving that you can make the most of the time you have for reflection. Researchers have carried out studies to help us understand how, for some teachers, experience is a great teacher, while others can make the same mistakes in their twentieth year as they made in their first year, and appear to be no wiser for their years of experience. Reflection seems to be fundamental to learning from experience. That means taking time to think about what you did, why you did it, the consequences of your actions, and the perspectives of all those who were influenced by your actions. It also means thinking critically about your purpose, whether it was achieved, how it could be better achieved, and what you took for granted. This kind of reflection is often prompted by discussions with people who hold slightly different views, who make us think by asking hard questions, and who passionately want to become better teachers.

Getting as much teaching experience as possible and learning to reflect on that experience both help to prepare you to teach. Research suggests that the study of cases with peers also contributes. Studying cases enables you to encounter a much wider range of students than you would expect to meet in preservice teaching practica.

The purpose of this book of case studies is to provide the basis for these stimulating discussions with your peers about the decisions and problems that confront "real" teachers every day. A case study is a written description of a problem, situation, or dilemma. Unlike other forms of stories and narratives, a case study does not normally include analysis or conclusions but only the facts of a story arranged in a chronological sequence. The purpose of a case study is to place participants in the role of decision makers, asking them to distinguish pertinent from peripheral facts, to identify central alternatives among several issues competing for attention, and to formulate strategies and policy recommendations. The method provides an opportunity to sharpen problem-solving skills and to improve the ability to think and to reason rigorously.

The cases in this book depict real situations. The details that might allow you to identify the characters and settings have been disguised and, in some instances, the events of two real situations have been combined. Cases are not intended to be comprehensive or exhaustive. Most cases are "snapshots" of a particular situation within a complex environment.

The focus of a case study is usually a main protagonist who is shown at the point of a major decision. The protagonist is facing a dilemma, with no clear course of action about the one right thing to do. Dilemmas tend to be those puzzles of practice that keep teachers awake at night. When you are "on the horns of a dilemma," every solution may be a partial solution that solves one problem and creates another. There may be no action that clearly resolves the situation; that is, two solutions may each be helpful, but both also have drawbacks or downsides. Typically, the information presented in a case is only what is available to the protagonist in the real situation on which the case is based. Thus, as in real life, important information is often unavailable or incomplete. Because a case study describes reality, it may be frustrating. "Real life" is ambiguous, and cases reflect that reality. A "correct solution" is rarely apparent.

The case study method actively engages you, the participant, in the following processes when you prepare before class and participate in your discussion group in class. You engage, first, in the analysis of the facts and details of the case itself; second, in identifying the most important dilemma or dilemmas; third, in the selection of a strategy or set of solutions; and fourth, in the refinement, defence, and questioning of the chosen strategy. The case method doesn't provide a set of solutions; rather, it refines your ability to ask appropriate questions and to make decisions about teaching dilemmas based upon the knowledge and judgment you bring to those questions.

This means that you can learn a great deal by thinking through and discussing cases, even if some are at grade levels different from the level at which you expect to teach.

This casebook contains exhibits following each case (normally three exhibits, but sometimes more). These exhibits usually contain two kinds of information that you can introduce into your thinking and discussions: first, relevant detail about the particular student, classroom, or curriculum (e.g., an exceptional student's Individual Education Plan [IEP] or the daily schedule for the class); second, information about best practices (e.g., how to teach strategies or how to do action research) or information about the characteristics of a particular exceptionality (e.g., the range of characteristics you might observe when a child has a learning disability). You will also find a list of suggested readings and Weblinks, with annotations, for each case. You may find that the exhibits for one case help with thinking about another case, and that two of the exhibits for one case suggest disparate solutions. This is because there may be a number of good solutions to a case. There may also be a number of poor solutions, so do not fall into the trap of thinking that all solutions must be equally good because there is not one best answer.

Do not be surprised if you and your peers arrive at different solutions to the cases. Be prepared to give reasons for your ideas and just as prepared to listen to the reasoning of others. When case study works well, there is intense but friendly discussion, much disagreement over ideas, but no disagreements among the participants. This is a good rule of thumb for case discussions and other discussions with teaching colleagues: Disagree with the idea, not with the person.

PREPARING FOR CASE DISCUSSIONS: READING A CASE, UNDERLINING HIGHLIGHTS, JOTTING NOTES, READING

The intent of all the steps, including written case notes and case analyses, is to help you prepare for the case discussions in class and to help you think like a teacher. The case study method is demanding and requires significant preparation time and active class participation by you. It is intended to build on your experiences and those of your peers and your professor. Differences in analysis among all these participants typically arise, and conflicting recommendations emerge as participants with varied perspectives, experiences, and professional responsibilities consider a case.

Box 1.1

I n general, when analyzing a case for class it is helpful to follow these steps:

1. Skim the case quickly to establish the broad issues of the case and the types of information presented for analysis.

2. Reread the case very carefully. Underline key facts as you go.

3. Jot down the key dilemmas or problems. Then go through the case again and sort out and list the relevant considerations and decisions for each dilemma. Consult your experience and your readings to help you. Look at the exhibits for this and other cases. Seek new information, if you feel you need it.

4. Prioritize the dilemmas and then under each dilemma order the decisions and considerations you noted. Jot down, briefly, your reasoning for the order.

5. Develop recommendations to address these dilemmas, beginning with the most important dilemma. Jot down your reasoning to support these recommendations, referring briefly to your experience and readings.

6. Evaluate your recommendations and the decisions that

Preparation of a case for class discussion varies with the background, concerns, and interests of participants. Professors may ask students to submit written case analyses for all the cases selected for study, for a few cases, or for only one case. Whenever a case discussion will take place, you should bring case notes representing your case analysis. You should be prepared to show these to the professor or teaching assistant and use them in case discussion.

In this book, general questions follow each case to guide your thinking. Use these questions in combination with the list of steps above to prepare for case discussion.

PARTICIPATING IN CASE DISCUSSION IN CLASS

Much of the richness of the study of cases comes from the small group and class discussion of the cases. The differences which emerge through discussion add texture and dimension to each individual's consideration of the issues. It is often helpful to meet with a small number of your classmates before class to review understandings of the case, compare analyses, and discuss strategies. This is a time to test and refine your choice of strategies and to explore and enrich your understanding of the issues in the case through the perspectives of others.

Your professor's role is to involve many participants in presenting, discussing, and defending their analyses and recommendations. The professor moderates discussion, calling on participants, guiding the discussion, asking questions, and synthesizing comments.

Discussion is intended to develop and test the nature and implications of alternative solutions. Professors sometimes ask groups and then individuals to moderate discussion, once everyone is familiar with case discussion. I have found this exciting for all concerned. Teacher candidates have an opportunity to practise a complex teaching approach in a safe place, and I have the pleasure of seeing understanding of case discussion translated into teaching and of being an observer of quality discussions.

Box 1.2

The success of a case study class depends largely on your active participation. Remember to:

- Express your ideas and be willing to give reasons for them.
- Listen to others, and evaluate their positions.
- Keep an open mind, and be willing to change it upon new insights or evidence.
- Make a decision. Don't avoid or equivocate.
- Enjoy yourself.

PREPARING A WRITTEN ANALYSIS OF A CASE IN THIS BOOK

If you are asked to prepare written case analyses, you will probably be given a set of criteria by which the analyses will be judged. I suggest you begin by completing the following steps:

1. Identify and discriminate the facts in the case.

    First, present the case from a descriptive perspective. Give an account, albeit brief, of the facts as you see them. Show that you know whose perspectives the facts have come from.

2. Support your identification of the major dilemma(s) or problem(s).

    Show that you have sorted out the issues, and indicate what the key dilemmas are. Your identification of the major dilemmas should take account of the facts you think are important in the case.

3. Thoroughly consider and present various perspectives on the case.

    Interpret the information, the facts of the case. How might the information presented in the case be influenced by other interpretations—how might it be seen from the student's perspective or the teacher's perspective, or from the point of view of the student's parents? Or how might it be understood in the context of a particular reading or educational theory?

4. Next, describe your solutions or recommendations, given the information presented in the first three sections.

    Be sure to support your solution with evidence to show why it is an appropriate and effective solution, including consideration of other perspectives in your solution. What evidence do you have to support what you propose?

5. Consider the consequences.

    If the protagonist were to follow your recommendations, what would the positive and negative consequences likely be for the major characters in the case study? Think of the solution as setting up ripples like a stone tossed into a calm pond. Follow the ripples as they move further from the people at the centre of the case, considering consequences for other characters, curriculum, the school, maybe even for society.

6. Think about what you have learned by working on this case. Then, critique your own analysis.

    What has this case taught you, or forced you to think and read about? Critique your reading of the case and your proposed solution. Most importantly, focus on the taken-for-granted assumptions you have made that become apparent as you critique your analysis. What beliefs do you hold that you recognized while working on the case? At this point, you are engaging in what John Dewey called critical reflection. This means recognizing that some ambiguities remain and that your solution is at best a partial one; it also means making explicit some of the implicit values, assumptions, beliefs, and knowledge that you hold. The best professionals continue to make these explicit by engaging in critical reflection throughout their careers.

REFLECTING CRITICALLY ON YOUR ANALYSIS

Regardless of how you analyze a case—whether you read and discuss a case, or develop a written analysis of it, or write a case based in your experience—reflect critically on your analysis. This is what pushes you ahead as a professional and ensures that you will be a teacher who learns from experience and creates opportunities to engage in discussion about these issues with colleagues. There is considerable evidence that when teachers talk about their practice and engage in critical reflection and professional development, they are more excited about teaching and their students are more excited about learning.

READING RELATED LITERATURE

Reading widely throughout your teaching career will keep you informed about changing values, policies, teaching approaches, and exciting new materials. While you are engaged in case study with this book, the exhibits provide a sampling of related literature; the suggestions for additional reading and the Weblinks, following each case, take you further afield. Consider analyses and solutions offered by readings for your other courses. If you can develop the habit of regular professional reading while you are a teacher candidate, you will have gone some distance to setting yourself up for success as a practising teacher.

WRITING CASES BASED IN EXPERIENCE

The closing chapter of this book describes the process of writing your own cases based in your experience. Such cases provide an opportunity for you to represent the dilemmas that occur in your practice, which brings case study even closer to practice. If you decide to learn by writing a case, keep in mind the ethical issues raised in the closing chapter.

ENJOY!

Studying cases is an active, involving, and thought-provoking way to learn to think like a teacher. It requires effort and goodwill on your part, and gives you a sense of accomplishment and autonomy in return. No one will tell you how to teach, but everyone involved in the class—professor and fellow students—will help you to embrace the dilemmas that make up teaching, and will listen to and question your ideas. So relax, be patient with yourself and your peers, and enjoy stimulating case discussions!

SUGGESTIONS FOR FURTHER READING

Brookfield, S. D. (1995). *Becoming a critically reflective teacher.* San Francisco, CA: Jossey-Bass.
    Brookfield reports studies of his own practice, called self-study, and inspires teachers to engage in reflective practice. A frank account of one teacher continuing to learn from experience after years of successful practice.

Dewey, J. (1933). *How we think: A restatement of the relation of reflective thinking to the educative process.* Boston, MA: D. C. Heath and Co.
    In this classic book, John Dewey tells us that critical reflection asks "Should I be teaching this? If I should, how can I do it better?" Three of the most important aspects of critical reflection, as developed by Dewey, are open-mindedness (recognizing and acknowledging the validity in other perspectives), responsibility (considering the consequences, including moral and ethical consequences, of choices), and wholeheartedness (identifying and addressing limitations in one's assumptions).

Hutchinson, N. L. (1998). Reflecting critically on teaching to encourage critical reflection. In M. L. Hamilton (Ed.), *Reconceptualizing teaching practice: Self-study in teacher education* (pp. 124–139). London, UK: Falmer Press.
    From this report of self-study, readers can "get a feel for" the case study approach to teacher education through the words of teacher candidates as well as those of the author.

Munby, H., Russell, T., & Martin, A. K. (2001). Teacher's knowledge and how it develops. In V. Richardson (Ed.), *Handbook of research on teaching* (4th ed.), (pp. 877-904). Washington, DC: American Educational Research Association.
    A thorough and insightful review of research on how teachers learn from experience.

Sarason, S. B. (1993). *You are thinking of teaching? Opportunities, problems, realities.* San Francisco, CA: Jossey-Bass.
    This venerable figure in educational writing makes a convincing case that there is more innovation, excitement about teaching, and learning by both students and teachers when teachers talk about their practice, ask questions of themselves and others, and direct their own professional development.

WEBLINKS

http://educ.queensu.ca/projects/action_research/
Tom Russell of Queen's University maintains this site, which provides access to a range of materials from action research activities designed to promote critical reflection.

http://www.tss.uoguelph.ca/onlineres/casemethod_studies.htm
Teaching Support Services at the University of Guelph supports this Webpage on teaching with the case method, what makes a good case, choreographing a case class, etc.

You Tell Me To Do Less
Because I'm Not As Smart

"See you tomorrow, Ms. Fine!" The Grade 3 students shouted good-byes to Marie Fine as they rushed off to the school bus in the spring rain. Marie watched Amber painstakingly transferring her books-on-tape and thick pages of Braille from the pile on her desk into her backpack. Marie always tried to stand nearby in case Amber needed help. But Amber did the same thing every day after school: she put everything into her knapsack herself and then asked, "Did I get everything? Everything I need to finish my work?" Marie thought about how hard Amber would work between the time she got home and the next morning to complete the day's tasks, just so she could start it all again the next morning. "Good night, Jeannie. Good night, Amber. Don't work too hard, Amber." As Amber lifted the heavy bag, she answered, "'Night. I'll try not. But I still have a lot of questions to do in math." Her voice sounded as heavy as her book bag. Amber knew from experience that everything took longer when you couldn't see.

Marie Fine watched the two girls leave the classroom. Jeannie and Amber had become friends by default this year. Before Marie had learned to assign the children to teams and pairs, Jeannie and Amber were always the two not chosen, or chosen last by their peers. Jeannie was shy and seemed to drift around the fringes of the classroom, like Amber. Marie was pleased that each girl had found a "best friend" and hoped their parents would not separate them because they wanted more socially acceptable friends for their daughters.

Marie worried about Amber. In a recent unit on friendship, she had asked all the students in her class to interview a peer and be interviewed by a peer. As she feared, Amber had described friends as people who helped her and let her work with them. Conversely, students who frequently helped Amber in getting around the school or in completing her assignments thought that meant they were her friends, but not her *good* friends. When the children described good friends, they talked about shared interests and trust. Many volunteered that they didn't really like working with Amber because she didn't look them in the eyes, her Braille pages were big and awkward, and Amber slowed them down. "She can't play games. It's because she's blind." Marie wondered whether the children really understood that Amber couldn't see them and that there was a good reason for her "looking" past their eyes when she talked to them.

Amber preferred help from her peers to help from the teaching assistant, but Marie thought, "They should want to read with her because she has great ideas and she is fun. They shouldn't just put up with her and see her as someone who needs help." Marie had thought she and the class were doing pretty well until she attended an in-service workshop about including students with a visual impairment: All the signs of social rejection and ignoring were happening in her classroom.

Marie's thoughts turned to the meeting of the in-school team that night, a meeting to begin planning for Amber's transition to Grade 4 next year from Marie's Grade 3 class. Amber was nine years old and had been blind from birth. Marie knew the facts from the file: Amber was born prematurely and was blind because of high-oxygen therapy sometimes given to low-birth-weight babies (the file said retrolental fibroplasia). Amber's mother had described to Marie how devastated she was to learn that Amber was blind. After she accepted the situation, she decided she would not work as a secretary for five years in order to be the mediator between Amber and her environment. During her preschool years, Amber took part in an early intervention program to enhance her language development, exploration of her environment, and ear-hand coordination. Amber's parents told Marie that they learned how to talk to her, to "show" her things by allowing her to touch and explore them, and to teach her to listen for clues about what was happening around her. Amber attended an integrated preschool program where she learned to play with other children and to take instructions in a group.

Marie had been looking at the Individual Education Plan (IEP) in the file that day. It said Amber had above-average intelligence (IQ test scores were slightly above 100 in verbal and non-verbal intelligence, on the Stanford-Binet). She was at or close to grade level in every academic subject according to Marie's curriculum-based assessments. When the CTBS (Canadian Test of Basic Skills) was administered to Amber in Braille near the end of Grade 2, Amber scored at grade level. But Marie knew the pressure that inclusion put on Amber. In most subjects Amber required more time than the rest of the class to complete daily assignments. Amber's assignments were usually in Braille, in tactile materials, or on tape. Amber was still learning Braille with the resource teacher. The equipment that Amber used required that she sit at a table by herself. This resulted in many missed opportunities for socializing.

Amber practised Braille daily with the resource teacher, and the support within the school for material preparation was generally good (Braille, taping, etc., were usually done on time), but Marie had to plan months ahead. "Hard to be spontaneous," Marie thought to herself. An educational assistant, Jane, was responsible for the preparation of materials for Amber (up to four hours per week) and spent up to eight hours per week in Amber's classroom. Marie, Jane, and Amber planned after school each Friday which eight hours of the upcoming week's lessons would be most important to schedule when Jane was in the classroom to support Amber.

In Grades 1 and 2, Amber's teachers and parents had decided that she should not be required to complete all the work that the rest of the class was required to do. When the rest of the class was assigned 20 questions in math, Amber was told to complete only the even problems on the page. In the first few weeks of Grade 3, Marie noticed that Amber would complain that the assigned work was too difficult, or that she couldn't complete it because she was blind. Marie met with Amber and her parents, the special education consultant, and previous teachers. Marie was worried about what she was doing wrong.

Amber's parents helped Marie to understand some of the changes that had accompanied Amber's development. During the preschool years, Amber had played with other children and was accepted by them. She felt part of the group. In Grades 1 and 2, when the educational assistant, Jane, spent more time with Amber, that meant Amber spent less time interacting with her peers. When Marie first put students in groups, Amber said, "My group will lose. Because I'm in it." For a couple of weeks, Amber had refused to take part in collaborative learning activities. Most of the children in the class had been with Amber since Kindergarten and they would help her if she was in their collaborative group. If anything, they helped her too much. Marie had observed that the children usually accepted Amber's contributions in a group, but Amber did not recognize this. Marie wondered if it was because Amber couldn't see the smiles and nods when she gave her ideas. Amber had recently started asking Marie or Jeannie how many children had raised their hands when Marie asked a question. It had never occurred to Marie that Amber couldn't see how well she was doing compared to the rest of the class. Jeannie seemed to understand Amber's hurdles, and ensured that Amber was not alone on the playground or during the social times in the classroom.

It was only April of Grade 3, but Marie had insisted on a meeting to plan Amber's Grade 4 program. She wanted the next teacher to be more prepared than she had been. The participants were Marie, Hema Patel (the Grade 4 teacher), Jane (the teaching assistant), the resource teacher, a district consultant, and a specialist teacher in Provincial Resource Services for the Blind. Marie knew that, beginning in Grade 4, more learning would be done from texts, and less from teacher-prepared activity sheets. More work would also be done in collaborative learning groups because this was an approach that Hema was committed to using. Marie knew that, at the meeting, they should decide what books and materials would need to be ordered for the fall term of Grade 4—in Braille, in tactile materials, and on audiotape. Marie had to impress on Hema the need to have materials for collaborative group learning ready in time for Jane to produce them in Braille.

Marie's real concern was still Amber's lingering attitude that she couldn't do the work because she was blind. "This attitude can reduce Amber's self-esteem and confidence," Marie told the other teachers. "The problem is that when I ask her to do fewer examples than the rest of the class, she says it is because she is not as smart as the other children. But when I ask her to do all the examples, then she wears herself out trying. And she usually can't finish the work, even for homework." The group thought that Amber would benefit from completing all questions on class assignments. They also discussed Amber's concerns that she was dragging down any group she was part of. They suggested Marie needed to include her in groups that were successful and in which she could make a genuine contribution. Marie said she had thought of these things herself, but didn't have any new ideas about how to do them.

Hema showed the group a book called *Designing Groupwork*. "Many of you know that I use cooperative groups a lot. I learned about this book in a course I am taking, and I have been trying out these ideas to ensure that every student's contribution is valued. One strategy is to prepare students who have low status to be group leaders by teaching them something that will be valued when the group does the cooperative activities. I bet Amber is good at visualizing what things look like from a description. I am guessing that if Amber and one member of each of the other groups were prepped ahead to lead their group in visualization of specific situations they read about, Amber would really feel successful in your heritage unit."

Just before the meeting ended, the group of teachers came up with a radical idea: "Why not re-examine the assignments given to the whole class? If you can decide whether Amber understands with 10 examples, then maybe you can decide after 10 examples for the other students." Marie thought the idea had begun with the consultant, but no one was sure. "Would it work? The reality was that it would take Amber longer than the other students to complete even 10 questions. Would it hurt anyone else?" Marie wasn't certain. She agreed to try fewer questions and a daily schedule in which some time was set aside each day for "completing work." Someone suggested Marie have students indicate on a sign-up sheet that they had taken work home, and sign the following day to show they had returned the work. Then she would know who was finishing assignments for homework. This would help Amber and some other students. As soon as the meeting finished, Marie phoned Amber's parents and drafted a letter to all the parents. That was a spring day in April.

In June the team of teachers saw what Amber had written on her self-evaluation for the heritage unit: "I was a leader in my group. I give myself 9/10 for group work." The in-school team still felt that it would be helpful for Amber to learn social strategies to initiate more interaction with her peers. This would mean removing Amber from the classroom for a planned period of time each week so that she could interact more effectively when she was in the classroom. The question Marie asked the team was "Can Amber afford to be out of the classroom for Braille and preteaching and social strategies?"

Everyone was aware that Amber would be competing in a sighted world for educational and employment opportunities, and that Amber would be a member of teams at school and at work. Not only would she need to be as independent and competent as possible, but she would also need to believe that she was as capable as others around her. The group recommended that the following be listed as goals for Amber at the fall IEP review meeting with her parents: initiating social interaction; being willing and able to collaborate with others.

QUESTIONS FOR REFLECTION AND DISCUSSION

1. What are the facts of the case?
2. What do we know about Amber? About her teacher, Marie Fine?
3. Describe the major dilemma(s) in this case.

4. What are some underlying issues in this case?

5. Describe Amber's experiences in Marie Fine's classroom, as Amber might describe them.

6. What does Marie Fine believe about inclusion for students with a visual impairment? How did Marie become aware of her beliefs about inclusion, and how did she try to act on her newly discovered awareness?

7. What can be done to resolve the dilemma(s) in this case? What will the consequences be for Amber, for Marie Fine, for others who are affected?

8. What generalizations can be made based on this case? Does this case lead us to question any long-held beliefs or to recognize assumptions we might be making about exceptional students, classrooms, and inclusion?

EXHIBIT 1.1	Tips for Teachers of Students Who Are Visually Impaired

This is a list of tips Marie Fine found in Amber's file, copied, and taped into her daybook.

1. Point out the classroom rules to which the student must adhere.

2. Expect the same quality of work, rather than the same quantity.

3. Don't move furniture in the classroom without warning the student.

4. Cut down on glare on boards, desks, etc.

5. Provide multisensory experiences, learning by doing, and support without dependence.

6. Stress legibility, not size, as students will tend to print or write in large size, if at all.

7. Remind individual speakers to name themselves (and remind the visually impaired student of who is speaking if individual students forget).

8. Help everyone in the class to provide non-visual feedback to the student with the visual impairment (like saying "well done" instead of smiling or nodding).

9. Encourage peers to be friends not helpers.

10. Encourage the visually impaired student to share his or her experiences with you, so that you can understand the student's perspective. Help the student to feel an integral part of the community in the classroom.

EXHIBIT 1.2	Guide for Ordering Materials for Print-Disabled Students

Lawrencetown Provincial School for Blind Students
Lawrencetown, (555) 759-5555

Information for Schools Ordering Materials for Print-Disabled Students:

1. The loan of materials is free of charge to schools for use by visually impaired or other print-disabled students.

2. For students with visual impairments, submit the Application for Consideration for Large Print, Braille, and Audio Tapes with signatures from an ophthalmologist and a resource teacher at the time of the initial IEP meeting. Each year, send an updated form (Re-application) following the IEP review. You will receive copies of the Materials Order form with your school name and identification number entered.

3. Order early. Allow two to four months to receive large print, tape, or Braille if The Provincial School does not have the materials on hand. In such cases, it will be necessary to prepare the requested materials. Allow two to four weeks for materials in our library.

4. Telephone orders to the Materials Support Office at (555) 759-5555, extension 5555, providing all the information requested on the Materials Order form.

5. Return the materials promptly by the date indicated on the Loan Record enclosed with the materials. Complete the Conditions of Materials form if the materials have been damaged in use.

6. Request copies of our Library of Holdings for Print-Disabled Students by telephoning (555) 759-5555, extension 5000, or visit our Web page.

EXHIBIT 1.3	**First Page of Individual Education Plan (Strengths/Needs Worksheet)**

Student: Amber Martin

Birthdate: March 19, 1993

Guardian: Bridget Martin

Address: 33 Stone St. E., Franksville

Phone (res): 777-9999

Phone (work): 777-8888

Teacher: Marie Fine

School: Shady Pines   **Grade:** 3

Exceptionality: Blind from birth (retrolental fibroplasia)

Placement: Regular classroom, 8 hours/wk with EA in class, 5 hours/wk with resource teacher for learning Braille, concept development, independence enhancement

Start date: October 2001

Review date: June 2002

PRESENT LEVEL OF FUNCTIONING: SUMMARY OF ASSESSMENT AND EVALUATION

Areas of Strength: Mobility and orientation; Willingness to participate; Independence; Memory; Hard worker; Number facts in mathematics; IQ verbal 104, nonverbal 100 (adapted Stanford-Binet, January 14, 2000); CTBS math 2.5, vocabulary 2.7, reading 2.5 (May 2001, Grade 2).

Areas of Need: Instruction in Braille; Social skills in classroom and on playground; Conceptual understanding in mathematics.

GENERAL NATURE OF ADAPTATIONS

Braille and taped materials from Lawrencetown Provincial School for Blind Students; Reduced number of examples completed; Support of educational assistant and resource teacher.

SUGGESTIONS FOR FURTHER READING

British Columbia Special Education Branch. (1995). *Students with visual impairments: A resource guide to support classroom teachers*. Victoria, BC: Ministry of Education, Special Education Branch.
>   This resource, written for teachers, contains basic information about visual impairments as well as examples of adapted curriculum activities.

Cohen, E. G. (1998). *Designing groupwork: Strategies for the heterogeneous classroom*. New York, NY: Teachers College, Columbia University.
>   In this resource, Cohen combines easy-to-follow theory with examples and teaching strategies for groupwork that can be adapted for any situation. Cohen has also developed status interventions that help students with low status in the classroom to make contributions that are valued by their peers.

Little, J. (1987). *Little by little: A writer's education*. New York: Viking Kestrel.
>   The engaging autobiography of a successful, blind, Canadian writer, written for children and young adolescents.

MacCuspie, P. A. (1996). *Promoting acceptance of children with disabilities: From tolerance to inclusion*. Halifax, NS: Atlantic Provinces Special Education Authority.
>   Based on interviews with five children with a visual impairment who are being educated in regular elementary classrooms and on interviews with their peers and teachers, this book contains many helpful suggestions within the interview data and in lists for classroom teachers and others.

Scott, E. P., Jan, J. E., & Freeman, R. D. (1995). *Can't your child see? A guide for parents and professionals about young children who are visually impaired*. Austin, TX: PRO-ED, Inc.
>   A practical guide that helps teachers as well as parents to recognize how children with visual impairments discover, explore, and learn in ways different from other children.

WEBLINKS

Provincial sources for books on tape and adaptive technology for students who are blind:

Alberta: http://www.lrc.learning.gov.ab.ca/scripts/cgiip.exe/links/links.htm

Atlantic provinces: http://www.apsea.ca/

British Columbia: http://www.prcvi.org/

Manitoba: http://www.edu.gov.mb.ca/ks4/blind/index.html

Ontario: http://www.edu.gov.on.ca/eng/document/nr/02.09/fs0920.html

Quebec: http://www.mab.ca/

Saskatchewan: http://www.sasked.gov.sk.ca/resources/

http://snow.utoronto.ca/technology/tutorials/
Special Needs Opportunity Windows (SNOW) Adaptive Technology Tutorial Resources: an online source of current information on adaptive technology, including online courses.

Our Children Are Getting Less Attention

Keith Lashyk was enjoying the tired satisfaction that comes with the end of the first week of school. It was a beautiful Friday afternoon—with warm September sun and the prospect of a weekend with his family and of some planning on Sunday evening to ensure he was ready for Monday morning. Keith was reflecting on how much he had learned already about including a child with a wheelchair in his Kindergarten class. He thought he would stop in to tell Kathleen Lester, the principal of Rolling Hills Elementary School, that Susannah was settling in well.

Just as he was packing his term plans and classroom observations into his briefcase, he heard a knock at the door. The mothers of two of the children in his Kindergarten class called out to him, "Got a minute to talk?" What they asked went something like this: "Why are you putting so much time and work into Susannah Weber's education? Everyone knows she will leave school as soon as she can, like all the Mennonite children do. And our children are getting less attention because of her."

After they left, Keith trudged down to Kathleen's office. "We need to talk. I feel like I was just attacked. Two parents were asking about Susannah. It looks like the real challenge this year won't be to accommodate Susannah. It may be to respond to the questions of the other parents. They suggested she has less right to accommodations because she will probably leave school early like many Mennonite children do. The Webers didn't make it clear, did they, about whether she would leave early?"

Kathleen asked Keith to describe his week with the Kindergarten class and the ways he and the children had accommodated Susannah. Then she added, "Didn't you ask one family to come in early and get to know Susannah? And we have started the school-based team process. I have been impressed with the way the children consider Susannah one of the group when I have been in the classroom this week." After they had shared the successes, she listened to Keith talk again about the parents' concerns. Kathleen suggested, "Let's think about this one and meet Monday afternoon to make a plan. Then you and I will meet with the two concerned parents. One of us will probably need to talk with the Webers. We know that they will not enter whatever debate ensues, that theirs will be what Mr. Weber called a 'pacifist response.' So let's try to come up with some calming strategies."

"I have an idea," Keith said. "Think about this—we could hold the 'Welcome to Kindergarten' Open Classroom Night a week earlier than usual. I will have artwork by then from every child to put on display. Maybe the two of us can share the load—providing information about the program and answering individual questions. That also provides us with an occasion to send home information about my program and about the school's inclusion policy."

"Great suggestions, Keith! I think I'll use the school's inclusion policy as the theme of my letter to parents in the first Rolling Hills newsletter this fall. Don't spend your weekend worrying about Susannah. Enjoy the last of the summer weather and we'll tackle this on Monday." Kathleen and Keith agreed to meet Monday afternoon at 3:45.

While he drove across the hills, Keith Lashyk thought about his five years of teaching at Rolling Hills, a small, rural school. Except for his preservice practica, he had never taught anywhere else. Because Rolling Hills had been new when he was hired, Keith had developed the Kindergarten program and even ordered the teaching materials. He was proud of his program, and had never felt criticized by parents.

Then he thought about all he had learned and accomplished in the past few weeks. Keith had been surprised to receive a call from his principal, Kathleen Lester, in the first week of August. "Sure, I can meet you at the school tomorrow afternoon. What's up?"

As usual, Kathleen took the most direct route. "Prepare yourself for a surprise," she said. "We need to make some plans tomorrow because on Thursday we meet with the parents of an exceptional student. Oh, by the way, I suggested they bring Susannah with them." Kathleen told Keith she had been wrestling with how break it to him that she had enrolled a child in a wheelchair in his Kindergarten class. She knew that Keith would rise to the challenge, but she also knew that it was late for him to begin thinking about the program adaptations that would have to be made.

Calmly, Keith Lashyk said, "Tell me about Susannah."

He listened while Kathleen described her conversation with Susannah's father. Susannah had been born without fully developed legs and with only two fingers on each hand. Her father had explained to Kathleen that "Susannah is bright, speaks well, and is happy to be going to school." At the end of the conversation, he had told Kathleen that the family were moderate Mennonites who farmed a large tract of land and belonged to a community that dressed conservatively but used powered equipment and vehicles.

The panic was rising in Keith's voice: "We sure better meet. I will have to do a lot between now and the beginning of school. What about a school-based team meeting and an IEP? What about the program I've already planned?"

Rolling Hills, the school where Keith teaches Kindergarten, is more accessible than the older schools in the area, and this makes it easier for children with sensory and physical disabilities to be included. It also means that the teachers at Rolling Hills are frequently called upon to change their program to accommodate exceptional children. Keith has taught a child with a visual impairment and many children with mild exceptionalities. Because the school is small, Kathleen Lester is the resource teacher as well as the principal. Kathleen considers this an ideal situation. She knows all the families in the school, works closely with all the teaching staff, and spends time in every classroom every week carrying out her responsibilities for administration and for overseeing the inclusion of the exceptional children in the school.

Both Keith and Kathleen had been nervous when they met Susannah Weber and her parents. Susannah was just as her father had described her: excited about school, and shy but well spoken. Her long hair was braided simply, and she wore a cotton dress printed with pastel patterns. The discussion was straightforward. The Weber family wanted Susannah to be literate and numerate. They had waited until August to enroll her because they were not certain that Susannah was ready for the social demands "and the stares" of school. Keith asked the Webers to bring Susannah back to the school the week before school started, so he could introduce her to the way the classroom would be organized in September. He also asked their permission to invite another girl from the class to meet Susannah that day, so she would know one of her peers before the first day of school. These were all part of the plan that Kathleen and Keith had devised between the first telephone call and the first meeting.

Already, Keith had found many ways to make classroom life easier for Susannah. For example, he had discovered that it was easier for Susannah to hold a large, three-sided crayon or pencil to colour or print letters than the usual crayons and pencils used in Kindergarten. During storytime, it was effective to lift her out of her wheelchair and sit her on the carpet like the other children. Everyone was more comfortable when Susannah was at the same height as the rest of the class. The consulting physiotherapist had recommended and ordered a scooter that Susannah could use to move around the gymnasium. Keith could see that at the time of the school-based team meeting he would have many suggestions to contribute about how to meet Susannah's needs.

Was including Susannah taking as much time as the unhappy parents suggested? Keith wasn't sure. He wondered about keeping a log of the time he devoted to meeting Susannah's needs. One of the parents had asked Keith how he would feel if his child was in a classroom with Susannah, and the teacher had less time to spend with his child as a result. It was still hypothetical because his son, Seth, was only three, but that question had made Keith think. Was he ignoring the other children?

Keith knew that he and Kathleen would have to prepare well to answer the parents' questions. As he pulled into his lane at home, Keith wondered, "What would be the best forum for getting the message across? And what should the message be?" He made up his mind to take Kathleen's advice and enjoy the weekend. Sunday night when he opened his briefcase, he would think through the questions the parents had asked and come up with suggestions for the Monday meeting with Kathleen. Right now, he would enjoy the successes of the week, and a weekend with his family.

QUESTIONS FOR REFLECTION AND DISCUSSION

1. What are the facts/key elements of the case?
2. What do we know about the student, Susannah Weber? About the teacher, Keith Lashyk?
3. Describe the major problem(s) or dilemma(s) in this case.
4. Describe Susannah's experiences in the class as her parents might see them, and as the parents who visited the classroom on Friday afternoon might see them.
5. What actions should Keith and Kathleen take to resolve the major dilemma(s)? What consequences are likely to follow from these actions for Susannah? For Keith? For Rolling Hills School?
6. What have we learned from this case? What long-held assumptions or beliefs about exceptional children, about equity, and about other issues are called into question after considering this case?

EXHIBIT 2.1	Information about Mennonite Communities

Both Kathleen and Keith had taught Mennonite children before. However, in order to be informed enough to know what questions to ask in Susannah's case, they decided to do some reading of the recommended sources (at the end of this exhibit) and they combined their notes and questions.

Information about Mennonite Communities and Questions for the Webers

Mennonite communities are worshipping communities, but members also support each other economically, socially, and spiritually. Are there children in Rolling Hills School who already know and support Susannah in their community?

Old Order Mennonites accept few of the advances of the modern world and often educate their children in their own schools. Mennonites known as Progressives usually participate in public schools and often value higher education. Susannah and her parents are Moderate Mennonites, which means that they are somewhere between these two groups. What modern conveniences do they use? Do the other children in their family and community attend a public school, or are the Webers making an exception for Susannah because of her disability? Do the children in their community usually leave school between 14 and 16 years of age to take their role on the farm, or do they usually continue their education?

On the Mennonite ideals of pacifism, care of others, and obedience to God, there is usually agreement. What will the Webers do and what will they want Susannah to do in response to the criticisms from other families and parental concerns that children in the class may repeat at school?

Sources: Notes and questions based on reading the following:
Kenna, K. (1998). *A people apart.* Toronto, ON: Somerville House Publishing.
Fretz, J. W. (1989). *The Waterloo Mennonites: A community in paradox.* Waterloo, ON: Wilfrid Laurier University Press.

| EXHIBIT 2.2 | **Draft Letter to Parents from the Principal about Inclusion** |

DRAFT Letter to Parents from Kathleen Lester, Principal of Rolling Hills Elementary School, to be placed in the first issue of this year's Rolling Hills School Newsletter:

September 11

Dear Parents:

Another school year is beginning, and I want to welcome you back to Rolling Hills or welcome you for the first time, if you are a new family to our school. I am Kathleen Lester, principal of Rolling Hills and also the school's resource teacher. This wonderful combination of responsibilities keeps me very busy and out of the office about four half-days of the week. It does mean that I am often away from my desk when you call. If you do not reach me, please leave a message with Ms. Singh, our school secretary, or leave a voice-mail message. I will return your call as soon as I can. Remember that I want to talk with you and get to know each family.

In this first newsletter of the year, I want to describe an important aspect of our work together—inclusion. At Rolling Hills we strive to be an inclusive school. The policies of this school, our school division, and our province all promote inclusive schooling. An inclusive school is a school where every child is respected as part of the school community, and where every child is encouraged to learn and achieve as much as possible, regardless of ability, disability, or ethnic background.

To help teachers achieve our goals for inclusive classrooms and an inclusive school, Rolling Hills has had a school-based team approach for the past three years. The school-based team is a problem-solving group that shares the responsibility for making educational decisions and providing educational support for the teachers and the exceptional children included in their classrooms. Each school-based team includes myself, the teacher of the exceptional child, a district resource teacher, and the parents of the exceptional child. When appropriate, the team may include other members, such as a consultant for gifted education or a physiotherapist.

As an inclusive school, we see parents as partners in the school community. Parents of exceptional children are members of the school-based teams. All parents are, after all, their children's first teachers and have a wealth of information that we should not ignore. I understand that some parents may have concerns about the gradual increases in inclusion in our school, and I welcome opportunities to talk with you about these and all other changes in education. My telephone number is on the letterhead of this newsletter. Do not hesitate to call and leave a message. Or come by the school to talk with me or your child's teacher.

I look forward to meeting each of you during our Open Classroom Nights in late September. Be sure to come to these evenings with your child, and introduce yourself to me as well as to the classroom teacher.

Sincerely,

Kathleen Lester, B.A., B.Ed., M.Ed.
Principal, Rolling Hills School

| EXHIBIT 2.3 | Steps in a School-Based Team Process |

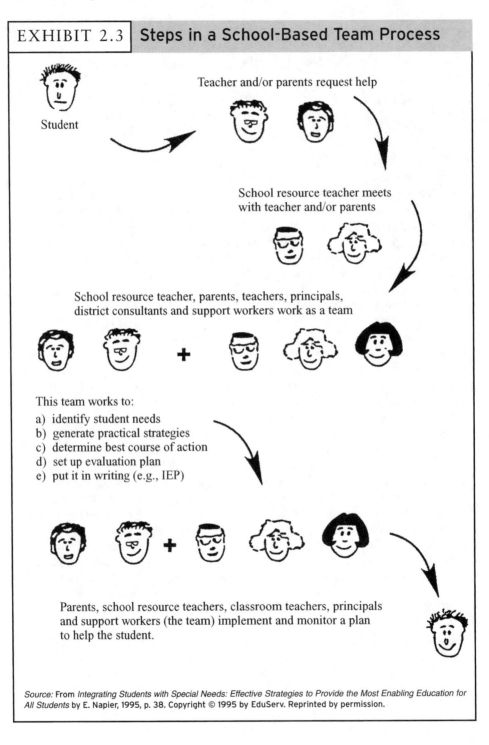

Student

Teacher and/or parents request help

School resource teacher meets
with teacher and/or parents

School resource teacher, parents, teachers, principals,
district consultants and support workers work as a team

This team works to:
a) identify student needs
b) generate practical strategies
c) determine best course of action
d) set up evaluation plan
e) put it in writing (e.g., IEP)

Parents, school resource teachers, classroom teachers, principals
and support workers (the team) implement and monitor a plan
to help the student.

Source: From *Integrating Students with Special Needs: Effective Strategies to Provide the Most Enabling Education for All Students* by E. Napier, 1995, p. 38. Copyright © 1995 by EduServ. Reprinted by permission.

SUGGESTIONS FOR FURTHER READING

Alberta Education, Special Education Branch. (1996). *Partners during changing times: An information booklet for parents of children with special needs.* Edmonton, AB: Alberta Education.
   A short but informative guide to help parents of exceptional children recognize the important role they can play with schools in ensuring that their children's needs are met.

Napier, E. (1995). *Integrating students with special needs: Effective strategies to provide the most enabling education for all students.* Vancouver, BC: EduServ.
   This 120-page, practical resource describes how policies and procedures were developed in one community and provides examples of the forms used to collect and record information important to the education of exceptional students.

Taylor, G. R. (2000). *Parental involvement: A practical guide for collaboration and teamwork for students with disabilities.* Springfield, IL: C.C. Thomas.
   This practical guide includes topics like how to improve collaboration between parents and schools, and should prove helpful for working with parents even though the examples are from the American context.

Watkinson, A. M. (1999). *Education, student rights, and the charter.* Saskatoon, SK: Purich Pub. Ltd.
   A thorough, but not overly technical, examination of recent court decisions that have an impact on education, which informs educators about student rights.

WEBLINKS

http://www.fhs.mcmaster.ca/canchild/
CanChild is a centre for childhood disability research that focuses on families and quality of life (e.g., transition to Kindergarten).

http://pages.sprint.ca/caringinmotion/
A Canadian organization that brings adaptive equipment that is no longer needed together with children who have a need.

http://www.learning.gov.ab.ca/parents/tips.asp
This helpful site prepared by Learning Alberta includes tips for parents about preparing children for transitions including the start to elementary school and the move to a new school.

http://canada.justice.gc.ca/loireg/charte/const_en.html
Contains the text of the Canadian Charter of Rights and Freedoms, which guarantees the rights and freedoms of all Canadians including people with disabilities.

I Want a Best Friend

The Grade 2 classroom looked beautiful—children's letters to their parents and self-portraits adorned the bulletin boards. A portfolio sat on every desk, each one containing samples of the student's work. "Parents' night always makes me nervous. What about you?" Bonnie Sipitis worried to her colleague, Joyce Meyer.

"Yeah, especially when we are running an individualized program for a student and we know that it is not doing the job," came Joyce's reply. Joyce had been a resource teacher for seven years at Oak Ridge Elementary. She and Bonnie Sipitis, the Grade 2 teacher, were reviewing the materials for their imminent interview with Casey Brewer's parents.

Casey's confidential file provided the details. Shortly after Casey was born, she was diagnosed as having Down syndrome and a congenital heart condition. Down syndrome, a genetic chromosome disorder, is usually accompanied by developmental disabilities (formerly called mental retardation). Casey's development has always been delayed, to roughly just a little more than half her chronological age. Her score on an intelligence test given last year was about 55. When Casey was three, surgery was performed, and her heart condition was corrected. The school picture in Casey's file shows that, like many children with Down syndrome, Casey has almond-shaped eyes.

Casey has always been included in all her family's activities, including shopping trips, weekly worship, and camping in the summers. Her older brother proudly walks her to and from school most days. Casey's parents believe that she should be a valued part of her community and her neighbourhood school. From the time Casey was four months, the family participated in a structured early intervention program that focused on helping Casey to relate to her environment and to communicate with the people around her. She learned skills that allowed her to manoeuvre around and to manipulate her environment.

After an integrated preschool program, she began attending Oak Ridge, two blocks from her home. The file notes suggested that preschool and Kindergarten had been fairly straightforward, except during Casey's hospitalization and recovery from surgery. One comment read, "Casey enjoys the other children and they accept her." However, the Kindergarten teacher felt Casey was not ready for the more academic demands of Grade 1 or for a full day of school. So Casey had spent a second year in Kindergarten, much to her delight. In her second year in Kindergarten, she made a best friend, Mara, and they were placed in the same Grade 1 class. Casey made progress socially in Grade 1 by spending every possible minute with Mara. She also worked hard on her hand-eye coordination and learned to print letters. She learned her mathematics in a small group with Joyce Meyer in the classroom. Joyce had arranged for an educational assistant, Tom White, to teach Casey beginning reading individually in the classroom at a slower pace than the rest of the class. In Grade 1 Casey had read environmental print for many words (e.g., Ford, Pizza Hut) and had made progress with matching the names of members of her family to their pictures and reading experience stories about members of her family. She had learned to read the labels for many objects in the classroom and could read all the names of her classmates to hand out student journals and assignments.

Bonnie and Joyce had brief notes on Casey's current program in Grade 2. Mara and Casey were no longer in the same classroom, and Casey was frequently grouped with another exceptional child, Albert. Albert had severe difficulties communicating orally and had learning disabilities that affected his math, reading, and written work. Casey was no longer learning math with the class; Tom was teaching Casey and Albert Grade 1 math in a group of two at a slow rate at the back of the classroom. Joyce taught Casey reading in the resource room with Albert, and Tom White was in the classroom most of the rest of the day. Bonnie had written, "Neither Casey nor Albert is making expected progress academically or socially." Joyce had noted that they were becoming too dependent on each other and "When one is away the other is lost."

When they arrived, Mr. and Ms. Brewer spread out their notes too. "We want to make sure we say what is most important," Mr. Brewer explained, "because we could talk all night about Casey's inclusion program, but we have one big thing on our minds."

The two teachers looked at each other. Bonnie began, "We have one big item, too, and I bet it is the same one." Everyone laughed—the nervous laughter of parent-teacher interviews. Bonnie said, "You go first."

Ten minutes later, the same issue had been aired from two perspectives. More nervous laughter. Everyone agreed that Casey was right when she said, "I want a best friend. I don't have friends, only Albert." This year in Grade 2 Casey was separated from her best friend. Joyce recalled the day she had made this recommendation last spring. "I take responsibility," she said. "I thought Casey was ready to make new friends, and I found that she refused to play or work with anyone other than Mara. It has really backfired. I hoped she would be able to work with Albert, another exceptional child, and make new friends this year."

Mr. Brewer picked up the story line. "She really misses Mara. And Mara has a new best friend. But Casey says that the only person who will sit with her is Albert. She talks only about the two of you and Albert. You would think there were no other children in this class.

Oh, she does mention Beth sometimes. She says Beth plays with her at recess." He continued, "She wants a best friend, a girl who will walk home with her, play with her at recess, and choose her as a partner. What can *we* do? We think this is something that has to be dealt with at school."

Casey's mother continued, "As you know, children with Down syndrome learn a great deal by watching. That is why it is so important for Casey to be included in a regular classroom with children who speak clearly and behave well and are working hard to learn. And rather than being with Albert all day, whose speech is a poor model and who looks to Casey for direction, she needs to spend some time with other students in the class. Also she needs the friendship of other girls close to her age."

Bonnie Sipitis thought back over the past few days in the Grade 2 classroom. She described the way Casey had refused to talk with the other girls during indoor recess. Then it struck her: "One day they were talking about the books they were using for their book reports, and conferencing their book reports. And Casey doesn't do book reports. Another day they were cutting out the figures you see around the outside of the bulletin board. Casey has a really tough time using scissors. She wouldn't want them to see how awkward she is. I remember that Casey was colouring both days." Bonnie turned to face Casey's parents. "I just realized something while we were talking. We have not been thinking about how closely academic learning and social acceptance are related for Casey."

Joyce elaborated, "We all know that the academic gap between Casey and her peers will increase as she grows older. The growing gap has already caused me to focus on teaching Casey reading in the resource room where there are fewer distractions. It has caused us to pull Casey and Albert aside for math, and in fact they learn math at a different time of day than the rest of the class. We have increased the intensity of teaching in these two areas. But at what cost?"

Casey's mother jumped in. "When I came to observe last Friday, I noticed that a lot of the time Casey was watching, but not taking part. When I asked her why she was not working on science, she said she did not have anything to do. The unit was on recycling. But Casey knows about recycling, just like all the other children. She puts her pop cans in the blue box and scolds us when we put recyclables in the garbage. I thought maybe she was left out because she had returned from reading in the resource room part way through the science class. Everyone needs to know about the environment. Couldn't Casey go to the resource room at another time? Or be included when she returns from the resource room? She wants to take part now. But I am afraid that if she gets used to sitting around while everyone else works, she will resist when we ask her to work. You know how stubborn Casey can be. She gets set in her ways, and being idle is not a way I want her to get set in. I think this is part of the reason Casey doesn't talk to the other children like she used to. She has less to talk about because she has almost no work in common with them. And little opportunity to practise socializing with them because she is only practising talking to one other child."

"Yes!" Joyce and Bonnie said together. Bonnie went on, "This is what I was trying to say when I said we weren't working on these two—academics and social development—together this year. We have noticed some of the same concerns as you, but we knew we were working hard on academics. And we have recognized that it looks like it was a mistake to separate Casey and Mara. But we haven't been able to come up with alternatives that looked like they would solve the emerging problems. I think this interview has made us think about things differently."

"Our time is almost up," Joyce said. "I hope you won't feel rushed if we close this interview now. We both have other parents to meet tonight. I think we have a better understanding of the problems and can see some possible solutions to try. Should we plan to meet again? Give us some time to plan ways to include Casey more in the classroom learning activities as a part of a group. What we will have to do is maintain as much intensity in her academic program as possible, and also increase her social role in the classroom. We will look at Casey's goals in her IEP in each curriculum area and think about how to teach her in that curriculum area at the same time as the rest of the class. Let's plan to meet in about two weeks. One of us will call to arrange a time. We will probably involve Tom White in the planning and the solutions, and the principal will have to approve our plans. Does two weeks give us enough time, Bonnie?"

Bonnie wrote the Brewers' final comment on the interview record sheet: "Casey needs to have friends *and* an academic program at school."

QUESTIONS FOR REFLECTION AND DISCUSSION

1. What are the important facts of the case?

2. What do we know about Casey? About her teacher, Bonnie Sipitis?

3. What did Casey's parents see as the dilemma(s) in the case? What did the teachers see as the dilemma(s)? What do you see as the major dilemma(s)?

4. Describe Casey's experiences in the classroom as she might describe them to her grandmother. Describe Casey in the classroom from the perspective of another student in the class.

5. What actions can the teachers take to resolve the dilemma(s)? What are the consequences of these actions likely to be for Casey? For her classmates? For Bonnie Sipitis? More widely?

6. Can we generalize from this case? What have we learned? Should we question any assumptions or beliefs that we brought to the case about people with Down syndrome? About inclusive classrooms? Should we question any other assumptions or beliefs?

EXHIBIT 3.1	Information about Down Syndrome

Down syndrome is a genetic defect causing limitations in physical and cognitive development. It is the result of a chromosomal error, not any fault of either parent. One in every 700–800 live births will be affected by Down syndrome. Though the likelihood of having a child with Down syndrome increases to some degree with the age of the mother, three-quarters of all children with the syndrome are born to mothers under 35.

A child with Down syndrome demonstrates a wide variety of characteristics—some of these are inherited family traits and others are specific to the syndrome. A syndrome is a condition distinguished by a cluster of features occurring together. In Down syndrome, certain physical features will probably be apparent, though these are not exclusive to Down syndrome and may appear elsewhere in the unaffected population.

Recent studies show that, though all children with Down syndrome have some degree of intellectual disability, other factors, such as environment, misinformation, and low expectations, have a considerable impact on their learning potential. Generally, progress will be slow, and certain complex skills may be difficult; each individual has unique strengths and weaknesses.

Physically, children with Down syndrome have low muscle tone and a generalized looseness of the ligaments. The Canadian Down Syndrome Society recommends that children be assessed by X-ray at age 3–4 (before Kindergarten) and again at age 10–12 to look for instability at the two top neck vertebrae. This instability must be carefully considered during any planning for physical activity to avoid serious injury. There is also a strong susceptibility to hearing and vision difficulties. Fifty percent of these children will require monitoring in these areas. At least one-third of the children will have heart defects.

Behaviour problems are no more specific to children with Down syndrome than to any other group of students. Any perceived reaction to a request may actually be only a difficulty in transition from one activity to another, going from the known to the unknown. Developmentally, these children will reach different stages at later times than the average child. Chronological age is not an indicator of achievement, but serves only to raise unrealistic expectations.

Remember this is a person, not a syndrome.

Classroom Strategies

General

- Prior to enrolment, meet with the parents and the student for assessment and mutual understanding of goals, possibilities and limitations.
- Consider placement on the basis of individual needs and program availability.
- Develop an IEP to include modified learner outcomes as well as essential skills.
- Maintain ongoing communication with other members of the team.
- Through continuing communication between home and school, ensure consistency of behaviour and expectations and understanding of setbacks and successes.
- Be aware of any specific medical problems or medication. It is the responsibility of the parents to keep the school informed.
- Communicate any marked changes, physical or behavioural, to the parents.

Teaching

- Discuss scheduling and activities before they happen: use wall charts, calendars, photos of a single activity or a single day. These activities reinforce structure and sequencing.
- Allow time to finish a task.
- Help the student to structure play as well as work—or the activity may become confusing.
- Break up tasks into small steps; use short blocks of time.
- Avoid the abstract in favour of the concrete and the visual.
- Phrase questions simply, and allow response time. Use short sentences.
- Encourage speech by having the student express wants, rather than forming simple "yes" or "no" responses.
- Gain attention by using simple commands, e.g., use eye contact. Be precise.
- Help the child focus on the task—remove items that might distract.
- Expect appropriate behaviour. All students are accountable for their behaviour.
- Cooperate with the parents in integrating learning activities, e.g., shopping, banking, renting a video, travel. Be mutually aware of what the student knows and is learning.
- Be aware of the available specialized computer software especially designed to facilitate reading and communication.

Physical

- Include the student in physical activities, following a medical assessment.
- Provide assistance, if necessary, to help overcome the muscular weakness and joint instability. Stairs and slippery floors may pose problems.

Social

- Help the student develop independence; this will both increase self-esteem and improve social relationships.
- Help the student and others understand Down syndrome. Initiate open discussion, considering individual differences and wide variations of abilities. Your own behaviour and acceptance will serve as a model.
- Encourage interaction and involvement with other students through play and classroom activities.

Professional

- Beware of outdated books and research.
- Read, research and investigate: contact the Canadian Down Syndrome Society for current material:
  Canadian Down Syndrome Society
  Box 52027, Edmonton Trail R.P.O.
  Calgary, AB T2E 8K9
  Tel.: 403-220-9224

EXHIBIT 3.2	Second Page of Individual Education Plan (Goals for the Year/Adaptations)

Student: Casey Brewer   **Teacher:** Bonnie Sipitis
Exceptionality: Developmental delay (Down syndrome)

LONG-TERM GOALS FOR THE YEAR: ADAPTATIONS:

1. Reading: Casey will continue to develop phonemic awareness and reading comprehension.

1. Materials at her level; individualized instruction (resource teacher).

2. Writing: Casey will improve her written expression using full sentences in her journal and curriculum areas.

2. Using drawings or pictures from magazines as necessary (support of educational assistant).

3. Listening: Casey will improve listening and following instructions.

3. Using comprehension check (repeating instructions to educational assistant or classroom buddy).

4. Speaking: Casey will speak clearly in social and learning situations, asking questions when she does not understand.

4. Asking educational assistant or classroom buddy about what to say.

5. Math: Casey will improve counting, use of money, addition and subtraction of numbers to 10.

5. Using coins, other concrete materials for addition and subtraction (educational assistant).

6. Social and environmental studies: Casey will participate in collaborative learning group.

6. Asking educational assistant or classroom buddy when unsure what to do.

7. Motor development: Casey will engage in games, increase independence in eating lunch, increase hand-eye co-ordination.

7. Assistance with eating lunch, using computer (educational assistant).

8. Art and music: Casey will gain experience with various art media.

8. Tasks at level.

9. Self-management: Casey will follow lunch routines, join an extra-curricular activity.

9. Adult volunteer to support in eating and cleaning up lunch.

10. Social: Casey will develop close positive relationships with several peers and participate in group activities.

10. Watching and following actions of peers (encouraged by educational assistant).

EXHIBIT 3.3	Planning the Curriculum and the Timetable to Include an Exceptional Child

Using a Common Timetable to Plan Casey's Day

Classroom activities and routines		**Casey's activities and routines**
8:40 AM	Entering school	8:40
8:45 AM	Using bathroom/lockers	8:45
8:50 AM	Getting organized and announcements	8:50
9:00 AM	Writing journals	9:00
9:20 AM	Journal sharing Class meeting	9:20
10:00 AM	Reading activities Group 1 – teacher-directed Group 2 – reading partners	10:00
10:40 AM	Break	10:40
10:45 AM	Reading activities continued Group 1 – reading partners Group 2 – teacher-directed	10:45
11:30 AM	Lunch and playground	11:30
12:20 PM	Getting organized	12:20
12:30 PM	Monday–Thursday Math Friday Environmental Studies all PM (project-based)	12:30
2:00 PM	M, W Physical Education T, Th Art and Music	2:00
2:45 PM	Current events and Sharing	2:45
3:10 PM	Dismissal	3:10

Strategies: cooperative learning; thematic and project-based learning; portfolio assessment; same curricular area and theme with adjusted-content, learning goals, and activities (e.g., write a sentence instead of a paragraph; use coins for counters, #s to 10 only).

Casey can work with Tom, the educational assistant, in the classroom. Joyce, the resource teacher, can help to plan the curriculum that Casey will follow in the classroom, and remove her for briefer periods, and less time overall.

Exhibit 3.3 *Continued*

Using a Common Framework to Understand Casey's Curricular Needs

Provincial Curricular Outcomes for Grade 3	IEP Goals (Specific, Short-Term) for Casey Brewer
To read, write, listen, speak	Reading – continuing development of phonemic awareness (segmenting and blending), of comprehension of reading material at her level
	Writing – keeping a journal, using approximate spelling, drawings or pictures from magazine as necessary; completing entry daily; taking turn to read and show journal entry to class; focus on writing full sentences in every curriculum area (as above)
	Listening – listening to announcements; following directions (repeating them to assistant, student, teacher when uncertain)
	Speaking – speaking clearly in social and learning situations; asking questions when she does not understand
To use basic operations to solve	Math – counting in a meaningful context; handling problems of measurement, money, time; money for purchases; using coins for addition and using multi-digit numbers; subtraction with numbers less than 10
To use scientific principles and methods To become knowledgeable and appreciative of people and society, other cultures, history To think creatively and critically	Social and environmental studies – to listen, enter discussion, participate as member of collaborative group; set goals consistent with above
To achieve physical well-being	Physical education and motor development – engaging in individual and team games; opening and eating lunch increasingly independently; increasing accuracy using pencil and striking appropriate computer keys
To express oneself artistically	Art and music – gaining experience with various art media; further developing skill in drawing; listening and moving rhythmically to music
To show awareness of and preparation for community participation, career possibilities, domestic responsibilities, and constructive use of free time	Self-management, school jobs, and leisure – using locker, outdoor dressing independently, following lunch routines with classmates, purchasing food with adult volunteer for classroom activities; joining extra-curricular group in school as leisure activity
To have positive attitude toward learning To show concern and respect for others To work cooperatively	Social – developing close relationships with several peers; watching and following positive actions of peers; following classroom rules and routines; participating in partner and group activities

| EXHIBIT 3.4 | One Strategy for Making Adaptations: Environmental Inventory Process |

When teachers choose teaching and assessment practices that are suitable for most students, they may want to teach and assess more functional skills in students with moderate to severe developmental disabilities. In these circumstances, they can use the Environmental Inventory Process, and ask themselves three questions to try to discern alternate testing practices:

1. What does a person who does not have a disability do in this environment?
2. What does a person who has a disability do in this environment? What is the discrepancy?
3. What types of supports and/or adaptations can be put in place in order to increase the participation level or independence of the person who has a disability?

Currently, the class is working in small groups depicting the steps in the recycling process for paper, metal, and plastic. Casey lacks the motor and cognitive skills to participate like everyone else. Ms. Sipitis decides to assign Casey to the same group as Beth, who plays with Casey at recess. The educational assistant, Tom White, will help Casey find pictures of sample recycled products. Ms. Sipitis will ask Beth to help Casey paste these onto the group's diagram. Casey's parents will help her identify recycled products in grocery stores and restaurants and sort the items for the recycling bin at home.

Environmental Inventory Process Form

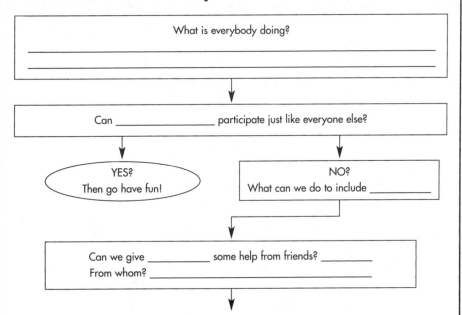

Exhibit 3.4 *Continued*

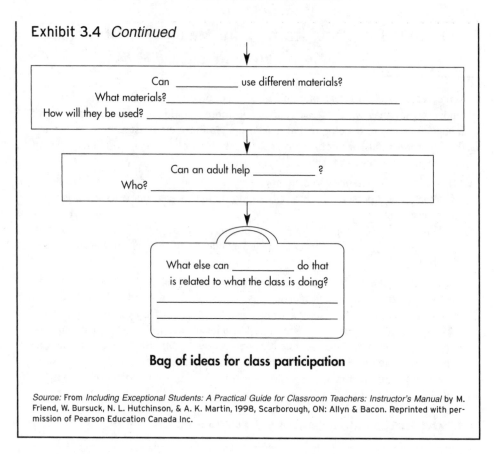

Can _____ use different materials?

What materials?_____

How will they be used? _____

Can an adult help _____ ?

Who? _____

What else can _____ do that
is related to what the class is doing?

_____
_____

Bag of ideas for class participation

Source: From *Including Exceptional Students: A Practical Guide for Classroom Teachers: Instructor's Manual* by M. Friend, W. Bursuck, N. L. Hutchinson, & A. K. Martin, 1998, Scarborough, ON: Allyn & Bacon. Reprinted with permission of Pearson Education Canada Inc.

SUGGESTIONS FOR FURTHER READING

Chamberlain, C. E., & Strode, R. M. (2000). *For parents and professionals: Down syndrome*. East Moline, IL: LinguiSystems.

> A resource containing basic information about how to help children and adolescents with Down syndrome learn at home and at school; includes resources on teaching these children to read.

DeGeorge, K. L. (1998). Friendship and stories: Using children's literature to teach friendship skills to children with learning disabilities. *Intervention in School and Clinic, 33*(3), 157–162.

> DeGeorge describes friends as people who know and like each other and describes a four-part program for teaching friendship skills to children in primary grades that includes a list of children's books about making friends as well as a sample lesson plan for using one of these books.

Gibbs, J. (2000). *Tribes: A new way of learning and being together*. Santa Rosa, CA: Center Source Publications.

> An excellent resource for establishing and maintaining a classroom where every student feels included; many strategies for teaching students to learn collaboratively.

Kingsley, J., & Levitz, M. (1994). *Count us in: Growing up with Down syndrome*. Orlando, FL: Harcourt Brace & Co.

> This moving book is based on the conversations of two young adults with Down syndrome. They talk poignantly about how their parents have helped them to get to where they are, about their need for independence from their parents, and about their experiences of acceptance and friendship.

Vermette, P. J. (1998). *Making cooperative learning work: Student teams in K–12 classrooms*. Upper Saddle River, NJ: Prentice Hall (Merrill).

> This practical handbook for teachers tackles all the classic problems teachers think they will encounter before they begin using cooperative learning. It includes dozens of classroom examples with practical, sensible solutions that teachers can use as well as brief, engaging summaries of important research studies on cooperative learning.

WEBLINKS

http://www.beachcenter.org/files/FRN-FS-002.pdf
A short paper on strategies to encourage friendships, such as one-to-one matching, existing/formal networks, community activities, and advocacy.

http://www.cdss.ca
Canadian Down Syndrome Society offers articles, Canadian resources, and information for families.

http://www.nads.org/
National Association for Down Syndrome (US) contains links to research, personal stories, and Web sites worldwide.

Always Challenging

Sam Bentley stood at the window and watched the children from his Grade 3/4 class playing tag on the schoolyard. He thought to himself, "It's a good thing they can make their own fun because there aren't many jungle gyms out there for them to climb on." Sam had been teaching at Red Lake School on the Red Lake Reserve for eight months. He continued to be impressed with the children's enthusiasm for toys they had made themselves. They didn't expect a park full of painted climbing apparatus, but Sam had suggested that the school and the community join forces to design and make some swings and climbing bars. Sam loved to build; it used to be his main hobby. He had brought some of his tools to Red Lake. But in the autumn he hadn't known the community well enough to make any suggestions. Even though Sam had taught for three years before deciding to move to Red Lake, he had felt awkward and shy in the autumn. He had taken courses in Native studies in university but had never taught First Nations children before, and there was a lot to learn. Like all isolated communities, Red Lake had to rely on its own resources. This appealed to Sam, but he also knew that it was important to find ways to bring fresh resources and ideas into the community.

Now Sam felt that he understood how Red Lake functioned and some of the roles he could play. Sam smiled when he thought about the success he had had recently in getting a friend of his who runs a bookstore "in the south" to fly in with boxes of books to Red Lake. The children had earned the right to choose new books for the school library by reading. For every book they had read in the month before the books arrived, they could select a new book for the school. Sam and the other three teachers had put half their supplies budget into the project. Every book in Red Lake—from school, home, and the teachers' collections—had been read and reread in that month by children eager to choose new books. Now the school had an exciting collection of new books for children and teachers to use and a simple system to keep track of who was borrowing them.

This simple system told Sam that Brian had already read half the new books. Sam thought about Brian—with his smudged glasses, his outbursts, and his love of reading. Brian would be the first student to have read every new book in the library. Indeed, it was because of Brian that Sam had come up with the plan to get the new books in the first place. Brian was the most challenging aspect of Red Lake for Sam. Brian questioned every idea Sam presented to the class, "And he's often right," Sam said out loud. In addition, Brian seemed to be always testing the limits. Or doing something he knew was wrong. When asked why, he would say, "Just to see what would happen." For example, this morning Brian had stuck out his foot and tripped Tim when he walked by Brian's table. Howling, bleeding, and reprimands had followed.

Sam looked around the classroom. The children's seating was in clusters of three and four at round tables. Piles of new books sat in the middle of the round tables. About five of the children were still in the early literacy stages, excited to be reading pattern books like *Drummer Hoff*. On Sam's desk was one of his favourite new books, *Windows on the World: Plays and Activities Adapted from Folk Tales from Different Lands*, open to a play Sam planned to read that afternoon. The walls were decorated with the children's artwork. Fresh paper was laid out at the painting centre because Sam expected that the children would paint the characters from the play he was going to read today. When he scanned the walls to see where they might put the mural, Sam was surprised to see the Classroom Rules poster that he had made on the first day of school was still up. He had forgotten about it.

As the children ran to the door of the school, Sam wondered what Brian would get up to that afternoon. And why. Brian was in Grade 3, but his results on intelligence tests and achievement tests suggested he functioned more like a sixth grader—in everything but citizenship. Suspecting that Brian was gifted, the teacher who had taught him in Grades 1 and 2 had requested an individual intelligence test when Brian was six. The itinerant psychometrist who had given Brian the test 12 months later was sure that it was not an accurate reflection of Brian's high ability. Even so, his score on the verbal test was 133; on the nonverbal, 129. Sam knew that the average was 100, and that in many school districts a score of 130 would qualify a student for a gifted program. There was no gifted program in Red Lake and, unless the teachers changed the entire organization of the school, Sam would teach Brian in Grade 4 next year.

The students were milling around. "Sit down, people," Sam said gently. As Sam recounted later to his friend and senior teacher, Doris Hill, "For 14 children they sure were making a lot of noise and chaos." Because Sam was soon to start an action research project in his classroom, he had decided to tape his discussion during language arts this afternoon. Hoping for a quiet afternoon, Sam reminded the children that he was going to read the Australian Aboriginal play, "The Great Frog." Sam read the play to them in an animated voice. As Sam later told Doris, "This Australian folk tale takes place in the Dreamtime long ago before humans came to earth. It tells of a frog who swallows all the water on earth. The other animals try to make him laugh so he will release the water. They all fail. The smallest animal, an eel, says that he can make the frog laugh. No one believes the eel. Undaunted, the eel dances, contorting his body wildly. The frog laughs and releases the water."

Sam told Doris that after he had finished reading, he stood by the window and began to lead a discussion about "The Great Frog." Of course, by this time he had forgotten about the tape recorder. After ensuring that the children understood what took place in the play, Sam turned his focus to the way the eel, the smallest animal, might have felt when no one believed him.

SAM: Sometimes parents, like those larger animals with the eel, just don't seem to believe what their children say. Have you ever had your parents not understand or not believe what you say or feel? [*Loud chorus of yeses.*]

SAM: [*encouraging*] Let's read between the lines in our story. I mean let's imagine what Eel must be feeling when nobody believes him. It did not say this in the story, but we can put ourselves in Eel's place, can't we?

ANN: [*eagerly*] I think Eel must have been sad, and maybe he cried.

BRIAN: [*from the table at the back of the room*] That's stupid. Boys don't cry! [*He laughs loudly. Some other boys laugh too.*]

SAM: Brian you have a point. Perhaps boys don't let people see them crying. But Ann is right too.

BRIAN: Ann is a crybaby. She thinks everyone's a baby like her. [*Under his breath.*] She's stupid.

SAM: [*ignoring his last comment*] What do other people think? How must Eel have felt? Yes, Charlie.

CHARLIE: Eel maybe thought they didn't trust him. Maybe he won't tell them things after that.

SAM: [*nodding*] Yes, I can see how Eel could do just that.

BRIAN: [*bursts out*] Eel would feel mad at his parents. And he'd just tell them he didn't care how they felt. If they didn't believe him, he'd just tell them they were dummies.

BARB: You aren't supposed to call your parents dummies.

BRIAN: [*loudly*] That's stupid. If they're dummies, they're dummies. [*His voice rises to a shrill note.*]

Sam realized he had to take this situation in hand, and thought, "I let it go too far."

When he told Doris about his emotion-filled afternoon, he started to laugh. "You won't believe that I captured the whole thing on tape. Only audio, thank goodness. Because I was trying out taping my teaching, getting ready to do action research. So I can listen to it, if I can bring myself to hear the way I let the class get away."

Doris asked in her quiet way, "Do you think the real problems started earlier than this afternoon?" She went on, "What a break. You have a tape of a class that can help you change the way you teach and figure out how to engage Brian in what you're doing. Your action research topic has fallen into your lap."

Sam knew she was right. "I wonder where I should start? They all seemed to listen to me and each other more in the autumn than they do now. And Brian seems, if anything, to challenge me more now. But this was a great play. It should have worked better than it did."

QUESTIONS FOR REFLECTION AND DISCUSSION

1. What are the facts/key elements of the case?
2. What do we know about Sam, the teacher? What do we know about Brian, the student?

3. Describe the major dilemma(s) in the case.

4. What are some underlying issues in this case that might arise from the context in which the case takes place?

5. What actions should Sam take to resolve the dilemma(s)? Consider the consequences of these actions for Brian, for other students, for Sam.

6. How can Sam use action research to help him improve his teaching?

7. What can we learn from this case? What widely held assumptions or beliefs might be called into question by this case? About groups of students, teaching, classrooms?

EXHIBIT 4.1	**Planning Guide for Teaching Gifted Students**

How can I adapt my teaching to meet this student's unique learning needs?

A. How can I change the content so it is more complex, more challenging?
   - Accelerate the student to a higher grade for appropriate subjects.
   - Compact the curriculum to free the student to extend learning in other areas.
   - Use broad-based themes with interdisciplinary connections.
   - Provide authentic problems or cases, or independent study of student-chosen topics.
   - Encourage the student to pursue personal interests and passions.

B. How can I change the learning processes so they are more independent, more meaningful for this student?
   - Involve the student in open-ended tasks that encourage critical thinking or problem solving.
   - Involve the student in research activities with primary and secondary sources of information.
   - Consider programs with intellectual peers like Odyssey of the Mind.
   - Listen to the student's ideas about processes that would be meaningful.

C. How can I change the learning environment to engage the student?
   - Make the classroom more engaging for everyone by consciously changing teaching (consider using action research).
   - Create a community of learners in the classroom; use collaborative learning.
   - Think of the learning environment as the classroom, the school, the community.
   - Consider mentorships or advanced placements for appropriate subjects.

D. How can I change the products that show what students are learning?
   - Focus on application, products made for real audiences (reports to town council, displays, works published in children's literary magazines).
   - Consider student choice of products (dramatizations, multimedia productions).
   - Encourage the student to negotiate products and criteria that meet personal learning goals.

EXHIBIT 4.2	Creating a Classroom Learning Community

Sam decided that he would begin to emphasize the importance of community in his classroom. He thought of community as the general feeling we create when we treat each other with respect. Sam read *Tribes* by Jeanne Gibbs. The following table was developed after reading *Tribes*.

Communication and Community Building

Norms for Communities	What to Do
Negotiation	Replace hostility and confrontation with give-and-take discussion. Don't assume all students know how to negotiate.
Cooperation	Increase the role of cooperation. Create situations that enable individuals to share goals, efforts, and outcomes.
Consensus	Use consensus to build community. Find areas of agreement. Use these to work toward consensus in new areas.
Decentralized management	Share decision making when that is feasible rather than practising authoritarian management.
Work teams	Use work teams to accomplish shared goals. Make work into fun by enjoying one another's company.
Shared responsibility	Foster more ideas, better ideas, strength, and continuity. No one has to feel overwhelmed when people work together.

Source: From *Inclusion of Exceptional Learners in Canadian Schools* by N. L. Hutchinson, 2002, Toronto, ON: Prentice Hall. Reprinted with permission by Pearson Education Canada Inc.

Resources to consult:
Gibbs, J. (2000). *Tribes*. Sausalito, CA: Center Source Systems.
Putnam, J., & Burke, J. B. (1992). *Organizing and managing classroom learning communities*. Toronto, ON: McGraw-Hill.

EXHIBIT 4.3	Strategies for Aboriginal Education

Strategy	Examples
Break down stereotypes	Start with the present; provide examples of Aboriginal Web sites, musicians, artists, professionals, urban and northern dwellers (*Shared Learnings*).
Engage students in Aboriginal culture through the arts	Invite storytellers, singers, dancers, painters, weavers, other artists from the Aboriginal community to collaborate (Butler, 2000).
Help students to understand Aboriginal perspectives	Provide readings, etc., at the students' developmental level: fiction, reports, films from an Aboriginal point of view (Reed, 1999). Invite speakers who are comfortable telling their stories and providing their perspectives (*Shared Learnings*).
Use Aboriginal communication and participant structures	The talking circle, where the right to speak is indicated by passing a concrete object such as a feather (Ward, 1996).
Explicitly discuss Aboriginal values	Teach environmental education through an Aboriginal perspective, "caring for the earth" (Caduto & Bruchac, 1988; Pohl, 1997).
Help students to think critically	Deal with sensitive issues and controversial topics about complex issues like racism, cultural identity in a caring and proactive way. (*Shared Learnings*). Use video series like *First Nations: The Circle Unbroken* to teach about current issues (Williams, Henderson, & Marcuse, 1998).

Source: From *Inclusion of Exceptional Learners in Canadian Schools* by N. L. Hutchinson, 2002, Toronto, ON: Prentice Hall. Reprinted with permission by Pearson Education Canada Inc.

References:
Butler, C. M. (2000). *Cultural awareness through the arts: The success of an Aboriginal antibias program for intermediate students.* Unpublished master's thesis, Queen's University, Kingston, ON.
Caduto, M. J., & Bruchac, J. (1988). *Keepers of the earth: Teacher's guide.* Golden, CO: Fulcrum Publishing.
Pohl, A. (1997, April). Teaching Natives studies. *OPSTF News.*
Reed, K. (1999). *Aboriginal peoples: Building for the future.* Don Mills, ON: Oxford University Press Canada.
Shared Learnings: Integrating B.C. Aboriginal Content, K-10. (B.C. Ministry of Education, 1998). (http://www.bced.gov.bc.ca/abed/shared.htm).
Ward, A. (1996). Beyond "sharing time": Negotiating Aboriginal culture in an urban classroom. *English quarterly, 28*(2/3), 23-28.
Williams, L., Henderson, M., & Marcuse, G. (1998). *The circle unbroken: The teacher's guide (videos 5, 6, 7).* Montreal: National Film Board of Canada.

EXHIBIT 4.4	Action Research

Action research is a way to study your own teaching practice. The intent is to change and improve your practice. Whether you focus on one student or your whole class, the question is, "How can I help my students improve the quality of their learning?"

The four steps to follow are:

1. Identify a concern in your practice.
2. Decide what you will do about this concern.
3. Select the evidence (one or more indicators) that will allow you to make a judgment about what is happening before, during, and after your action research.
4. Think about how you can validate any claims you might make about the success of your action research. Select evidence to show that you have done what you claim to have done.

Typically, action research is carried out over several weeks or a few months. Some improvements in teaching practice take longer to accomplish than others and some require more time for you to demonstrate improvement. Teachers usually start with a concern that they can do something about, something that is important to them and to their students. Talking about your action research with one or more colleagues is a good idea.

What you will do about this concern could be a small change, anything that will be likely to improve the quality of learning for students or even for one student. Starting small and achieving success is more likely to mean you will continue to use action research to improve your practice. When you try to find out if your actions have made a difference, look for indicators of improvement that you can see in what the students do, or what they learn, or in how they treat one another during discussions in the classroom. In the fourth step, always prepare a written report, even if it is very brief. It should summarize the four steps you have taken. Always protect the identity of your students and colleagues in your report. You can use pseudonyms or initials. If you carry out your action research in a university course, you may have to submit your proposal to an ethical review committee in the university. Discuss the report with other teachers and ask for suggestions. Perhaps you and your colleagues will find that you want to support one another in action research as each of you sets out to study your own teaching practice to improve it.

Sources: Adapted from: (1) *The August Week: A Guide for Teacher Candidates* by R. Luce-Kapler and colleagues, 1998. Unpublished manuscript. Kingston, ON: Queen's University Faculty of Education. (2) *You and Your Action Research Project* by J. McNiff, P. Lomax, and J. Whitehead, 1996. London, UK: Routledge.

SUGGESTIONS FOR FURTHER READING

Brant Castellano, M., Davis, L., & Lahache, L. (Eds.). (2000). *Aboriginal education: Fulfilling the promise.* Vancouver, BC: UBC Press.

A thoughtful and thought-provoking volume based on research conducted to inform the education section of the Royal Commission on Aboriginal Peoples report. The emphasis is on models of education that seek to address the needs and dreams of Aboriginal peoples in Canada.

British Columbia Ministry of Education. (1995). *Gifted education: A resource guide for teachers.* Victoria, BC: Queen's Printer for British Columbia.

> A practical classroom guide to understanding what giftedness is, and how you can recognize it, that describes many approaches for teaching gifted students in the regular classroom.

Gibbs, J. (2000). *Tribes: A new way of learning and being together.* Sausalito, CA: CenterSource Systems.

> This practical resource not only includes dozens of community building activities, but also shows teachers how to use collaborative learning in the curriculum subjects.

McNiff, J., Lomax, P., & Whitehead, J. (1996). *You and your action research project.* London, UK: Routledge.

> These three authors share their experiences with action research to produce a highly readable source. Many examples help to show the wide range of aspects of professional practice that teachers could choose to improve in action research.

Putnam, J., & Burke, J. B. (1992). *Organizing and managing classroom learning communities.* Toronto, ON: McGraw-Hill, Inc.

> An unusual resource on classroom management that focuses on the challenges of creating a learning community in the classroom. Practical yet idealistic.

Renzulli, J. S. (2001). *Enriching curriculum for all students.* Arlington Heights, IL: SkyLight.

> This readable source describes the Schoolwide Enrichment Model, one approach to increasing the challenges at school for all students.

Winebrenner, S. (2002). *Teaching gifted kids in the regular classroom: Strategies and techniques every teacher can use to meet the academic needs of the gifted and talented.* Minneapolis, MN: Free Spirit Publishing.

> This great book describes many strategies that teachers have used successfully, including "Most Difficult First," "Compacting the Curriculum," learning contracts, reducing the amount of time students spend on a unit when the general pace is too slow for them, independent study, and more challenging activities.

WEBLINKS

http://www.firstperspective.ca
An online newspaper called *The First Perspective: News of Indigenous Peoples of Canada* that reports on community events, news, culture, and the arts.

http://www.schoolnet.ca/aboriginal/
This government-sponsored Web site includes lesson plans for teachers and links to programs, research, news, and services.

http://edu.yorku.ca/caas
A site intended to help teachers introduce all students to Aboriginal-perspective curriculum content.

http://www3.bc.sympatico.ca/giftedcanada/
A forum for Canadian teachers and parents of gifted children, as well as researchers, to share information, resources, and ideas.

case 5

Striving For Balance

Wang has had a tough day! Another one! "Well actually," he realizes, "it is only noon. Technically it was just a tough morning!" How can one student make such a shambles of a class? "I can't think like that. It doesn't help to blame the student. I know that. When will I ever get assigned a teaching assistant to help me with Jim?" Wang looks over the plan he had made for teaching Jim this week. None of it has happened, yet. It is only noon on Tuesday. But it feels like Friday afternoon. Wang looks at the IEP for Jim. It recommends that Wang use computer-assisted instruction until the school district gets approval to hire another teaching assistant.

It used to be so easy. Wang remembers when the principal requested a teaching assistant in the spring and everything was ready to go in August. With all the recent changes, those days are gone. Approval takes forever and getting the requested paraprofessional is never certain. Or someone could be assigned for a month or two to "solve the problem" and then move on, leaving the teacher alone again.

It is March, already. Last June Wang learned that Jim was deemed to have made enough progress in the behavioural program at Larch Centre that he could return to an inclusive classroom. Jim's aunt lived within walking distance of Main Street School where Wang taught Grade 5. "And that is how I became Jim's teacher," Wang says to no one in particular.

The file said that Jim had been transferred to Larch Centre in November of Grade 1. In Grade 1, Jim started at one school where he lasted for three weeks. After putting his hands around the neck of a Kindergarten girl in the hall and squeezing, Jim was moved to Main Street School. Wang did not remember Jim's short tenure at Main Street. But the file said that Jim had walked in front of cars six times before Halloween of Grade 1. He had told his teacher he wanted to kill himself. During this period, Jim's father had been hospitalized for depression. For the first year Jim was at Larch, he lived in the residential program. Then before New Year's of Grade 2, Jim had moved to the home of his aunt.

Try as he might, Wang could not understand how a family could live like Jim's family seemed to. Wang's family was closely knit and caring. When he had gone away to university, he and his parents had missed each other terribly. Wang and all his siblings had returned to work in the city where they had grown up and his parents still lived. Wang's friends told him his Asian family's tight bonds were unusual, but they were all Wang knew. And a family like Jim's didn't seem like a family at all, to him.

Wang knew that, in the Centre, Jim and seven other children, all boys, had spent half a day in therapy and half a day in the Centre's primary classroom. Usually students returned to their home school at the end of Grade 3. But, because both the therapist and teacher had recommended he was not ready to leave Larch Centre, Jim had stayed an extra year and completed Grade 4 there.

Jim's current home life was a bit of a mystery to Wang. When Jim first came to Main Street School for a meeting last June, he had come with his aunt. The aunt had put considerable pressure on the school to "do the right thing by Jim." A young woman, studying at the community college, with a two-year-old daughter, she seemed to really care about Jim. She had spoken to Wang about the possibility of adopting Jim and asked him not to discuss this issue with Jim, even if Jim brought it up.

For the past month or so, Jim's life had seemed different. It seemed to Wang that during the week Jim still lived with his aunt. It was the weekends that confused Wang. Wang wrote in a communication book and sent it home with Jim, whenever Jim could find the book. It was still signed by his aunt when it came back to school. However, it was rare for Jim to return the book to school the morning after he had taken it home. While Wang had used this strategy successfully with other students, it had not been working for Jim in the past month or so.

Recently Jim had been wild in the classroom, running and spinning around like a top. He was running into other students, shouting at them, and storming out of the classroom. Jim hated to be laughed at and would lash out with his fists at any student who made fun of him. Last week he had punched an older boy on the schoolyard and yesterday he had fought with one of the boys in Wang's class—shouting, pounding with his fists, kicking, and knocking the boy to the ground. Wang hated to think what would have happened if he had not shouted at Jim and distracted him from his tirade.

According to Jim, he had recently begun spending weekends with "my real mother and father, so they can show them!" When Wang asked him what they would show them and who "them" was, Jim's response was confused and angry. Wang's guess was that Jim's parents were being given a chance on weekends to prove that they were fit parents. What pressure for a disturbed child and parents, one of whom has been hospitalized for depression! Wang supposed that if they were successful in convincing the authorities, they would regain custody of Jim. This seemed a cruel test. But what would be a better way? This arrangement made Jim confused and angry. He acted like his parents were on trial. And Wang wondered how it must make Jim's aunt feel.

Judging by Jim's recent outbursts at school, all this new tension and uncertainty was not helping him remain stable and in control of himself. One of Jim's behaviours that had always been troublesome, but had recently grown worse, was his noises. Apparently Jim used to bang his head on the desk in Grade 1 as well as groan, grunt, and "blow raspberries." Now, when asked to complete written work, Jim would begin to groan, grunt, and make loud, wet "raspberries" by blowing air through his lips. At first, Wang had tried to ignore them, hoping they would go away. Then he moved Jim to a desk by himself, turned to face the wall. Then the principal had suggested that, when Jim made noises, Wang ask him if he would like to leave the room to work in the library. During the three weeks when Wang had offered this option to Jim, Jim had never declined. But at the end of three weeks, the librarian said, "No!" She was not Jim's teacher, she did not know what he was expected to do in the assigned work, and Jim only paid attention to the written work when the librarian stood beside him. From the seat he had been assigned in the library, he could see everyone who entered and left the library and all the computer stations. So much to be distracted by!

So, Jim was back, having exhausted his welcome in the library. Wang was disappointed because he had hoped to set Jim up to work at computer-mediated instruction on a computer in the library. That option was pretty well ruined now. The librarian, who provided computer support for the teachers, had offered to help Wang and Jim choose software, tasks, and an organizational strategy to use computer-mediated learning in the classroom. At least she had become aware of Jim's needs during his sojourn in the library.

Just last week, Wang had learned a great deal. He decided to talk with Jim directly about the noises. He had been giving an explanation of a math question to a student who sat near Jim. When Jim began to make noises, Wang went to Jim and told him, "I am having trouble concentrating on explaining this problem to Jean. Do you know that you make loud noises that interrupt other people's concentration?"

Jim seemed surprised. "You can hear me?" Since then, Wang had used a hand signal to show Jim that he was too loud and needed to stop making noises. Wang felt silly. He wondered whether Jim really didn't realize how loud he was. So far, the direct approach had helped more than anything else.

If Jim was quieter, maybe he could concentrate better. But Wang suspected that it was much more complex than that. Jim seemed so highly distractible. He didn't follow through on written work, he didn't hear oral instructions, and he lost everything he touched, it seemed. Mathematics was particularly difficult for Jim. Wang knew that the Larch Centre primary teacher emphasized language arts in her half-day program, but Wang wondered how much math and science she managed to fit in.

Wang had found it difficult to enact the recommendation for Jim to work on a computer. The classroom computers had many programs loaded on them. Unless Wang monitored him, Jim gave up on the math programs after a few minutes and played games. Some of the other students complained that Jim received privileges on the computer when he had not done his work, while they had put more effort into their assigned work, and did not get computer opportunities. Wang had tried to explain that we are all different. But it was difficult to defend anything that would appear to be rewarding Jim, because Jim caused chaos in the classroom.

Right from the beginning, Jim's aunt had been fearful about his acceptance by the class and fearful for the safety of the other children. She understood that he seemed to deliberately annoy people and reported that her own family and friends had asked her not to bring Jim to their homes. Wang had seen Jim cry when other children did not invite him to their birthday parties. But Wang understood the other parents' concerns about taking responsibility for a boy who threatened other students on his bad days and annoyed them on his good days.

Right from the start, Wang had expressed to Jim's aunt his concerns about how much support for Jim he could realistically promise—while at the same time he had reassured her that he could meet Jim's needs and still ensure the safety of the rest of the class. It was a tall order, and Wang still felt overwhelmed some days, like today. If he was not careful, Wang knew he could spend 10 minutes out of every hour helping Jim to focus, ensuring Jim understood the instructions, encouraging Jim to stay with the computer-mediated math instruction instead of playing a computer game, and so on. Before he realized what he was doing, Wang had jotted down a list of questions:

1. Is the educational assistant going to be assigned to this class?
2. When?
3. If not, who can help me balance my responsibilities to the rest of the class and to Jim?
4. If there is an assistant or a volunteer to pay individual attention to Jim, what am I allowed to ask this person to do?
5. Can I ask for a meeting of the in-school team to help me with Jim?
6. How do I ensure that all the other children are safe in my classroom?
7. How do I find out what is going on in Jim's life?
8. How do I get control of my class again?

QUESTIONS FOR REFLECTION AND DISCUSSION

1. What are the facts/key elements of the case?
2. What do we know about Wang, the teacher? What do we know about Jim, the student?
3. Describe the major dilemma(s) in the case.
4. What are some underlying issues in this case?
5. Describe Jim's experiences in Wang's classroom, as Jim might describe them to his parents. Describe the situation from the librarian's perspective.
6. What actions should Wang take to resolve the major dilemma(s)? Consider the consequences of these actions for Jim, for Wang, for the other students in the class.
7. What can we learn from this case? Does this case cause us to question any beliefs or to recognize assumptions we might be making about exceptional students, teachers, or classrooms?

EXHIBIT 5.1	**Excerpt from Individual Education Plan (IEP)**

Student name: Jim Mills
School: Main Street School

Grade: 5
Teacher: Wang Chin

BACKGROUND INFORMATION: Jim's academic functioning on individually administered assessment instruments is at grade level (language arts) or near grade level (mathematics), which is consistent with individually administered cognitive test scores that show average potential. His performance in classroom work is below grade expectations and difficult to assess because it is incomplete. Jim refuses to complete academic work in group settings, preferring individual instruction. Behavioural observations and assessment instruments show improvement in social-emotional functioning: more self-regulation, absence of self-injurious behaviour, and some participation in group activities following Behavioural Program at Larch Centre.

RECOMMENDATIONS:

1. Regular classroom placement with full-time educational assistant.
2. Computer-assisted instruction in absence of educational assistant.
3. Regular observations of classroom behaviour by school psychologist.

| EXHIBIT 5.2 | Working with Students with Behavioural Problems in the Regular Classroom |

The rationale for placing students with behaviour problems in the regular classroom is based on research demonstrating that the most effective way to teach students behaviours they are lacking is to expose them to others who demonstrate the behaviours. In the case of prosocial skills, it seems logical that a student lacking age-appropriate interpersonal skills would learn these skills better from students who demonstrate them than from students who lack these skills. There is, however, no guarantee that exposure will result in learning.

Direct instruction of desired target skills is often required to ensure that students learn them. This usually requires collaboration between a classroom teacher and a highly skilled professional or paraprofessional who can work individually or with a small group of students with behaviour problems.

Making the regular classroom as effective as possible for the student with behavioural problems and the rest of the class requires:

- an organized classroom and learning environment
- successful experiences for all students
- high expectations + high support
- a structured behaviour management program
- collaboration with special education staff and paraprofessionals
- data about the impact of programs implemented
- a focus on self-management and self-monitoring

When developing a structured behaviour management program, it is important to:

- ask the key question: "What do I want the student to do in place of the problem behaviour?"
- ask the second important question: "What is the most effective and efficient means to help the student reach his or her goals?"
- conduct an assessment that tells you the rate at which the student engages in the desired replacement behaviour, and that provides you with records of events and actions prior to and following the desired replacement behaviour
- develop behaviour objectives; negotiate these with the student
- develop an intervention; teach the student the desired behaviour and reward the student when the new response is used
- evaluate how well the intervention is working

Source: Developed after reading *Teaching Students with Behavioral Disorders* by T. J. Lewis, J. Heflin, and S. A. DiGangi, 1991, Reston, VA: Council for Exceptional Children.

EXHIBIT 5.3	A Letter about Using Technology for Learning

In his frustration with the current situation, Wang wrote a letter to a friend who was teaching in Albuquerque, New Mexico, on a teacher exchange. Wang knew that one of the purposes of the exchange was for his friend, Maxine, to work in a school with a model computer program. This is the letter Wang received from Maxine:

March 20th

Dear Wang,

It sounds like you have your hands full. Let me tell you about Albuquerque. It is almost 20°C here already. The flowers are blooming, and the sunsets are incredible. I can hardly believe that it is already past the middle of March. Three months from now, the school year will be finished here, and my long-awaited exchange will be over. I have learned so much! I am so pleased you asked! Now I have a chance to tell you all about this amazing class! I expect to be back in Saskatoon next year, but maybe you can come and visit my classroom. I am going to set it up just like this class.

Remember I told you that there was a published paper about the class? You can find it in *Teaching Exceptional Children,* the summer issue of 1994, pages 56 to 60. The class is still very much like the article. Technology is used as a tool for learning. The teacher invites the children to discover how the software and hardware work through play for about two months at the beginning of the year. That way the children have ownership of the classroom and the technology. This school is in a poor neighbourhood, and about half the children are exceptional learners; but when new software comes, we give it to a group of children to figure out, and they do. Once they master it, they are the resident experts and teach the rest of us. I have seen them asking other kids to help them read the manual when all else fails. We usually use themes for our teaching. Frequently, groups of kids will create learning activities, often at a computer, for the rest of the class. Or create a big book for everyone to read. When anything new comes, we have to remember to give time for play and exploration. There are many problems to solve—technological, interpersonal, and academic. The students become amazing little problem solvers. One day the principal came into the room and saw some children figuring out how the laser disk worked. He asked them to show him. Were they proud!

I just came across another article that might be more pertinent right now for your challenges with the student with behaviour difficulties. It is in *Intervention in School and Clinic,* volume 33, issue 3, September 1997, pages 65 to 69. It describes a technique for using peer tutors to deliver computer-based instruction. You would need to choose appropriate software for your student's needs in math and choose a willing and patient tutor competent in math and experienced with computers. I suggest you make a contract, a point sheet, and a poster showing the tutor's and the "tutee's" roles. The tutor and tutee can each award a point for a successful session, and you can award points when you see particularly good cooperation, learning, and tutoring. It is all explained in the article. Hope you can find it. Some teachers here have used the Math Blaster computer program for peer tutoring. You might want to look at that one.

Well, I had better go. It is getting late, and I want to try out a new program tonight that I loaded into my home computer this afternoon. I can't keep ahead of these kids!

Write again! Good luck with your challenges, and see you in the summer,

Maxine

EXHIBIT 5.4	Preventing Fights

Teachers can take actions to prevent fights from breaking out. These preventive actions can be taken well ahead of any incident occurring.

Rules—clear to students. State rules frequently in a positive manner, in language that all students understand. Spell out rewards and negative consequences and then apply them consistently.

Classroom climate—positive and respectful. Make the classroom appealing and ensure that all students feel safe.

Teaching—engaging and relevant. Make the ideas clear to all students and ensure that they understand. Teach students to be in control of themselves and their learning, while teaching the academic content by providing opportunities for them to exercise voice, choice, and self-regulation.

Student conflicts—handle them immediately. Better still, anticipate what is coming. This way conflicts can be kept at a low level, and escalation prevented.

Sometimes students feel themselves losing control. You can teach students to calm themselves and prevent conflicts.

Teach students to **recognize** the signs of anger. Physiological signs include increased rate of breathing, pressure in the chest, and feeling flushed and hot.

Students can **slow** down (e.g., count to 10) and **assess** the nature of the problem (what am I doing?).

They should list the **alternatives** to anger and fighting and choose a peaceful alternative.

Help students to **evaluate** the consequences of their problem solving and to **repeat** the process if necessary.

Sources to consult:
Hutchinson, N. L., & Freeman, J. G. (1994). *Pathways: Anger management on the job.* Scarborough, ON: ITP Nelson Canada.
Meese, R. L. (1997). Student fights: Proactive strategies for preventing and managing student conflicts. *Intervention in School and Clinic, 33*(1), 26-29, 35.

SUGGESTIONS FOR FURTHER READING

Cartledge, G., & Johnson, C. T. (1996). Inclusive classrooms for students with emotional and behavioral disorders: Critical variables. *Theory Into Practice, 35*(1), 51–57.

This helpful paper begins with the premise that, to be socially integrated, a child must be socially accepted by peers, have at least one reciprocal friendship, and be an active participant in the activities of the peer group.

Meese, R. L. (1997). Student fights: Proactive strategies for preventing and managing student conflicts. *Intervention in School and Clinic, 33*(1), 26–29, 35.

Meese explores some of the reasons students fight at school and suggests proactive strategies with the emphasis on creating a positive classroom atmosphere, consistently rewarding all students for positive classroom interactions, and consistently administering logical consequences for infractions of the agreed-upon rules.

Pudney, W., & Whitehouse, E. (1996). *A volcano in my tummy: Helping children to handle anger.* Gabriola Island, BC: New Society Publishers.

This creative resource is about helping 6- to 15-year-olds to handle their anger; includes activities for groups and individuals, as well as guidelines for incorporating the activities into curriculum teaching.

Sitko, M. C., & Sitko, C. J. (1996). *Exceptional solutions: Computers and students with special needs.* London, ON: Althouse Press.

Describes the application of computers and telecommunications to facilitate communication by exceptional students, with chapters focusing on a range of topics, including supporting oral language for young children with communication handicaps, and improving written language of adolescents with learning disabilities.

Smith, R. G. (1997). Integrating computer-based instruction and peer tutoring. *Intervention in School and Clinic, 33*(3), 65–69.

Smith describes methods teachers can use to combine Class-Wide Peer Tutoring (CWPT) and computer-based instruction (CBI) to match software and learning from a computer to the instructional objectives in a student's IEP.

Woodward, J., & Cuban, L. (Eds.). (2001). *Technology, curriculum, and professional development: Adapting schools to meet the needs of students with disabilities.* Thousand Oaks, CA: Corwin Press.

A comprehensive resource on the current state of the art in using technology to meet the needs of students with a wide range of disabilities.

WEBLINKS

http://www.schoolzone.co.uk/teachers/jft/GoodPractice/classroom/Special_needs/ Behaviour.htm
A British site that includes a brief article on how teachers can set up effective behaviour contracts.

http://www.peacemakers.ca/
Peacemakers Trust is a Canadian, non-profit organization dedicated to research, education, and consultation on conflict resolution. The bibliography of resources is excellent.

http://www.cln.org/subjects/general_inst.html
"Collections of Lesson Plans" within the Web site of the Open Learning Agency of British Columbia. Includes lesson plans for using information technology in creative ways to meet student needs.

Why Hasn't Someone Told Me About This Before?

It was only the last week of September, but Sally Yandon felt like she had been back at school for months. Summer vacation now seemed like an ancient dream. When the slowest members of the Grade 1 class had finally left for the day, she went to the staff room to brew a pot of tea and carried it back to her classroom.

There were two children in Sally's class of 20 who had IEPs and one who had been tested by a psychologist in August. Mae Abbott, the principal, had explained to Sally before school started that these parents had asked for their children to be placed in Sally's class because they knew she would ensure that their children were learning. Sally was first flattered and then annoyed. It wasn't fair that she was being punished for her success. Was this still an inclusive classroom when so many children had special needs? Sally had known she couldn't go into the year with that attitude. Either she agreed to teach these exceptional children and did it enthusiastically or she asked for a change of student list in August. She had asked herself, "Do I have enough time and energy to teach all these children well?" Although there were no children with IEPs in the other Grade 1 class, Sally had decided against asking for a change in the class lists.

The irony of the situation made Sally laugh to herself. The two children with IEPs had made a great start to the year. Abdul wore a hearing aid and was a bit shy, but so far he seemed to be keeping up. Patsy had suffered traumatic brain injury a year ago and had an educational assistant with her at all times. She seemed to be still recovering and was primarily with her peers for social benefits and language development. Both these children's disabilities had intimidated Sally at first. But the real puzzle now was Mitch, who had not worried her at all in August when she had received his psychological report—Mitch, who was bright and talkative and still only knew a few letter names and sounds. In the last week, Mitch had refused to come to the carpet for Big Books, thrown a book at Sally, and run away at recess. When she asked him why, he said, "I can't read!" and burst into tears.

Sally studied the report for Mitch Cherniak one more time. The last sentence made her smile grimly: "Mitch is a bright boy who wants to learn and with some additional help with the basics should soon begin to succeed in school." Sally thought about all the children she had taught to read. Nothing in the report she had received the week before school (see Exhibit 1) had prepared her for Mitch. Contradictions abounded. This talkative little boy who often knew the meanings of words that other children had never heard of—how could he not know the names and sounds of the letters? But he didn't. And he was growing more frustrated every day. Sally had taught his older sister, and she knew the family. The Cherniaks cared, they read to their children, and they had warned Sally that Mitch was easily frustrated by books and letters and everything that had to do with reading.

But he was not the only one who was frustrated! Sally could match him and raise him in the frustration department! Like many Grade 1 teachers, Sally loved the August ritual of coming into the classroom early, unpacking the boxes of books that had been packed up hurriedly in June, and starting fresh. She looked now at the wonderful collection of children's books and at the reading bathtub and at the reading centres and activity cards. She had made great progress with her gentle introduction of centres and patterned books...and if it weren't for Mitch she would feel like it had been a good start-up. But Mitch! What Sally had described on Parents' Night as her balanced reading program seemed anything but balanced right now. For most of the students, it was fun and they would be reading in no time. But Mitch was different. He tried, he wanted to read, but he simply could not remember the words or even the patterns and rhymes in the repetitive books.

Sally had not found any solutions in the psychologist's report that was dated August 22. It certainly described all the problems she had seen, but that was about it. What was she supposed to do about it? When she had telephoned the psychologist who carried out the testing, the psychologist had suggested Sally would need to teach Mitch phonemic awareness. "But why didn't you say that in the report?" Sally asked. "You said he would need help with the basics. I have a balanced reading program, and it works for most of the students. Many years, there are one or two who develop slowly and can't get onto reading, like Mitch. But they usually come from homes where there are no books, the parents don't read, and they have not been talked to, let alone taught the alphabet. But Mitch's parents are both teachers, and he has had every opportunity to learn. This shouldn't be happening. I really don't want to tinker with a successful program for the sake of one student. What about everyone else? Won't this interfere with their learning to read? And I can't give him much individual attention—this is Grade 1. They get away quickly when the teacher isn't hands-on with them!"

Sue Doran, the psychologist, suggested that balanced reading programs emphasized meaningful reading; after all, that was their main goal. But increasingly such programs were being supplemented by experiences that drew children's attention to the phonemic basis of language. She suggested Sally work on developing phonemic awareness with the whole class and find a way for someone, perhaps a volunteer, to continue this with a small group made up of Mitch and his peers who were not responding to her existing reading program. Sally reflected on all this: So what was phonemic awareness and how come a veteran Grade 1 teacher didn't know these things? Who could do the individual or small-group tutoring? Sue had suggested retired persons. "Try recruiting at McDonald's; I'm serious, a retired crowd goes there for coffee every day. High school kids who want to do cooperative education in a classroom and college and university students who want to help are good, too. If it takes too long to recruit them, consider for this term using those few volunteers who still come into your school weekly."

Sue had then offered to send a package of articles to Sally. The package arrived in today's inter-school delivery—the usual blue pouch that said "Lakeland School District." And Sally was eager to see if there was anything helpful. (Contents of the pouch are listed in Suggestions for Further Reading.)

First out of the blue pouch was a paper that included an annotated bibliography of books that played with speech. Many of these books were already in Sally's collection, but the article emphasized how to draw children's attention to the sounds, systematically, and to get them to play with the sounds. There was another paper by the same author, Yopp, that suggested four kinds of phonemic awareness activities. Sally was surprised to see that it suggested these activities should be done with groups rather than individuals. Other papers that were harder to read summarized the research that showed phonemic awareness was most often the missing link for students who struggled to learn to read or who developed reading disabilities.

What about all the students who normally succeeded in Sally's classes? Where had they learned phonemic awareness? She had taught these skills only incidentally in her literacy program. Would they be bored and restless if she tried to introduce these activities that she thought they didn't really need? And would group activities be intense enough for Mitch and Rae-Anne and Billy, the three who really needed phonemic awareness? Sally struggled: she understood how Rae-Anne and Billy had missed learning about letter names and sounds, and had not played with language. These parents couldn't name their child's favourite book, a question Sally asked each family when they came to the school, or on the telephone when she was talking to them. But she knew that Mitch had been read to, and his parents did play with language and sang nursery rhymes to him.

As Sally worked her way through the papers in the blue pouch, she realized that Mitch was at risk for learning disabilities. This was probably why he had been tested. And because Lakeland School District did not identify learning disabilities until Grade 3, Sally realized how important it was for her to help him. Her reading had told her that Grade 3 would be really late to start interventions for Mitch. Sally thought out loud, "Why does so much responsibility fall to the classroom teacher? I have two students with IEPs. Then there's Mitch, whose testing didn't tell me what to do. And even if Mitch has a learning disability, it won't be identified for two more years in Lakeland. If I hadn't phoned Sue, I wouldn't have this pouch of papers. And if I had been as busy with my own family as I usually am, I wouldn't have had time to read all this stuff. There must be a lot of Mitches and Rae-Annes and Billys falling through the cracks, without IEPs, and with high needs. Who should be doing something about this? Phonemic awareness—why hasn't someone told me about this before now?"

QUESTIONS FOR REFLECTION AND DISCUSSION

1. What are the facts/key elements of the case?

2. What do we know about Sally Yandon, the Grade 1 teacher? What do we know about the student, Mitch Cherniak?

3. Describe the major dilemma(s) confronting Sally Yandon.

4. How else can the problem be framed? From the perspective of a student who is thriving in Sally's class or from the perspective of that student's parents? From Mitch's perspective, or the perspective of his parents?

5. What should Sally do to resolve the major dilemma(s)? What are the consequences of these solutions for Mitch, his classmates, Sally?

6. What generalizations can be made from this case? What assumptions or beliefs should be questioned that are widely held about teaching reading, about Grade 1, about exceptional students like Mitch?

EXHIBIT 6.1	**Psychologist's Report**

Name: Mitchell Cherniak
D.O.B.: June 10, 1994
Age: 6 years, 2 months
Date of Assessment: August 18, 2000

BACKGROUND INFORMATION

Mitchell is a six-year-old boy going into Grade 1 this following September. He is the younger of two children. His sister has not experienced any difficulties in school. Mitch has had some behaviour problems in Kindergarten and has not experienced much success. On the recommendation of both his parents and the classroom teacher, a decision was made to assess Mitch prior to the start of Grade 1.

PRESENT ASSESSMENT

During the present assessment, Mitch tried very hard to do all that was asked. He was very disappointed when he didn't succeed but continued to try hard.

On the WISC, which is a measure of general intelligence, Mitch scored at the 93rd percentile (in the superior range) on the Verbal Scale, at the 81st percentile (in the high average range) on the Performance Scale, and at the 91st percentile (in the superior range) on the Full Scale score.

Mitch's highest scores were on the subtest of Similarities, which is a measure of verbal reasoning, and on Vocabulary. These two tests are a very good measure of potential for school success. Mitch also did very well on the subtest of Block Design, which is a measure of non-verbal reasoning. The only areas on which Mitch scored below average were Digit Span and Object Assembly. The score on Digit Span is a measure of short-term memory for numbers. It can reflect distractibility, but Mitch scored above average on Coding, which is a measure of visual memory and also reflects attention to detail.

On the academic assessment, Mitch was able to recite only the first seven letters of the alphabet orally and, when asked to write it, experienced a great deal of difficulty. He printed only five letters, some in upper case and some in lower case. When asked to print the numbers from 1 to 10, he printed only four numbers and he reversed the numbers 3 and 7.

Mitch was also able to name three sounds of the alphabet and he was able to read a four-word sentence after it was read to him first. He has a great deal of difficulty colouring pictures and keeping within set limits.

SUMMARY

Mitch is a very pleasant, attractive six-year-old boy who is rather immature for his age. He is the younger of two children. His older sister has never experienced any difficulties in school. Mitch has had some difficulties this past year with his behaviour in kindergarten and has not succeeded academically. Mitch scored in the high average range or better on the Verbal, Performance, and Full Scale scores on the WISC, which is a measure of general intelligence. His highest scores were on Similarities and Vocabulary, which are good indicators of potential for school success. He also scored very high on Block Design, which is a measure of non-verbal reasoning. His poorest scores and the only ones below average were on Digit Span, which is a measure of short-term auditory memory for numbers, and Object Assembly, which measures the ability to reconstruct a whole from parts.

On the academic assessment Mitch had great difficulties reciting the alphabet orally and great difficulties writing it. He knows a few sounds of the alphabet and can read a short sentence of four words after it has been read to him. He was not able to write the numbers from 1 to 10 and reversed two of the numbers he did write. Mitch's fine motor co-ordination is poor. He had great difficulties colouring pictures within limits.

Mitch is a bright boy who wants to learn and, with some additional help with the basics, should soon begin to succeed in school.

Report written by: Sue Doran, B.A., M.Ed.
Dated: August 27, 2000

EXHIBIT 6.2	Teaching Phonemic Awareness

Sally Yandon's Notes Made While Reading about Phonemic Awareness

Phonemic awareness

- It is a sensitivity to, and explicit awareness of, individual sounds that make up words.
- It demands that children analyze or manipulate the sounds rather than focus on the meaning.
- Early skills include recognizing rhyming, and later skills include segmenting the sounds in words and synthesizing the sounds in words.

General teaching ideas

- Read widely about phonemic awareness.
- Start with easy tasks and build up gradually.
- Teach explicitly, because children who lack phonemic awareness do not usually generalize well and are at risk of developing reading disabilities.
- Develop 15- to 20-minute daily activities for a group that supplement, and are a natural extension of, shared reading activities.
- Use literature and play with the sounds in language; make it fun!

Instructional Guidelines for Planning Phoneme Awareness Activities

1. Identify the precise phonemic awareness task on which you wish to focus, and select developmentally appropriate activities for engaging children in the task. Activities should be fun and exciting—"play" with sounds, don't "drill" them.
2. Be sure to use phoneme sounds (represented by / /) and *not* letter names when doing the activities. Likewise, remember that one sound may be represented by two or more letters. There are only three sounds in the word *cheese:* /ch/-/ee/-/z/. You may want to target specific sounds/words at first and "practise" beforehand until you are comfortable making them.
3. Continuant sounds (e.g., /m/, /s/, /l/) are easier to manipulate and hear than stop consonants (e.g., /t/, /g/, /p/). When introducing continuants, exaggerate by holding on to them: rrrrrring; for stop consonants, use iteration (rapid repetition): /k/-/k/-/k/-/k/-/k/atie.
4. When identifying sounds in different positions, the *initial* position is easiest, followed by the *final* position, with the *medial* position being most difficult (e.g., *t*op, po*t*, le*t*ter).
5. When identifying or combining sound sequences, a CV pattern should be used before a VC pattern, followed by a CVC pattern (e.g., pie, egg, red).

Note: CV = consonant-vowel; VC = vowel-consonant; CVC = consonant-vowel-consonant.

Source: From "How Now Brown Cow: Phoneme Awareness Activities for Collaborative Classrooms" by P. J. Edelen-Smith, 1997, *Intervention in School and Clinic, 33*(2), 103–111. Copyright © 1997 by PRO-ED, Inc. Reprinted with permission.

Awareness of Onset and Rime

Onset and Rime:

In families of words (like lend, send, tend), the initial consonant (l, s, t) is the onset, and the following vowel/consonant combination (end) is the rime.

Word Families:

1. Play games and put the resulting words on charts. For example, say /b/ + it = *b*it. Ask the children to name other words that sound like *bit*.
2. Use literature. For example, *Tog the Dog* (Hawkins & Hawkins, 1986) places various onsets in front of the rime /og/. Many of the books recommended by Yopp could be used to create reference books of families of words. These could be used in making new rhymes. Remember to say the words and draw attention constantly to the sounds.

Literature:

Choose books with rhyme patterns (many by Dr. Seuss), and with alliteration (e.g., *Aster Aardvark's Alphabet Adventures* by Kellogg, 1987), and with assonance (e.g., *Moses Supposes His Toeses Are Roses* by Patz, 1983). Raffi's tapes contain many songs with these patterns.

Direct Teaching:

1. Say pairs of words and ask if they sound the same or different (e.g., run, sun and hit, pan).
2. Say a list of words and ask which is the odd one out (e.g., kite, site, pen, right).
3. Create card games, songs, and picture collections that provide opportunities for children to say words, attend to their sounds, and decide whether specific sounds are the same or different.

Simple Phonemic Awareness

Targeted Skill	Example
Isolated sound recognition	Sammy snake sound says _____. (/s/)
Word/syllable/phoneme counting	How many (words/syllables/sounds) do you hear in this (sentence/word)?
Sound synthesis	It starts with /l/ and ends with /ight/, put it together and it says _____. (*light*)
What word am I saying?	Put these sounds together to make a word— /f/-/i/-/sh/.
Sound-to-word matching	Is there a /k/ in cat? What is the first sound you hear in dog?
Identification of sound positions	Where do you hear the /g/ in *pig* (at the beginning, middle, or end of the word)?
Sound segmentation	What sounds do you hear in the word *ball*? Say each one.
Letter-sound association	What letter goes with the first sound in this word—*book*?

Source: From "How Now Brown Cow: Phoneme Awareness Activities for Collaborative Classrooms" by P. J. Edelen-Smith, 1997, *Intervention in School and Clinic*, 33(2), 103–111. Copyright © 1997 by PRO-ED, Inc. Reprinted with permission.

EXHIBIT 6.3	Characteristics of Learning Disabilities in Young Children

Problems in Reading

- often lacks awareness of sounds that make up words; does not "attack" a new word but guesses or waits for the teacher to say the word.
- loses meaning of sentence before getting to the end; loses sequence of what has been read.
- is painful to listen to, finds reading painful and finds creative ways to avoid reading.

Difficulty in Copying

- copying from a page beside him is better than copying from the board; appears careless.
- loses his place frequently and ignores organizational cues.

Difficulty With Alphabet

- difficulty remembering sounds of letters and names of letters.
- confuses letter names and sounds if learning both at once.
- poor penmanship, frequent reversals, distorted shapes and sizes of letters (and numbers).

Strengths

- often shows strengths in some areas and weaknesses in others, and really benefits from recognition for his strengths.
- often expresses ideas better orally than in writing.
- often highly motivated by small successes and willing to work very hard to succeed again.
- often shows imagination and complex ideas when asked to draw or act out his ideas, but reverts to simpler ideas when writing, to avoid errors or embarrassment.

SUGGESTIONS FOR FURTHER READING

Cummings, R., & Fisher, G. (1995). *The school survival guide for kids with LD.* Minneapolis, MN: Free Spirit Publishing.

    Written for young people with learning disabilities, at a low reading level, this illustrated guide contains tips and strategies in many areas including coping with tests, getting help, and staying out of trouble for children eight and up.

Edelen-Smith, P. J. (1997). How now brown cow: Awareness activities for collaborative classrooms. *Intervention in School and Clinic, 33*(2), 103–111.

    Highly recommended. Readable and clear enough to serve as a guide for implementing a phonemic awareness program.

Ericson, L., & Fraser Juliebo, M. (1998). *The phonological awareness handbook for kindergarten and primary teachers*. Newark, DE: International Reading Association.

> In a short, readable handbook, two Canadian teachers have introduced the research and developed a teaching sequence that includes activities and tests.

Winebrenner, S. (1996). *Teaching kids with learning difficulties in the regular classroom*. Minneapolis, MN: Free Spirit Publishing.

> Begins with how to make everyone feel welcome in the classroom, and includes many activities and forms that can be photocopied.

Yopp, H. K. (1995). Read-aloud books for developing phonemic awareness: An annotated bibliography. *The Reading Teacher, 48,* 538–543.

> Provides teachers with lists of excellent children's books and with many suggestions for how to supplement the meaning-based reading program with fun phonemic awareness activities.

The Readings in the Lakeland Blue Pouch that Sally Received:

Edelen-Smith, P. J. (1997). How now brown cow: Awareness activities for collaborative classrooms. *Intervention in School and Clinic, 33*(2), 103–111.

Jerger, M. A. (1996). Phoneme awareness and the role of the educator. *Intervention in School and Clinic, 32*(1), 5–13.

Yopp, H. K. (1992). Developing phonemic awareness in young children. *The Reading Teacher, 45,* 696–703.

Yopp, H. K. (1995). Read-aloud books for developing phonemic awareness: An annotated bibliography. *The Reading Teacher, 48,* 538–543.

WEBLINKS

http://www.ldac-taac.ca/english/ldac.htm

The Canadian Association for Learning Disabilities site has a great deal of general information on learning disabilities with links to research, scholarships, and provincial and local organizations.

http://www.ldonline.org

Helpful for teachers, parents, and other professionals; contains personal stories as well as recent research findings.

http://ca.geocities.com/phonological

This site provides phonological awareness tests, activities for developing phonological awareness, and links for children and adults to many other resources.

case 7

Why Can't Annie Listen and Finish Her Work?

Marge Wilson looked over the report card one more time. It said Annie, but it could have been Mason's report card three years ago. Now in Grade 6, Mason was tall and confident. He didn't mind attending the resource room or having the resource teacher teaching in the classroom alongside his classroom teacher. When Mason was in Grade 3, his teacher had called Marge around the end of September to say that she thought Mason should be assessed by a psychologist. Marge was surprised and hurt at the time. What could be wrong with her wonderful, caring little boy? But now she appreciated the careful assessments and Individual Education Plans that had helped Mason navigate successfully through the assignments, tests, and report cards from Grade 3 to Grade 6.

"Annie is different," Marge thought to herself. "Annie doesn't want anyone to help her. Annie who draws and sings and wants to put on plays." But the report card was not different.

Marge smiled when she looked at Annie's reflections form that she had filled in to be attached to her report card. Annie had said she did her best work when "it is quiet," and that she needed to improve in "math," and was good at "gym because I run fast." She had said that she liked to "read." The report card contained letter evaluations for a number of items under social and personal skills, language, mathematics and science, and the arts. Few of these letter evaluations showed Annie was "making expected progress." Most suggested she was "showing improvement" or was "progressing with close supervision." Marge wondered why Annie's teacher had not contacted her during the fall term. This was a poor report for a bright young girl who liked to read, liked to get her friends to take part in plays, and showed an intense curiosity at home about the world. "I think I had better take the initiative and phone Ms. Way," Marge decided.

The next morning Marge phoned the school. When Marge had met Ms. Way, Annie's teacher, in September she had been surprised to hear that it was her first year teaching. Ms. Way was about Marge's age. She told the parents that she had returned to university after her third child had started school. When Marge phoned, Ms. Way was quick to return her call, but sounded surprised.

Student Achievement Record – Supplementary Report

Annie, you are a friendly and caring student. You are beginning to listen in class discussions. You need to listen attentively to instructions and complete your written work more independently. You are easily distracted, and you find it difficult to complete your work without supervision. You have a difficult time organizing your work and your belongings. We will focus on improving these areas next term.

I am pleased with the improvement in your reading skills. Please continue to read every night to develop your fluency and speed. I encourage you to practise your spelling and phonic skills as well. When you take your time, you can produce neat work.

You have a good grasp of some concepts we have learned in math. You are making slow but steady improvement in your math abilities. Please continue to work on addition and subtraction facts to 18 at home. Subtraction with regrouping is a challenge for you. We will continue to work on this concept this term. You are an active participant in the arts. You produce pieces that are original and creative. Keep up the improved effort next term!

Three days later Marge was meeting with Ms. Way. "I am frustrated by Annie's report card. She didn't do very well." Marge went on: "Let me tell you about my son. Like Annie he made it through the first couple of years, probably on his personality. Then in Grade 3, his teacher phoned me. She said, 'Mason just cannot listen attentively to instructions and complete his written work independently. He is easily distracted and finds it difficult to complete his work without supervision. He has a difficult time organizing his work and his belongings.' Doesn't this sound familiar? This is what you wrote on Annie's report card. But you didn't call me or suggest that she may have attention deficit disorder, like her brother. Maybe we need to do something."

The two discussed their reading about attention deficit disorder, more like friends than parent and teacher. Ms. Way felt that because so many more boys than girls had attention deficit disorder, it was unlikely that this was Annie's problem. She thought Annie needed to work harder and that putting additional pressure on her through a formal assessment and labelling would not help, but rather make matters worse. Marge wanted Annie to receive the kind of tutoring that had helped Mason. "I don't care if she is identified. I just want the extra help for her. I could hire a tutor at home, but tutoring at school can be so much more aligned with classroom work. I know because I have watched Mason benefit from small group teaching, in the resource room and in the classroom."

Marge reminded Ms. Way that Annie did not know the addition or subtraction facts, even to 10, reliably, not to speak of multiplication tables. When she copied an addition or subtraction problem onto her page, she often failed to line up the numbers in columns and then added whatever happened to be closest, not necessarily in the same column. Ms. Way added, "Copying from the board is even worse. And she never seems to notice the signs. If the first question is addition, she adds them all. Maybe a bigger problem is that she really dislikes math, is almost afraid of it. And I don't think she understands the first thing about the reasons we need math in our lives. She basically waits, restlessly, for it to be over every day."

Ms. Way thought about Annie. "She never hears me the first time. I have to repeat everything I say to her. She just doesn't seem interested: she fidgets, interrupts, and bosses other kids around. The other day we played a game in social studies, and Annie was really involved. I thought, 'Good for her!' but then she couldn't settle down afterwards. And I had to send her to the quiet place in the room. When I looked up, she was at the aquarium, the garbage can, the pencil sharpener. I didn't know what to do with her." Ms. Way looked out the window. "Students like Annie make me feel like teaching is so...hard. And there are two other children in here with similar difficulties, maybe even more difficulties than Annie. I have to think about them too. Maybe she will mature. Do you think we should wait?"

Marge argued, "The longer we leave this, the harder it will be for Annie. I think the real problem will be that she doesn't like to be helped. Whereas Mason loved going to the resource room and still enjoys the attention of the resource teacher, Annie will assert her independence. I think we need to get moving. If Annie has ADD like her brother, what are we waiting for?"

Ms. Way was quiet for a long time. She looked like she was going to break into tears. "To tell you the truth, as a first-year teacher, I have not referred any children for assessment and in-school tutoring. Our resources are few, and I am unsure about how much need is a great enough need. And I have been urging Annie to work harder and to pay attention, but it isn't helping. She seems so restless. When I give the instructions, she is never with me. She is looking in her desk, or in her book, or looking for her pencil so she can write them down. I don't know what to do with her. I can't get her to write anything, and when I finally coax her until she writes, she doesn't edit it at all. Sometimes no one can read it but Annie. Is this like your son, what did you say his name is?"

Marge took her time responding, "This is so much like Mason, but as I said, he liked having extra help. Annie will resist, I think."

"Will you give me a chance to see what I can do to improve the situation myself, and to talk with the principal and resource teacher? Can we talk again in a month or so?" Ms. Way asked.

Later that week, Ms. Way talked with the other Grade 3 teacher in the suburban school. "I have to do something, don't I? What should I do? Will the principal think I am lazy or incompetent if I ask for help for Annie and two other children? I don't trust him enough to show my uncertainty. What if Annie refuses the help? Do teachers have to refer kids because parents ask them to? What about the other children in my class who are having even more difficulty than Annie? Does the squeaky parent necessarily get the grease? When I talk alone with Annie's mother, I understand why she feels so strongly, but then I look around my class and I say, 'If I am going to refer Annie, I had better do something about these two other children, too. And I don't know where to start with them. And their parents aren't calling me.' I have been reading a book about attention deficit disorder. It happens in girls, but is just less common than in boys. I might be able to get her more focused on my instructions and her work, but how can I teach her to read, and to remember the basic addition and subtraction facts? What should I do?"

QUESTIONS FOR REFLECTION AND DISCUSSION

1. What are the facts/key elements in this case?

2. What do we know about Annie? About Ms. Way?

3. Describe the meeting to the principal, first from the perspective of Ms. Way, then from Marge Wilson's perspective.

4. Describe the major dilemma(s) in this case.

5. What actions should Ms. Way take to resolve the dilemma(s)?

6. Consider the consequences of these actions for Annie, for the other students in the class, and for Ms. Way.

7. What have we learned from this case? What assumptions and widely held beliefs are thrown into question by our work on this case?

EXHIBIT 7.1	Characteristics of Children with Attention Deficit Disorder

After her meeting at the school, Marge Wilson dug out a list of characteristics she had received at a parents' meeting about ADD.

A. Does your child:
- often make careless mistakes in schoolwork or other activities?
- often have difficulty sustaining attention in tasks or in play?
- often seem to not be listening when spoken to directly?
- often fail to finish schoolwork or chores even when she means to and understands what to do?
- often have difficulty getting organized?
- often act forgetful or become easily distracted?

These are all signs of inattention.

B. Does your child:
- often squirm in his seat or fidget with his hands?
- often leave her seat when she is expected to stay seated?
- often run around and climb when it is inappropriate, or act as if "driven by a motor"?
- often have difficulty playing quietly?
- often talk excessively, blurt out answers before it is time, or interrupt others?
- often have difficulty waiting his turn?

These are all signs of hyperactivity-impulsivity.

C. Have these characteristics:
- been present in your child since before the age of seven?
- appeared in your child's behaviour both at home and at school?
- prevented your child from participating fully, either socially or academically?

If you answered yes to many of these questions, discuss your concerns with your pediatrician, your family doctor, or your child's teacher. They can help you obtain a professional assessment by doctors and psychologists to identify whether or not your child has either attention deficit disorder (ADD) or attention deficit hyperactivity disorder (ADHD). Do *not* make a home diagnosis.

| EXHIBIT 7.2 | Math Strategies for Teaching Children with ADD |

After her meeting with Marge Wilson, Ms. Way borrowed a book from the teacher resource shelf in the staff room (*How to Reach and Teach ADD/ADHD Children*). She wrote some notes after reading Section 12 on Math Strategies and talking with the other Grade 3 teachers:

- Use a problem solving approach; think out loud; ask children questions like: "Can you tell me what this means?" "Can you draw a picture to show us what is happening here?"
- Encourage the children to persist, rather than emphasizing getting the correct answer quickly.
- Put children in pairs and devise tasks in which they listen to each other, ask questions, share ideas, and grapple with the problems together.
- Remember calculators can do the operations, but there is no calculator that can tell the children which operation to do; emphasize thinking, not calculating.
- Teach strategies like:
  * look for a pattern
  * make a table
  * draw a picture
  * work backwards
  * guess (and figure out how to check whether it is a good guess)
  * use objects
  * use money to learn place value (pennies for ones, dimes for tens, loonies for hundreds)
  * act out the problem or make a model.
- Encourage children to use many approaches; find a way that works for the children who are having difficulty.
- Use computer programs for drill and practice to hold the child's attention.
- Use portfolio assessment, and encourage children to make brief journal entries about their portfolio artifacts.
- Use estimation.
- Allow children to turn lined paper on its side so they can line up their numbers in the columns.
- For children who have difficulty starting, help them with the first question, and ask them to show you the first three problems completed (perhaps within a specified time).
- Assign fewer questions if children are discouraged; work them up to the full assignment gradually; let the child in on the game plan.
- Allow extra time on tests and remind the child to take her time.
- Use a coloured highlighter to distinguish signs for the operations (+ − × ÷).
- Get or make overhead transparencies of clock faces, number lines, calculators, etc., and model thinking out loud (make the invisible visible to students who can't see it in their heads).

Sources to consult:
How to Reach and Teach ADD/ADHD Children, 1993, New York, NY: The Center for Applied Research in Education.
The ADD/ADHD Checklist: An Easy Reference for Parents and Teachers, Sandra Rief, 1998, Paramus, NJ: Prentice Hall.

EXHIBIT 7.3	Using Portfolios in Assessing Mathematics

What is a portfolio? A portfolio is a systematic way to collect and display student work over time. Portfolios usually show how students learn and show their strengths as well as providing a basis for discussion about what and how the student is learning.

Why should students show their portfolios to their parents? Portfolios help parents to see students' progress over time. They also make it easier for parents to understand teachers' evaluations. Children can talk about their "regular" work and about their "best" work.

What goes into a portfolio? Usually portfolios include samples of students' best work along with their regular work. If there are dated samples of the same kind of work done over time, it is easy to see progress. Work that shows unusual ideas, creative uses of materials, sustained projects, and independent endeavours are all suitable for a portfolio.

What are suitable math activities or artifacts for a portfolio? In addition to written work, students could include videotapes or photographs of their group building a kite or discussing an authentic problem. Survey data, calculations of costs of food for the class camping trip, observations made at the local creek, or measurements of the schoolyard are all appropriate.

Who chooses the items for a portfolio? Some items may be chosen by the teacher. A sticky note with the date, context, and a comment will refresh everyone's memory. A more permanent record is a form suitable to the grade level, completed by the teacher and stapled to the back of the item. Some items should be chosen by the student. (Some teachers think all portfolio items should be selected by the student.) Encourage students to select work carefully and for a reason, especially work they are proud of or believe represents high quality work. Encourage students to polish this work, to make corrections, to reach the standards or rubrics you use in the classroom.

How much time do portfolios take? It will be necessary to set time aside, perhaps weekly, for students to review their recent work and choose an item for their portfolio. Ensure that it shows their best effort.

How can parents be kept informed about portfolios? Introduce portfolios in a meeting with parents. Explain to parents that the portfolio is a means of urging children to do their best work, take pride in their work, and receive encouragement at school and at home. Then at regular intervals ask children to show you a piece of work they would like to show their parents. Help the child prepare to explain the work and to complete a brief report about the item.

Below is a form developed by Susan Winebrenner on which children can report to their parents, and parents can respond.

Portfolio Product Report

To be filled out by the student:

Name: ______________________________ Date: ______________

Name/title of product: ______________________________

Description of product:

____

Why did you choose to include this product in your portfolio?

____

____

____

How does this product demonstrate that your schoolwork is improving?

____

____

____

____

To be filled out by the parent/guardian/caregiver:

How did your child share information about this product with you?

____

____

____

____

How did you acknowledge/celebrate your child's progress?

____

____

____

____

Student's Signature: ______________________________

Parent's/Guardian's Signature: ______________________________

Please give this form to your child to return to school. Thank you!

Source: Excerpted from *Teaching Kids with Learning Difficulties in the Regular Classroom: Strategies and Techniques Every Teacher Can Use to Challenge and Motivate Struggling Students* by Susan Winebrenner,

SUGGESTIONS FOR FURTHER READING

Barkley, R. A. (1995). *Taking charge of ADHD: The complete, authoritative guide for parents.* New York, NY: Guilford Press.

   In this book, a prominent researcher writes for parents with compassion and clarity and helps them to be better informed and more confident in their dealings with teachers, doctors, and psychologists.

Hebert, E. A. (2001). *The power of portfolios: What children can teach us about learning and assessment.* San Francisco, CA: Jossey-Bass.

   Shows the power of portfolios to motivate students to assess their own work, set goals, and take responsibility for future learning, with examples from 10 years of portfolio use in one school.

Rief, S. (1993). *How to reach and teach ADD/ADHD children.* New York, NY: The Center for Applied Research in Education.

   In this book of practical strategies and interventions for parents and teachers to help children with attention problems and hyperactivity, strategies are placed in the context of particular curriculum areas and functional skills required for day-to-day living.

Reif, S. (1998). *The ADD/ADHD checklist: An easy reference for parents and teachers.* Paramus, NJ: Prentice Hall.

   Impressive for its clarity, this guidebook is an excellent source for understanding ADD and ADHD as well as for adapting teaching and activities in the home to help children and adolescents focus and experience success.

WEBLINKS

http://www.odyssey.on.ca/~elaine.coxon/Reporting/portfolio_assessment.htm
Site called The Staff Room for Ontario Teachers includes practical resources and article reprints on a wide range of topics including portfolio assessment.

http://www.occdsb.on.ca/~proj1615/portf1.htm
The Ottawa Carleton Catholic District School Board site includes pages by classroom teachers on topics including portfolio assessment. Many forms teachers could use to ease the implementation of portfolio assessment are available.

http://www.chaddcanada.org/
Children and Adults with Attention Deficit Disorders Canada offers information, articles, and contacts on this site.

When the Usual Approaches Don't Work

Cassie sat at her desk and cradled her cup of cold coffee. When she looked up to the window, she saw that the snow was drifting down again. It was dark outside. "How long have I been holding this cup of disgusting coffee?" She looked at her watch. "How can it be five o'clock already? I've been sitting here for over an hour. And what have I resolved?" She looked down at the notes she had written and the samples of children's work she had piled on her desk. "Actually, quite a lot. I am going to raise this at the next staff meeting. I have to admit that I can't solve everything by myself. Especially when I'm new in this school."

Last March Cassie Nilsson had been very excited to be hired by this northern school district. After two years of successful teaching in a suburban school district, she could hardly wait to make the move to a school where she would be really needed. Cassie loved a challenge and the two interviewers had assured her she would find challenges at Big Bay School. As Cassie had learned, just getting to the community of Big Bay was a challenge. The little plane that had brought her the last leg of the trip only flew when the weather was good. And the weather seemed to be too windy, too rainy, or too snowy more often than not. Taking the advice of the interviewers, Cassie had left home a week earlier than had seemed necessary and had spent three of those extra days waiting to get into the community. But she loved it! Most of the time.

Cassie's thoughts drifted back to the reason she was sitting here watching the snowflakes coming down. She said to herself, "His name is Darren. He is in Grade 6. But...he is really like a second grader...sometimes." It was the "sometimes" that had been driving Cassie crazy. On Monday, Darren had known the two, three, and five times multiplication tables and had been so pleased with himself. Today, Tuesday, when he didn't know any of them, he had thrown his book at Cassie, narrowly missing her head. When she raised her voice to him (always a mistake, she realized, as she heard herself) he flew around the room, throwing things and screaming, until he wore himself out. Whenever this happened—today was the eighth time since September according to Cassie's journal—she moved the other children out of the room. She knew that when he finished, Darren would take no responsibility for what he had done. And what really mystified Cassie was that the more she held him responsible and handed down consequences for what he had done, the more he lashed out. She had never known a child like Darren. In four months' teaching practicum while in the Faculty of Education and in two years' teaching in a suburban school, Cassie had never seen anything like this!

Cassie knew what the file said. Darren had been receiving resource room services since Grade 1. He had always had difficulty meeting the behaviour expectations and academic outcomes for his age and grade. Cassie knew what she had seen this fall: Darren couldn't decode or understand the Grade 6 textbooks independently, and he often didn't understand the instructions Cassie gave to the class, even when he appeared to be listening. He paid attention only for short periods of time and frequently got into power struggles with other students and with Cassie. His behaviour was unpredictable, yet he needed routine. He knew something one day, and the next day he acted like he had never heard of it. At first, Cassie thought maybe he was playing a joke. The file said, "Has a great sense of humour, some days." Cassie had seen that Darren loved to act and could make everyone laugh by mimicking his peers and, especially, mimicking Cassie. Even though she didn't like it, she had to admit he could be pretty funny. Cassie used to think, after she had decided Darren wasn't joking, that maybe he was having a lazy or a stubborn day. But after a few months with Darren and his peers, she believed that he really couldn't do the work on some days and could do it on other days.

Cassie thought back warmly to her first day with the Grade 6 class. She had been more nervous than the students, as she stood at the door and welcomed each one into her classroom. Because the teachers had used instant cameras extensively the previous year, there was an album of photographs in the staff room. Cassie had called the students by name as they entered the classroom. The short boy, Darren, had looked as unusual in person as he had in his photographs. In the photographs, Cassie had been struck by how flat his face was and how small he was. In person, he could be engaging and funny, but he certainly seemed younger and smaller than everyone else in Grade 6.

Last week, Cassie had attended the first professional development event of the year. What a great two days! She had made some new friends and met people who had taught in the north for years. Teachers had come from schools in communities all over the northern school district. But there had been more than one serious moment, for Cassie, in the proceedings. In a Question and Answer session with an itinerant school psychologist, Cassie heard one of the teachers from another school ask about a student. The student could have been Darren! Even though the teacher was describing a girl in Grade 3 the similarities were striking. The teacher wanted the psychologist to tell her whether or not the child had Fetal Alcohol Syndrome or perhaps Fetal Alcohol Effects. The psychologist, who had obviously been asked these questions before, was treading carefully. He put on an overhead transparency showing characteristics of children with FAS and FAE. He showed the steps that teachers can take. And in what Cassie called "a large print voice," he read out "FAS and FAE must be and can only be diagnosed by a medical doctor." He encouraged the teacher to suggest that the parents take the child to a doctor. He also urged the teacher to provide classroom observations to aid the doctor in making a diagnosis. But again and again he warned teachers not to expect too much parental cooperation when they suspected a child had FAS or FAE. The psychologist reminded the group, "Saying a child has FAS or FAE means pointing a finger at the mother. There is only one cause, and that is alcohol abuse during pregnancy."

When the psychologist suggested that the teacher could refer the child for assessment for suspected learning disabilities and attention deficit disorder, the teacher jumped to her feet. "But some of the recommendations, things we usually do with children with LD and ADD, like using more structure and pointing out consequences—those don't work. Those make the situation worse!"

The psychologist agreed that that appeared to be the case with some children with FAS/FAE and suggested that these specific characteristics could be noted on the identification. "After all, almost all children with FAS and FAE do have learning disabilities or attention deficit disorder, and most will suffer emotional problems as they grow older. So it's not an inaccurate diagnosis, just an incomplete diagnosis." The psychologist pleaded for teachers to get the support they needed with these challenging children by making referrals. And to make changes in their teaching based on what they observed and knew, using their professional judgment.

Barb, the teacher sitting beside Cassie at the Question and Answer session, had taught in the community for five years. When Cassie whispered to Barb that she was glad she had chosen this session instead of the one on the new language arts curriculum, Barb replied, "I'll tell you more later." What Barb said at the break went something like this: "We had this discussion a few years ago, shortly after I came to the community. It puts teachers in such a tough position. Do you want to tell a mother she is responsible for the difficulties her child is giving her and everyone else? But if you don't say anything, everyone goes along thinking it is a learning disability, and not identifying the real cause. When you know that if everyone understood...well...this is preventable. There don't have to be any more Darrens."

Cassie had picked up the theme then, and now she replayed it in her head: "What can I do, essentially on my own, without prejudging Darren? This is so hard. We don't know Darren has FAS; he probably doesn't; if anything, he probably has FAE. His physical characteristics are certainly less extreme than those described for FAS." Although Darren had some of the facial features the other teacher had described, Cassie could not be sure. His nose was not really short, and she didn't see any folds on the inside of his eyes. His eyes weren't that small. His nose just looked unusual, and he was so small all over, and short for Grade 6. She asked herself, "Can't we just continue to change his program? People have done that for years. Can't we just think of him as having FAS/FAE without anyone identifying him? Don't we have to do that anyway? What is lost by doing that? Surely people don't expect teachers to report this so we can have better community education? What about nurses and doctors?" Cassie went around and around the issues without a resolution.

QUESTIONS FOR REFLECTION AND DISCUSSION

1. Identify the facts of the case briefly.
2. Describe what we know about the teacher, Cassie Nilsson, and about the student, Darren.

3. Use your statement of the facts (including what you know about Cassie and Darren) to support your statement of the major dilemma(s) in the case.

4. Describe this class the way Darren might describe it to his grandparents. Describe this class, with Darren in it, the way another student might describe it to her grandparents.

5. What are some underlying issues that might arise from the context in which this case takes place?

6. What would you advise Cassie to do if you were one of her fellow teachers in this northern community?

7. What actions should Cassie take to resolve the dilemma(s)? Consider the consequences for Cassie, for Darren, for the other students, for the community.

8. What have we learned from this case? What taken-for-granted assumptions and beliefs does this case cause us to question?

EXHIBIT 8.1	**Diagnostic Characteristics of Children with FAS/FAE (Psychologist's Overhead)**

FAS/FAE: Cluster of irreversible birth defects including: (1) facial malformations; (2) growth retardation; (3) central nervous system (CNS) abnormalities.

Characteristic Facial Features
- short eye slits
- thin upper lip
- flat mid-face
- long, indistinct space between nose and upper lip

Prenatal and/or Postnatal Growth Delay
- height below 10th percentile and/or weight below 10th percentile

CNS Abnormalities
- small head circumference (below 3rd percentile)
- intellectual impairment
- learning disabilities
- attention deficit hyperactivity disorder

For Diagnosis of FAS: Child exhibits three diagnostic criteria above and there is known significant prenatal exposure to alcohol.

For Diagnosis of FAE: Child exhibits some, but not all three, diagnostic criteria above and there is known significant prenatal exposure to alcohol.

Diagnosis of FAS/FAE must be made by a doctor with expertise in recognition of birth defects.

EXHIBIT 8.2	Teachers' Observations and Roles with Students with FAS/FAE (Psychologist's Overhead)

What Teachers See in the Classroom: Cluster of learning problems including: (1) language delay; (2) memory difficulties; (3) behaviour problems; (4) learning disabilities; (5) attention deficit hyperactivity disorder.

Language Delay or Disorder
- immature speech and literal understanding of language
- difficulty following directions

Memory Difficulties
- learns one day, forgets the next
- difficulty with sequential information and short-term memory

Behaviour Problems
- difficulty connecting cause and effect
- inability to handle change and immature social skills

Learning Disabilities
- reading disabilities and spelling difficulties
- math difficulties

Attention Deficit Hyperactivity Disorder
- restless and impulsive
- outbursts

Teacher Observations: Can lead to referral. Write down your observations. Write down the questions you asked and parents' answers in parent-teacher meeting. Sensitively suggest to parents they consult family physician to discern if there is a medical reason for child's difficulties.

Teaching Strategies for Children with FAS/FAE:
- Provide a lot of structure and explain any changes before they occur.
- Overteach and keep using the same language.
- Break assignments into small pieces and/or provide extra time.
- Teach them how to ask for help.
- Ask them to tell you the consequences of behaviours.
- Remember the behaviours are symptoms of FAS/FAE and the children are not purposely trying to annoy you.
- Keep records.
- Remember they have difficulty relating cause and effect in their own behaviour, so use preventive strategies to minimize disturbances.

EXHIBIT 8.3	Sample Questions to Ask during a Meeting with Parents or Guardians

As with all good working relationships, the first time you meet is very important. Lasting impressions are made, so it is useful to prepare for this meeting and arrange the most comfortable space and time possible for all concerned. A warm welcome and invitation to work together will quickly establish rapport between you and the parent. A few sample questions have been provided to help you.

General Information

- What do you think is important for me to know about your child (e.g., specific health problems such as seizures, vision/hearing problems, heart problems, medications)?
- What educational and social goals do you have for your child?

Communication and Adaptations

- What are some strategies you have found useful in working with your child?
- Does your child require special therapy outside of school such as speech/language, occupational/physical, counselling?
- Did your child receive services from the Infant Development Program or attend a special needs preschool?
- Has your child previously received special services within school?

Behaviour

- Could you tell me about your child's challenges and what this might mean in my classroom?
- What interests, activities, or hobbies does your child enjoy?
- What causes your child to get overloaded?
- When other children ask about your child's differences, how do you handle this?

Assessment and Evaluation

- What reports or other information about your child do you feel are important for me to have?
- Is your child able to work independently? For how long?
- In what areas has your child experienced particular success?
- In what areas would you particularly like to see your child succeed this year?

Home and School

- Is there further information you feel I should know about the child (e.g., recent changes in child's life, history of child's living arrangements)?
- How can we provide a consistent home/school approach in teaching your child?
- Are there any questions you would like to ask me (such as my classroom expectations, assignments, materials, activities, assessments of progress, projects, portfolios, or tests)?

Source: From *Teaching Students With Fetal Alcohol Syndrome/Effects: A Resource Guide for Teachers* by the British Columbia Ministry of Education, Skills and Training, 1997, Victoria, BC: Queen's Printer for British Columbia. Copyright © 1997, p. 72. Reprinted by permission.

SUGGESTIONS FOR FURTHER READING

Beddard, J. M. (1996). *Fetal alcohol syndrome: Educators' knowledge and needs.* Unpublished master's thesis, Queen's University Faculty of Education, Kingston, ON.

This master's thesis showed that teachers from northern and southern Canada felt that they needed to know more about FAS, especially about how to recognize and teach children suspected of having FAS.

British Columbia Ministry of Education, Skills and Training. (1996). *Teaching students with fetal alcohol syndrome/effects: A resource guide for teachers.* Victoria, BC: Queen's Printer for British Columbia.

In less than 100 pages, this guide is practical, thorough, and very relevant for classroom teachers. It focuses on what teachers can do when teaching students with FAS/FAE including sections on characteristics, teaching, and developing an IEP, as well as checklists for teachers and lists of Canadian resources.

Burgess, D. M., & Streissguth, A. P. (1992). Fetal alcohol syndrome and fetal alcohol effects: Principles for educators. *Phi Delta Kappan, 74*(1), 24–30.

A classic paper that shows the issues and lays out clear areas of intervention for teachers: teaching communication skills, functional living skills, and social skills. Also suggests a set of five steps school districts can pursue to enable teachers to work effectively with students with FAS and FAE.

Lasser, P. (1999). *Challenges and opportunities: A handbook for teachers of students with special needs with a focus on fetal alcohol syndrome (FAS) and partial fetal alcohol syndrome (pFAS).* Vancouver, BC: Vancouver School Board.

Written by teachers for teachers, this handbook is highly readable and very practical.

Streissguth, A. P. (1997). *Fetal alcohol syndrome: A guide for families and communities.* Baltimore, MD: Paul H. Brookes.

A multidisciplinary resource written in accessible language by a prominent researcher in the field.

WEBLINKS

http://www.nofas.org/main/index2.htm
Home page of the National Organization on Fetal Alcohol Syndrome; provides links to many resources (mainly American).

http://educationcanada.com
Contains job search information for teachers interested in teaching in the Canadian north.

http://www.hc-sc.gc.ca/hppb/childhood-youth/cyfh/fas/resources.html
Health Canada Resources page containing information on many aspects of Fetal Alcohol Syndrome and Fetal Alcohol Effects as well as helpful links. (Can also be accessed by going to the Health Canada Web site at **http://www.hc-sc.gc.ca/**)

My Learning Problems Won't Quit

Marcy Wong drove to work going over the case of Daniel in her head again, as she had many mornings. Marcy had taught Grade 7 for five years at Highview School and was distressed to find that her experience, continuing education courses, and professional reading had not prepared her for dealing with the dilemmas posed by Daniel. Marcy had established a reputation as an imaginative, hardworking teacher who expected a lot of her students and supported her students so they met her high expectations. This year was proving to be the most challenging and frustrating of Marcy's career. This morning before school she was meeting with Frank Dunbar, the special education consultant for the Spirit School District. Marcy and Frank had worked together in the past, and Marcy was hoping that they could come up with some solutions that were good for Daniel, the other students, "and me."

In August the principal, Mona Good, had telephoned Marcy at home to invite her to a meeting with Daniel and his parents. Daniel was new to the neighbourhood and school. He had cerebral palsy, used a nonmotorized wheelchair, and was quite small for his age. Daniel's parents were adamant in the conversation: "We want the school to do everything it can, and involve us as much as necessary, to support Daniel in Highview. This is our neighbourhood school, now. We worked it out with the last school, and we expect to work it out here." They talked about Daniel's physical needs and were pleased, when they toured the school, to see that it had been made accessible in the renovations two years ago. Marcy understood their concerns about accessibility and inclusion, and assured Daniel's parents she would do everything she could. After all, she would want the same thing if Daniel were her son.

Two years ago, Highview School and the Spirit School District had made a public commitment to inclusive education for meeting the needs of exceptional learners. At the same time, the Ministry of Education had been introducing new reforms, asking teachers to use integrated learning approaches, portfolio assessment, and more small-group learning. Marcy held strong opinions about inclusion, both as intended and as carried out. When teachers received the support and cooperation of administrators, consultants, and parents, she knew from experience that children with disabilities could thrive, and that other students could learn acceptance and understanding. She had seen wonderful friendships develop and exceptional students learn beyond anyone's expectations. But these success stories had required a lot of pulling together. "I hope Frank and I can get started today turning this situation around so Daniel starts *learning in* my class, and is not just *being in* my class." Marcy laughed to herself, "This must be really getting to me; I'm starting to talk to myself in italics!"

When asked to tell about himself in that August meeting, Daniel had talked about his passion for sports statistics and described his need to eat frequently to keep his energy up. At that first meeting Daniel had also said, "My learning problems just won't quit."

Marcy had thought this was an odd way to talk about a physical disability, but had decided not to ask about it. She had told herself in August, "There is lots of time." But a few weeks into the term, Marcy was discouraged. Although Daniel was cheerful, communicated well, and was responsive in conversations with teachers and fellow students, he rarely volunteered information or comments in class discussions. And he had restated on a couple of occasions that his learning problems wouldn't go away. Now Marcy needed to know, "What does he mean?"

Frank Dunbar arrived on time, and greeted Marcy warmly. "Good to see you, Marcy. How was your vacation in the mountains this summer?" Marcy knew Frank had been a classroom teacher for 12 years before accepting the position of consultant. Everyone in the school district knew the true stories of Frank's wonderful successes as a classroom teacher and resource room teacher, and the way he had been able to include students with all kinds of disabilities long before the Spirit School District had made integration the official policy. Marcy thought, "If anyone can help me to include Daniel, it's Frank!"

Frank invited Marcy to describe the situation from the beginning, saying he would listen and ask questions later. Marcy took her time getting started and then gave her account, knowing Frank would not interrupt her.

> Marcy had welcomed Daniel warmly when school started and tried not to treat him differently than she treated her other students. But he seemed to need more attention than the typical student. He was hesitant about his work and asked questions regularly to seek assurances that he had the right answers or was doing the right task.
>
> Daniel pulled up his chair to a work desk near the door because access to the rest of the room was limited with so many desks in such a small room. He rarely moved among his fellow students. The storage areas were too high for him to use comfortably, so that he could not even see into the bin in which he stored his 'things.' Marcy and Mona had submitted the request for a carpenter in August, but a month later Spirit School District had still not sent a carpenter to lower Daniel's storage bin.
>
> Daniel related well to his peers, joined in, and was included in student conversations. He was often helped by his friends. His closest friends were the most popular and socially outgoing students in the class. Daniel was careful to protect these relationships and spent a lot of time socializing during class. He shared his snacks with his friends even though he knew this broke the classroom rules. Marcy had wondered whether the snacks were a way for Daniel to maintain

friendships. Daniel had continued to speak in a loud and disruptive voice despite Marcy's warnings. He frequently requested washroom breaks which he stretched into 10-minute tours through the halls of the school. He liked to take messages to the office, maybe because he could move freely in the halls. After three other new students had arrived on the first day of school, the extra tables made the aisles so narrow that Daniel could not move around much in the classroom.

Daniel had found himself in a class of 26 students with a wide range of backgrounds and abilities. There were two students who were academically advanced compared to the others, and three who had been identified with learning disabilities. The class could be unruly and several students could be disruptive. Marcy had always thought of herself as firm and effective in managing her classroom. She thought, "I am working hard to keep control of a difficult class, but I don't feel very successful."

In Marcy's class, Daniel and his classmates were involved in a long and complex project in September. They worked in groups of six at square worktables. Daniel started work well each day, but soon lost interest, spending long parts of the work periods talking and snacking. He seemed easily bored and tired. When Marcy helped Daniel individually, he returned to the project for short periods of time. The first collaborative group he was placed in had said that Daniel didn't do his share. Marcy had tried assigning a partner to Daniel for the current three-week project. But the partner had begun to complain that Daniel let him do all the work on the project while Daniel chatted. Daniel had suggested to Marcy that he be exempted from the project. Daniel hadn't answered a single question on the pop quiz yesterday. He chose books for independent reading that were popular with the Grade 4 class who were reading buddies for Marcy's class. She thought that her main tactic in dealing with Daniel had been keeping him in the integrated setting, no matter what he was accomplishing.

Marcy said, "I have been very sympathetic and friendly without being patronizing. Daniel has seemed comfortable and at home in the class. He has even volunteered to take the attendance information to the office. But maybe that was a way to escape. I have given him so much encouragement, but he has given up quickly whenever the activity has been long or complex. I've been wondering whether we are doing him a favour by keeping him in this class. Removing him and putting him in a remedial situation would have meant he left a group with whom he had become socially accepted. Maybe entertaining his friends, maintaining his relationships with these friends, and avoiding becoming socially isolated was more important than completing every project." Marcy said, "Whew, I'll stop there, for now. I want to know more about cerebral palsy. Other things will come to me as you talk, and then I'll describe some more of my frustrations later."

Frank Dunbar, the special education consultant, started by describing cerebral palsy. "Cerebral palsy is one of the most common crippling disorders in children. It affects between one and five children per hundred. It is nonprogressive; that means the condition stays the same, does not deteriorate. It begins in childhood because it is due to a malformation or damage to the brain. The technical term is cerebral dysfunction." Frank went on to add that 10 to 20 percent of persons with cerebral palsy had paraplegia. Most children were likely to exhibit one or more additional disabilities. These included learning disabilities and behavioural disorders. Frank had brought three resources for Marcy that he had prepared for classroom teachers: information about cerebral palsy, about multi-level teaching and assessment, and about cognitive behaviour management programs.

Frank suggested a multidisciplinary assessment. Marcy was already beginning to consider that perhaps some of Daniel's difficulties, especially with the projects and reading and writing, might not have been caused only by his physical disabilities. Marcy said, "I had been thinking that perhaps Daniel's arms and hands were affected but not as obviously as his legs. He is a bit awkward and slow with his handwriting. I had entertained the idea that he gets fatigued, and that's why he wants to get out of work. I thought maybe the worktable was the wrong height. I even wondered if it was tiring to sit in the same posture in the chair for long periods. But I had not seriously considered that he has a learning disability. I thought it was his way of getting out of work, to say 'my learning problems just won't quit.'" Marcy recalled, "When I gave the students a surprise quiz, Daniel did not answer any of the questions. Do you think he couldn't read the questions? He does few of the reading and writing activities, and in the group projects, the other students rarely ask him to contribute to the academic aspects. If I am going to alter my teaching for Daniel, does that mean I should be adapting assessment too? It seems like I should, to be fair."

"This has really been bothering me. You know I have high expectations for my students. They know that and would be disappointed if I started to expect less. But continuing to ask more from Daniel is going to really frustrate him. At the same time, I can't decrease my expectations for the class as a whole or for the small groups. If I give him individual assignments, will I be defeating the intent of inclusive education by setting him up as different and less able? At the moment he is not learning much, and is not meeting my expectations in reading, writing, and project work. He is happy enough and has made great friendships. But that isn't enough. He needs to be learning. And I cannot allow him to eat in class, treat his friends, and talk out. So far the other students seem to recognize that Daniel is adjusting to a lot of change, but soon they'll be doing these things too. A couple of students already are. I like the idea of a multidisciplinary assessment. But that will take a while, and I have to start doing things differently right away. What should I do? Let's get down to specifics."

QUESTIONS FOR REFLECTION AND DISCUSSION

1. What are the facts/key elements of the case?
2. What do we know about the student, Daniel? What do we know about the teacher, Marcy?
3. Describe the major problem(s) or dilemma(s). What may have been overlooked in the past?
4. How else can the problem be framed? From Daniel's perspective? From the perspective of Daniel's parents?
5. What should Frank recommend and what should Marcy do to resolve the dilemma(s)?
6. What would the consequences of these actions be for Marcy, Daniel, the class, beyond the classroom?
7. What have we learned from this case? What assumptions and beliefs about exceptional children, about inclusion, about cerebral palsy are called into question by this case?

EXHIBIT 9.1	Cerebral Palsy: Information for Teachers
	by Frank Dunbar

Cerebral palsy is a disabling condition. "Cerebral" refers to the brain and "palsy" refers to a lack of muscle control. The condition is not hereditary, contagious, progressive, or medically curable.

Cerebral palsy results from damage to the brain, usually caused by a lack of oxygen. The damage interferes with messages sent from the brain to the body or from the body to the brain and may cause involuntary movement and/or speech, hearing, or sight disorders. A positive attitude and acceptance of the condition by others will enhance the quality of life for the child with cerebral palsy.

The extent of cerebral palsy can vary from mild speech impairment or no obvious signs to no speech at all and a severe lack of muscle coordination. The lower limbs or one side of the body may be more affected than the other. The severity of the disability caused by cerebral palsy will determine the expectations and lifestyle of the student.

Many children with cerebral palsy have normal learning skills and intellectual development; they are able to care for themselves and to walk unaided. Others require very specialized treatment, including multidisciplinary care from physicians, physical therapists, occupational therapists, speech pathologists, and teachers with special training in learning disabilities. Many children with cerebral palsy also have learning disabilities.

Key Behaviour Patterns

- spasmodic, uncontrolled or jerky movements
- spells of staring
- inconsistent attention span

Classroom Strategies

- Meet with the parents and the child as early as possible in the school year to determine individual needs. Student records should reveal special programming in previous years.
- Work with other professionals as a team to help the child lead a productive life.
- Determine specific learning requirements on the basis of a current educational assessment.
- Develop an IEP if necessary to meet the child's needs.
- Encourage the child to complete assignments by assigning fewer parts or providing extra time. A feeling of accomplishment will enhance self-esteem.
- Expect acceptable and appropriate behaviour. Students with disabilities are accountable for their behaviours in the classroom.
- Assist the student to form and maintain meaningful interpersonal relationships. A sense of acceptance is important to students of all ages.

Exhibit 9.1 *Continued*

- Encourage the student to participate in as many classroom activities as possible. Some students will need a modified form of the curriculum in some or all subject areas. Be aware of attendant disabilities like speech impairments and learning disabilities.

- Be familiar with specialized equipment like wheelchairs, adapted typewriters, pencil holders, and special desks.

Source: Adapted from *Awareness of Chronic Health Conditions: What the Teacher Needs to Know* by the British Columbia Ministry of Education, 1995, Victoria, BC.

EXHIBIT 9.2 | Multi-Level Instruction and Assessment: A Guide for Teachers by Frank Dunbar

It is not necessary for teachers to prepare and teach a number of different lessons within a single class. Rather, teachers can develop a framework for planning that allows for **one main lesson** with varying methods of presentation, practice, and assessment. Multi-level instruction includes a variety of techniques aimed at reaching all students. This may mean adjusting expectations for some students. It may mean providing for student choice in the means of demonstrating understanding of the concept being taught. For multi-level instruction and assessment to be successful, teachers must accept that these different methods are of equal value.

Four Steps to Multi-Level Instruction and Assessment

Identify the underlying concepts or skills of the lesson or class. Translate these concepts into meaningful objectives for students, including those with IEPs.

Decide on the teacher methods of presentation—how concepts will be presented or skills demonstrated. For students with IEPs, this may require a more structured format or an alternate format of presentation (e.g., visual as well as auditory).

Decide on the methods of practice students will use to enhance their understanding of the concepts or execution of the skills. For students with IEPs, this may require a more structured format or an alternate format for practice (e.g., Braille).

Decide on the method of student assessment. For students with IEPs, this could require an oral presentation, drawing, or writing a shorter account.

Key Concepts: Form of Participation and Degree of Participation

While planning, the teacher decides the degree and form of participation appropriate for all students, with particular emphasis on exceptional students. In thinking about the degree of participation, the teacher considers whether some students might do a segment of the activity based on current knowledge level, IEP goals, and current patterns of needs and strengths. Sometimes, in group work, it is appropriate to assign each student a different but complementary task.

Developing a choice of activities may be more helpful than asking all students to complete the same activity in the same way. Also, a student who works more slowly may be asked to complete fewer items or to complete the same number of items as his or her peers in a longer time.

Universal Design

Universal design can enhance curriculum access. Universal design refers to designing instruction and activities with alternatives so they can be accessed in a wide range of ways by students with considerable differences in their abilities to see, hear, speak, move, read, write, understand English, organize, and engage.

Four Essential Qualities of Universal Design for Learning

1. Curriculum provides multiple means of representation.
2. Curriculum provides multiple means of expression.
3. Curriculum provides multiple means of engagement.
4. Curriculum provides multiple means of assessment.

Resources:
Collicott, J. (1994). Multi-level instruction: A guide for teachers. *Keeping in Touch* (a quarterly newsletter from the Canadian CEC Office, Ottawa, ON).
Hutchinson, N. L. (2002). *Inclusion of exceptional learners in Canadian schools: A practical handbook for teachers* (pp.195-226). Toronto, ON: Prentice Hall.
Orkwis, R., & McLane, K. (1998). *A curriculum every student can use: Design principles for student access.* Reston, VA: Council for Exceptional Children.

EXHIBIT 9.3	Implementing a Cognitive Behaviour Management Program by Frank Dunbar

Cognitive behaviour modification (CBM) is a broad term. It describes a number of specific techniques that teach self-control. They all work by increasing a student's awareness of cognitive processes and knowledge of how behaviour affects learning.

CBM interventions require student evaluation of performance rather than teacher evaluation. This means that they are practical for busy teachers and parents.

Self-instruction is one technique that helps students to regulate their own behaviours—social and academic. It uses self-statements to help students recall the steps required to solve a problem—social or academic. Examples of problems include: rushing through assigned work, looking around instead of focusing on assigned work, talking out in class, eating or giving food to others in the classroom. Initially students say the steps out loud to a teacher or parent, then to a peer or themselves. Gradually they say the steps covertly.

The actions a teacher and student follow include:

1. They agree on a problem—social or academic—that is getting in the way of learning.
2. The teacher makes a cue card to prompt the student to use the steps of self-instruction.
3. The teacher models using the self-instruction steps to solve a problem like the one impeding the student.
4. The student practises using the self-instruction steps aloud with the teacher to solve the problem.
5. The student practises with a peer and then alone using the steps to solve the problem.
6. The teacher arranges booster practice regularly to review the strategy with the student. For booster practice, they use verbal rehearsal as well as practising in familiar and new situations.
7. They arrange a signal for the teacher to let the student know this is a time to use the steps. This is phased out because the student is supposed to do the monitoring. For the SNAP strategy, snapping fingers may be a good signal.

Sample Cue Card to Tape to Student's Desk or Book

SNAP out of it!

See my problem.

Name my best plan.

Act on my best plan.

Pat myself on the back. I solved my problem!

SUGGESTIONS FOR FURTHER READING

British Columbia Ministry of Education. (1998). *Awareness of chronic health conditions: What the teacher needs to know* (2nd ed.). Victoria, BC: Queen's Printer for British Columbia.

Written for teachers, it uses a minimum of jargon and provides characteristics, classroom strategies, and resource lists about many physical disabilities and chronic health conditions. Every school should have a copy.

Hutchinson, N. L. (2002). *Inclusion of exceptional learners in Canadian schools: A practical handbook for teachers*. Toronto, ON: Prentice Hall.

A current, Canadian source of practical ideas for classroom implementation and information about exceptionalities. Shows many examples of ways teachers can adapt their learning outcomes, teaching, assessment, and classroom organization to accommodate exceptional students. Includes full chapters on adapting teaching and on adapting assessment.

Lauren, J. (1997). *Succeeding with LD: 20 true stories about real people*. Minneapolis, MN: Free Spirit (Works for Kids).

This engaging set of biographies is written for young people who are experiencing learning difficulties. Adolescents could read the accounts themselves while children would enjoy hearing them read aloud.

Mecham, M. J. (1996). *Cerebral palsy: PRO-ED studies in communicative disorders* (2nd ed.). Austin, TX: PRO-ED, Inc.

This accessible book focuses on the communication disorders that often accompany cerebral palsy, and explains for parents and teachers how assessments are conducted and interventions designed to enhance communication in all contexts, including the classroom.

Swaggert, B. L. (1998). Implementing a cognitive behavior management program. *Intervention in School and Clinic, 33,* 235–238.

A readable account of three strategies for implementing cognitive behaviour management programs in the regular classroom that teach the student to monitor his or her use of the program, making these strategies practical for busy teachers.

WEBLINKS

http://www.cerebralpalsycanada.com/
This comprehensive Canadian site on cerebral palsy offers opportunities for parents to link with parents, kids to link with kids, professionals to link with professionals, and much more.

http://www.ldac-taac.ca
Home page of the Learning Disabilities Association of Canada with links to provincial and local associations; informative.

http://snow.utoronto.ca/access/ud/toc.html
On the SNOW (Special Needs Opportunity Windows) Web site, this page focuses on universal design instructional environments.

http://www.cast.org/about/
CAST (Center for Applied Special Technology) is a not-for-profit organization that uses technology to expand opportunities for all people, especially those with disabilities. Contains extensive information on universal design.

http://idea.uoregon.edu/~ncite/
National Center to Improve the Tools of Educators (NCITE) at the University of Oregon states that its purpose is to advance the quality and effectiveness of technology, media, and materials for individuals with disabilities.

How Much Do I Have To Change For One Student?

Marla started attending Brook School in the village of Cotnam when she was five. Brook School consisted of an old brick building with seven classrooms and six portables beside the baseball diamond. Marla's Kindergarten teacher thought Marla was immature. She encouraged Marla to play with the other children and to speak more clearly. As the year went on, she worried that perhaps Marla's difficulties went deeper than immaturity. Marla seemed to ignore the other children most of the time. She followed the teacher around the classroom, and she never learned to follow directions. Usually, Marla watched the other children, and then she did what they did.

When the Kindergarten teacher invited Marla's parents to meet with her, only Marla's mother came to the school. She brought three younger children with her. Calm conversation was almost impossible. Marla's mother pointed out that she did not have much time to worry about Marla being shy with other children. "She helps me a lot with the little ones. And that's what I need. I can understand her most of the time. She will talk clearer when she gets older, won't she?" Marla's father travelled for a small manufacturing company and was home one week each month. The Kindergarten teacher documented her concerns in the file, and Marla went on to Grade 1.

For Grade 1, Marla was placed with Ms. Trew. She had been teaching six-year-olds for 20 years, and was a keen observer of the children in her class. Ms. Trew observed each child carefully and wrote detailed observation notes. The first set of observations of Marla appear below. All through September of Grade 1, Ms. Trew kept wondering about Marla. She told Marla's mother, "It's the confused expression on her face. And the way she never seems to hear me. I want someone else to observe her, and see if they share my concerns." In October, the district special education consultant came to observe Marla. They shared notes. The consultant asked Ms. Trew what she thought. "I think she needs her hearing checked," the classroom teacher ventured.

OBSERVATIONS of Marla / Sept. 12, 1:45–2:00
- Marla is at the painting centre
- turned her head when I called her name for the third time
- asked me what I had said
- her voice seemed too loud
- her speech is like a three-year-old; sounds are garbled
- ignored me when I asked her if she needed clean water for her paint brush
- then told me her paint was green; what did she think I asked?
- when I returned to the painting centre she was staring into space; daydreaming?
- told me about her painting; she knew the colours, but did not know the name for mailbox (we posted letters yesterday in the mailbox outside the school)

Leone Trew

The consultant smiled, and recommended Ms. Trew call Marla's parents. "Suggest they ask their family physician to refer Marla to the audiology clinic."

Six weeks later, the suspected hearing loss was confirmed. Audiological assessment diagnosed Marla as having a 55 dB conductive hearing loss in her left ear and a 40 dB conductive hearing loss in her right ear. Marla was fitted with an in-the-ear hearing aid in her left ear. An audiologist came to the classroom to show Ms. Trew and Marla how the hearing aid functioned. He showed them how the on/off switch worked, how to change the battery, and how to check the volume control. Marla and Ms. Trew learned how to ensure that the hearing aid was performing properly and how to clean it. They received a list of "don'ts": don't get it wet, drop it, put hairspray on it, or leave it on any hot surface (like the classroom radiator).

Marla began to work on language activities with an itinerant specialist who came to the school for two hours each week. The specialist's goal was to support children with hearing loss in their neighbourhood schools in the Lakeside School District. She taught Ms. Trew and a volunteer, a retired teacher, how to carry out these language activities in the classroom. The specialist showed Marla's parents how to extend the language activities into the home with a daily 20-minute program. By the end of Grade 1, Marla had made friends and had begun to join in activities in the classroom and on the playground. Her language development was delayed, but continued to progress in Grade 2 and Grade 3.

Grade 4 was a struggle for the first few weeks, with harder textbooks and more demands for independent work. Then the itinerant specialist met with Marla and her teacher and made some suggestions. Ms. Grande, the Grade 4 teacher, placed a carrel in the "Quiet Corner" of the room. Marla could take her work from any learning centre in the classroom to the carrel. In the quiet corner, she could usually concentrate. Ms. Grande often paired the students, so Marla, and everybody else, had a buddy. She used chart paper to list the day's agenda and wrote the homework on the board.

By Grade 5 Marla was accustomed to her hearing aid and had learned to speech-read the teacher fairly well. She sat with her friend Patricia whenever she could and wished she had more friends outside school. Marla's entry in her journal on the first morning of school in Grade 5 reflected her outlook: "I hope we learn cool things. I think I like Grade 5 this year." One week later, Marla wrote in her journal, "I can't do it. Everyone's talking all the time." Marla's Grade 5 teacher, Mr. Fraser, did not use centres as much as he used collaborative groups. There was no carrel this year where Marla could retreat to relative silence and fewer distractions (auditory and visual). This classroom was a portable with no carpet, an echo, and lots of reverberating noise. Mr. Fraser could see by the middle of September that Marla was giving up on the small group. Instead of straining to listen and scanning the group every time a different member spoke, she tuned out. She didn't know whom to look at and she couldn't hear the voice over the other noise. In her journal, Marla wrote almost daily, "I can't do this. This is too hard."

One boy whom Marla particularly liked started to call her "Marvellous Marla." At first, Marla thought he was being nice, but she changed her mind when he laughed at her one day and called out, "Earth to Marla, Earth to Marla." Mr. Fraser knew that Marla's hearing loss made it more difficult for her to socialize and be accepted. She spoke in a less mature way than her peers, and her voice was sometimes too loud, sometimes too soft. He decided to take a more active role in the social organization of the classroom. Although he preferred groups, he formed pairs and placed Marla with Patricia. He knew Patricia was an understanding girl who had befriended Marla and sometimes offered to help her with her assignments.

Mr. Fraser tried to focus on the problems Marla was experiencing by observing her, conferencing with her, and reading her journal carefully. He was talking to himself, puzzling over the problem: "I remember that the principal said, 'Maybe you should move out of that zany portable into a carpeted classroom.' Something about improving the 'signal-to-sound' ratio for Marla. But I observed Marla last spring in her Grade 4 classroom. I saw how well she was doing. Totally disrupting the way I teach seemed so unnecessary." Now he reflected, "She must have been doing well because of what the teacher was doing."

A talk with the Grade 4 teacher confirmed Mr. Fraser's guess. "I learned how to adapt my teaching and reading demands for her. Remember I showed you the report I put in her file about what works. Now that you know her and her problems, you might want to read it again. I say in the report that she has a hard time getting meaning from textbooks. But the changes I made for her also helped some of my other students who did not read with good comprehension. I had a whole group of students who benefited from the reading adaptations. As well, call the itinerant specialist. She helped me about this time last year; what is it, the third week of school?"

The specialist brought a list for Mr. Fraser. She explained that adapting instruction means changing the teaching actions you take when communicating with students and the way students communicate with one another. Articles by Ciborowski and Graves showed how to adapt reading materials for students who cannot read the textbook. The specialist told Mr. Fraser that Marla depended on speech-reading to supplement her hearing, even though she wore an aid in one ear. Mr. Fraser's large, floppy moustache was interfering with Marla's speech-reading, so she was getting almost no information from his face and mouth.

Now Mr. Fraser feels caught. What a dilemma! He has a list that suggests he try to move into a regular classroom when he loves his zany portable. He is supposed to shave off his moustache, which he thinks is his trademark. He should use more visuals, but he loves language, and relies on students listening to him and to one another. He has already changed from groups to pairs to accommodate Marla. If he wants to use group work, he will have to find a way to place the students into groups that work for everyone including Marla. In the back of Mr. Fraser's mind is a nagging thought that some of these changes are consistent with suggestions made by a little delegation of parents last January. But Mr. Fraser knows how hard it is for teachers to change their practice. Talking with the principal, Mr. Fraser agonizes, "How far does a teacher have to go to adapt instruction for one student?"

The principal surprises him by asking, "But is it only for one student?"

"How do I make sure that I keep the best parts of my usual teaching style? And still include Marla?"

The principal replied, "It sounds like you have made up your mind to try to make the changes. Good! Maybe you should write about it when the students are writing in their journals every day. Then you and Marla can share your journals with each other. She will know you are trying to help her learn. We can talk whenever you want. Now what are we going to do about a quiet classroom for you and Marla?"

QUESTIONS FOR REFLECTION AND DISCUSSION

1. What are the facts/key elements of the case?

2. What do we know about the teacher, Mr. Fraser? What do we know about the student, Marla?

3. Describe the major problem(s) or dilemma(s).

4. How else can the problem(s) be framed? Look at the problem(s) from the principal's perspective. How might he frame the problem(s)? Other perspectives on the dilemma(s)?

5. What actions should Mr. Fraser take to resolve the dilemma(s)?

6. What will be the consequences of the actions you suggest for Marla, other students in Mr. Fraser's class, students in other classes, Mr. Fraser?

7. What questions does this case raise about beliefs and taken-for-granted assumption-that you recognized while you worked on this case?

EXHIBIT 10.1	Ten Ways to Adapt Instruction for Students with Hearing Loss
	Prepared by Hearing Specialists of the Lakeside School District

- Use visually oriented materials, demonstrations, and aids (slides, diagrams, videos, charts); write information when necessary.
- Make sure students are attending; provide short, clear instructions; use a buddy system.
- Speak clearly and normally; do not exaggerate the pronunciation of words.
- Keep your face visible to the students; avoid frequent movement around the classroom, turning your back on students while talking, and standing in front of a bright light source.
- Use gestures and facial expressions; trim beards and moustaches if such facial hair interferes with speech-reading.
- Check with students to confirm whether they are understanding what is being discussed or presented; encourage students to request clarification and to ask questions.
- Identify other speakers by name so that students can more easily follow a discussion; repeat the comments of other students who speak, if necessary.
- Paraphrase or summarize discussions throughout and at the end of a class session.
- Provide students with advance organizers, such as outlines of lectures and copies of overhead transparencies; provide summaries or scripts of videotapes or films.
- Preview new vocabulary and concepts prior to their presentation during a lecture.

EXHIBIT 10.2	Report on Successful Practices with Marla Kosovic by Her Grade 4 Teacher (Martine Grande, Brook School)

After struggling at the beginning, I learned how to teach Marla. I followed the principal's advice and chose a carpeted classroom. Then I placed a carrel in the Quiet Corner beside the reading chair. I encouraged Marla to take her work to the carrel whenever she was having trouble concentrating. Everyone had a buddy for activities. That way Marla did not feel like she was "the only one." The day's agenda was on chart paper and I wrote the homework on the board.

Helping Marla to read her textbooks was a big challenge. I made changes in what I did before reading, during reading, and after reading. Before reading a new chapter or section of a chapter, I asked five pairs of buddies to meet me at the round table. Marla and her buddy were usually one of these pairs. The others with reading difficulties took turns. We guessed the meanings of words and predicted what we would be learning. During reading, I offered all students partially completed chapter maps to fill in. A popular strategy involved students retelling to a buddy what they had read silently. Following reading, the students worked with their buddies to complete an activity, prepare for the test, and predict what would be in the next chapter. Most of these reading ideas came from the papers by Ciborowski and Graves [see Exhibit 10.3].

Marla works best when she can see me and hear me, and when she knows which student is speaking. She uses the carrel to complete her learning centre activities. We have had a thumbs-up/thumbs-down signal system. When I showed thumbs-up, Marla would respond with the same sign if she understood and with thumbs-down when she was confused. Marla has done well this year and is proud of herself.

EXHIBIT 10.3	Using Collaborative Learning and Guided Learning to Teach Content

Teachers can use collaborative learning and guided or scaffolded learning to allow students to complete tasks, with support, before they would be able to complete them independently. This way, students gradually gain control, independence, and content knowledge. When using textbooks for students to read to learn, there are usually three components: prereading activities, during-reading activities, and postreading activities.

Prereading Activities

These usually take place in the classroom, but can also occur in the resource room for exceptional learners.

It is effective to relate the reading to students' lives so they begin thinking about relevant experiences and background knowledge.

You can capture their interest and create motivation to learn.

Preteach vocabulary and concepts.

Raise questions to which students can seek answers and suggest or review strategies they can use.

During-reading activities

Assign part of the reading and writing in class, so that guided reading can occur. Have students collaborate.

Read to students and show them how to make connections explicit between ideas in the text, from the text to their own lives, and from the text to their assignments.

Use oral reading by the students, taped reading of the text with students following along, and other modifications as appropriate.

Postreading Activities

Use questioning, discussing, and planning of writing in large or small groups.

Students can collaborate to make chapter maps, study for tests, and check their comprehension.

Include writing, drama, artistic, and nonverbal activities.

Reteach as necessary in a supportive, non-punitive manner.

To learn more, consult the following sources:
Ciborowski, J. (1995). Using textbooks with students who cannot read them. *Remedial and special education, 16,* 90-101.
Graves, M. F., & Graves, B. B. (1996). Scaffolded reading experiences for inclusive classes. *Educational leadership, 53*(5), 14-16.
Graves, M. F., & Braaten, S. (1996). Scaffolded reading experiences: Bridges to success. *Preventing school failure, 40*(4), 169-173.

SUGGESTIONS FOR FURTHER READING

Ciborowski, J. (1995). Using textbooks with students who cannot read them. *Remedial and special education, 16,* 90–101.

Suggests adaptations that are feasible for whole-class implementation, minimizing the need to prepare separate lessons for students of varying abilities and strengths.

Graves, M. F., & Braaten, S. (1996). Scaffolded reading experiences: Bridges to success. *Preventing school failure, 40*(4), 169-173.

A clearly written, helpful paper that enables teachers to adjust the amount of support provided during, before, and after reading activities so that students can complete tasks successfully.

Hutchinson, N. L. (1994). Promoting social development and social acceptance in secondary school classrooms. In J. Andrews, (Ed.), *Teaching students with diverse needs: Secondary classrooms* (pp. 160–180). Scarborough, ON: Nelson Canada.

This chapter takes teachers through the process of teaching students to work in pairs and gradually to carry out units of study in jigsaw formations and other complex arrangements of collaborative learning.

Watson, L. R., Gregory, S., & Powers, S. (1999). *Deaf and hearing impaired pupils in mainstream schools.* London, UK: David Fulton.

Addresses a wide range of issues from the teacher's perspective, including how to adapt teaching for children with hearing aids and deaf children who sign.

WEBLINKS

http://www.chs.ca
The Canadian Hearing Society provides courses in sign language, information for teachers, and services to people who are deaf or hearing impaired.

http://www.deafcanada.com
DeafCanadaOnline provides a means of communication and a virtual community for persons who are deaf and hard of hearing in Canada.

http://www.voicefordeafkids.com
Voice for Hearing Impaired Children, a Canadian organization that promotes auditory-verbal therapy (learning to speak) for all deaf and hearing impaired children.

I Simply Don't Know
What To Do

I am Kelly Mullen. I teach Grade 1 at Briar Hill School in a middle-class neighbour-hood in a small city in the Central School District. And I simply don't know what to do. Today, October 14, I had a tough day. Today I stopped making excuses and promised to come to terms with a bad feeling I have.

I have been keeping a reflective journal for five years, since my first year of teach-ing. I have just reread my journal entries for the months of September and October of this year, and I've come to a frightening realization. As I write this at my kitchen table, I'm crying. Rereading what I have written has shown me that I have gradually come to suspect that one of my students is being physically abused. But it is not a simple case. That's why I don't know what to do.

From the first day, I was drawn to Melissa because she was shy and spoke quietly on the few occasions when she said anything. I often stood near her desk, trying to draw her into the discussion. About the third week of school, I was surprised to find Melissa shouting at the other children in the cloakroom at the back of the class. And she shoved another student, Bonnie, when Bonnie tried to calm her. After that I began to notice that, whenever I approached her or stood near her desk, Melissa cringed or leaned away from me. I tried not to take it personally. I even joked with her that I didn't bite. She never smiled or showed that she understood the joke. Now, of course, I feel insensitive, but I didn't suspect anything then. At first I thought she was just having a bad day or a bad week. But gradually I realized that Melissa had changed since the start of the school year. I began to hear her talk about "my mother and him." I came to understand that "him" referred to her mother's new boyfriend. Suddenly Melissa stopped talking about "him." I just thought, "Some children don't like competing for their parent's attention."

I guess I really didn't think much about all of this at the time. Melissa was always well dressed, and this is such a good neighbourhood. I had always thought child abuse was more common in families living in poverty.

When Melissa talks she tends to whine. One day she didn't have a pencil and I told her to go to the green box at the front of the room and borrow a pencil for the day. Instead of going to the box, she sat at her desk, pouted, and whined that no one would give her a pencil. Then she poked Franny, the girl beside her, while Franny was doing her printing. Franny refused to answer. Franny has since asked to be moved away from Melissa, saying, "I don't like her much. Can't I move to sit near someone else? She has the nicest dresses and brings the most toys to school, but I don't like sitting beside her." While I chided Franny for her comment, I had to agree silently that Melissa was not much fun as a seatmate anymore. She rarely smiled or participated in classroom activities. Melissa interrupted Franny when she wanted something, and neglected Franny when Franny tried to engage her in conversation.

I have a volunteer in the classroom each afternoon. I feel so fortunate that there are three community college students, a retired teacher, and a parent of one of my students who can come in to help in the classroom. I had asked the volunteers to have each child dictate a story titled "My Favourite" and to print each child's story on chart paper. Melissa wanted to be first. Most children described their favourite toy or trip or movie. However, Melissa dictated a touching story titled "My Favourite Sister." In her story, she described how her sister Grace was the most important person in her life. She said that Grace, who is nine years old, protects her when life gets hard, makes sure that she is safe, and is always there when Melissa's Mom can't come home from work until late. She ended her story, "The worst thing that could happen is if I could not be with Grace. Grace is my favourite person in the whole world. I love Grace and she loves me."

I think that I almost forgot about the gradually developing problem because it was out of sight—Melissa was absent for most of a week soon after she wrote her touching story about Grace. After the last weekend in September, Melissa had not come back to school on Monday. Her mother, the only parent mentioned in the school records, did not telephone the office to report the absence. At recess, somewhat worried about Melissa, I phoned her home. A woman answered after about ten rings and, when I said I was from Melissa's school, she told me to mind my own business and hung up. It all happened so fast that I was not sure what I had heard. When the school secretary asked me how Melissa's mother sounded, I wasn't sure, but I thought maybe I had awakened her.

When Melissa returned to school on Thursday afternoon, it was a hot day for early October. She was wearing a beautiful wool pullover sweater. I suggested that she remove it to be cooler. Melissa yelled at me and threw a tantrum. So I urged her to at least push up the sleeves as much as she could. On her right arm I saw a red, oozing sore, perhaps the result of a burn or an untreated cut. When Melissa saw me looking at it, she quickly pulled the sleeve down again. But that brief glimpse brought to mind the partially healed bruises that I had seen on Melissa's arms, legs, and back when she had been wearing shorts and T-shirts in September. I remembered that in September Melissa had walked away from me when I asked her how she had hurt herself. I guess I was looking for a reason for the bruises.

The next day, after what I think of as the tantrum-and-sweater incident, Melissa was absent again. Her mother phoned the school with a brief message that Melissa was sick. Then this afternoon Melissa finally returned. She crept into our classroom shortly after the bell rang, and sat in her chair with her head on the table. She had a black eye and bruises around her nose. She spent most of the early afternoon staring into space, and after recess I found her crying in the cloakroom. I asked her what was wrong, and she told me that she couldn't go home after school. Through her sobs she said that her mother's boyfriend was there, and her mother wouldn't be home from work until six o'clock. When I asked about Grace, Melissa said that Grace had to mind their cousins and would be away until the evening.

Not sure what to do, I took the direct approach. "Melissa, what happened to your nose and eye?"

She sobbed, "I had an accident. It was my own fault. I had an accident." Then she huddled on the floor of the cloakroom looking at the wall, refusing to look at me, and pleading, "You can't phone my house. You can't tell my Mom. You'll just make it worse." Tears ran down her face. "Leave us alone. Grace and me are OK. It's just that when Grace isn't there...[floods of tears] You don't understand!"

What to do? I carried Melissa's favourite book into the cloakroom, brought a pillow for her to sit on, and gave her a snack. She read in the cloakroom and then returned quietly to her desk. As soon as the bell rang, she scooted out of the classroom without saying goodbye or taking her backpack.

I helped the stragglers collect their books for reading at home, zippered students' jackets, and made a decision to talk with the principal. But when I got to the office, the secretary reminded me that the principal was at a professional development meeting at the district office, "It can probably keep 'til tomorrow morning. And, even if it can't, it will have to."

So here I am at home, reading over my journal and coming to a hard decision. I have looked in my *Central School District Policies Handbook* and I know my responsibility. If I suspect child abuse (that is, if I have reasonable grounds for suspicion), I have to make a report immediately, whether or not I have the support of my principal. I am not sure what Mr. Drucker will say tomorrow. But I know that Melissa will hate me. I may be responsible for her being separated from Grace, the most important person in her life. I don't have much confidence in the system. I'm not sure that anything will be done that will actually help Melissa. But how does it help her to let this situation go on? Something is wrong here—I think a child is being hurt physically, I know she cannot concentrate at school, and she has told me that she is dependent on another child to protect her. My guess is that Melissa's mother's boyfriend treats Melissa roughly when she annoys him. And I know Melissa can be annoying when she whines and complains.

Will reporting my suspicions help Melissa? Or make her situation worse? How will it affect Melissa's relationship with the other students? The whole Briar Hill community will know. So much for parent-teacher collaboration! What will it do to my ability to focus and teach my class? In spite of my misgivings, I am making a list of the dates and what I saw, and a summary of my phone call to her home, and my conversation with Melissa today. I don't know how much suspicion is enough to be "reasonable" when I know the chaos and pain that I could cause. This is the hardest thing I have ever done. But I feel that I have a moral responsibility to report my suspicions to Mr. Drucker tomorrow. From what I just read, I think I have a legal responsibility too. And once I start, I can see that I will have to keep going down this road, whether it helps Melissa or not.

*   *   *

Two days after the above journal entry, Mr. Drucker and Kelly are sitting in Kelly's classroom after school. The school is finally empty and silent. Over cups of tea, Mr. Drucker describes for Kelly the scene after he explained to six-year-old Melissa and nine-year-old Grace that a woman was coming to ask them some questions about their home life:

"When the caseworker arrived from the child protection agency, she told them that you had been worried about the 'accidents' that Melissa reported were the cause of her bruises. The caseworker said that she wanted to speak with each girl alone. They huddled together with Grace reassuring Melissa. Grace kept saying, 'It's OK, Missy, everything is going to be all right.' Melissa cried quietly, and Grace kept hugging her and reassuring her. Grace asked to speak first. She told the caseworker about the two girls being left in the care of her mother's new boyfriend, who would tell Melissa to 'Stop whining!' and, when she didn't stop, would hit her with anything he could find—a newspaper, an electrical cord, a belt, and even a coffee mug. She did not report him burning or cutting Melissa.

"Grace cried when she talked about how her mother believed her boyfriend rather than Grace and Melissa. 'She tells us we have to be good or else we deserve what we get when we bug him.' Grace described how she and her mom had tried to stop the bleeding after he threw a coffee mug that hit Melissa in the nose. That time, Grace said, her mom let Melissa stay home, but Melissa insisted on coming back to school the day that her mother had to work after school. Grace was upset because she said she wasn't doing a good job of taking care of Melissa. She didn't know the reason, but she did know the pattern—her mom's boyfriend only hurt Melissa, not her. Grace begged the caseworker, 'I can't save her, but please don't take her away. She is afraid of everyone now except me.'"

Mr. Drucker sighed, "No kids should have to deal with this. And no teachers either. I'm sorry, Kelly."

Entry in Kelly's journal, later the same day: It has been a really tough couple of days for everyone, and it is only beginning. The other children want to know where Melissa is—they have heard rumours. I will have to face Melissa soon when she comes back to school. Grace cried all day in her classroom and refused to acknowledge me. Melissa's mother phoned the school and made threats against the principal and against me. I may never know whether I did the best thing for Melissa. I think I did the morally right thing, and I guess legally I had to do it. I certainly know that I did the hard thing, in making my report. But I still have the feeling that Mr. Drucker wishes I had not been so insistent. So far, he has supported me. But…oh well, it is too late for going back now. Good luck, Melissa!

QUESTIONS FOR REFLECTION AND DISCUSSION

1. What are the facts/key elements of the case?

2. What do we know about Melissa? About Kelly Mullen?

3. Describe what Melissa might tell her pillow about what is happening to her at home. Describe what Grace might tell her cousin about what is happening to Melissa at home.

4. Describe the major dilemma(s) in this case.

5. What actions would you have advised Kelly to take to resolve the case? What role should the principal take in resolving the case? How much more difficult would this have been for Kelly if her principal had not agreed with her that there were grounds for reporting suspicion of abuse?

6. Consider the consequences of Kelly's actions for Melissa's relationship with Grace. Consider the consequences for Kelly's teaching and for the rest of the students in her class.

7. What can we learn from this case?

8. What assumptions and beliefs are called into question by this case?

EXHIBIT 11.1	Signs of Abuse

Note: These lists need to be used with caution as some of these indicators may reflect problems other than child abuse.

Signs of Physical Abuse

If a child is being physically abused, you may see the following **physical indicators**:

- Unexplained bruises, welts, and abrasions, especially on the face, back, buttocks, and thighs, sometimes in the shape of a belt or hairbrush; most often after the child has been absent or after a weekend
- Unexplained burns from cigarettes on hands, feet, buttocks, and back; burns in the shape of an iron or electric burner; immersion burns from scalding water
- Unexplained fractures and dislocations to the skull or facial structure; spiral fractures of the long arm or leg bones
- Inappropriate dress, especially long sleeves or pants in hot weather to cover bruises, burns, etc.
- Unexplained head injuries, including patches of hair pulled out
- Delays in seeking medical attention for any kind of injury

If a child is being physically abused, you may see the following **behavioural indicators**:

- Reports (by child) of injury by parents
- Extreme wariness of parents
- Extreme wariness of adults in general
- Wariness of physical contact, especially when initiated by an adult
- Resistance to being touched; pulling away when someone approaches or extends a hand
- Extreme watchfulness
- Fear of going home
- Unexplained prolonged absence (may be kept home while healing)
- Unlikely explanations for bruises, burns, etc., or denial of these injuries
- Resistance to undressing to change clothes for physical education
- Poor social relations with peers
- Apprehensiveness when other children cry
- Appearing unhappy, anxious
- Extremes of behaviour from aggressiveness to withdrawal

Exhibit 11.1 *Continued*

Signs of Neglect

If a child is being neglected, you may see the following **physical indicators**:
- Attending school hungry or fatigued
- Poor hygiene, dirtiness; lice or skin disorders associated with poor hygiene
- Inappropriate dress; exposure symptoms including sunburn, frostbite, frequent colds, pneumonia
- Unattended health problems
- Inadequate supervision or abandonment
- Frequent absence from school

If a child is being neglected, you may see the following **behavioural indicators**:
- Theft
- Begging or stealing food
- Verbal reports of no caretaker in the home
- Arriving early, staying late
- Sleeping in class
- Delinquency, alcohol or drug use

Signs of Emotional Abuse

If a child is being abused emotionally, you may see the following **physical indicators**:
- Lags in emotional, mental, or physical development
- Extreme lack of confidence or withdrawal
- Inability to concentrate, continual procrastination
- Excessive desire for teacher's attention
- Has-to-win attitude
- Extreme aggressiveness or passivity when playing with other children
- Participation in too many activities

If a child is being abused emotionally, you may see the following **behavioural indicators**:
- Conduct disorders; antisocial and destructive behaviour
- Extreme depression; attempted suicide
- Constant apologies, even when not responsible
- Speech disorders; sleep disorders; inhibition of play
- Fear of failure
- Inappropriate "adult" behaviours, including "bossing" or disciplining others
- Inappropriate childish behaviours, including throwing tantrums, crying, and sulking
- Sucking; biting; rocking
- Fear of failure; giving up; unwillingness to try after even small setbacks

EXHIBIT 11.2	What Is Required of Teachers Who Suspect Physical Abuse

Kelly learned that, across Canada, Child and Family Services legislation requires individuals who suspect child abuse to report their suspicions. Her school board had prepared both a set of steps for teachers to follow (called *When You Suspect Child Abuse*) and a form for them to complete (titled *Suspected Child Abuse: Report Form*).

When You Suspect Child Abuse

Be alert to the signs (physical and behavioural) of child abuse and neglect.

Take note of any child who shows some of the signs and write down your observations of the child in the school setting.

If a child discloses abuse to you, take the child to a quiet place, allow the child to tell what happened in his or her own words, and listen. Comfort the child by saying that telling you was a good thing for the child to do. Do not overreact; tell the child that it is not her or his fault. Reassure the child that you know what to do to get help and that you will tell people who can help the child.

Right after a child discloses abuse to you, or as soon as you suspect it, you have a legal obligation to report the disclosure or your suspicions immediately. Make an oral report to your principal the same day.

If your principal agrees, the two of you together follow the school district policy, calling the local child protection agency. If your principal disagrees, you are still required by law to make an immediate report to the local child protection agency yourself. Complete the form, *Suspected Child Abuse: Report Form*. (Note: If you do not make this report of suspected child abuse, you may be fined; for example, in Ontario the fine is $1000.)

The agency worker will require that you provide information, including the child's name, address, home telephone number, and the nature of the abuse you suspect. Refer to the objective observations you have made. As well, you will have to describe the statements made by the child (or other person) at the time information was disclosed to school personnel, including the name of the suspected abuser. Have your notes in front of you when you telephone the agency.

The child protection agency will investigate. They are expected to report their findings to the school. If they suspect a parent of abuse, they will not require parental consent to proceed and will access the child, in school, without the consent or prior knowledge of the parents. If they suspect abuse by persons outside of the family, they will conduct an investigation in consultation with the parents.

Remain attentive, responsive, and sympathetic to the child after making the report. The child may wish to continue talking with you.

Exhibit 11.2 *Continued*

Central School District

Suspected Child Abuse: Report Form

Child's Name: _____ Date of Birth: _____

Address: _____

_____

Telephone Number: _____

School: _____

Telephone Number: _____

School Address: _____

_____

Reasons for Referral: _____

_____

Suspected Abuse Reported By: _____

Name: _____ Position: _____

Date and Time: _____

Action Taken: _____

_____

_____

Consultations Held: _____

_____

Reported To (name agency, worker, position, time and date): _____

_____

_____

Teacher (printed name and signature): _____

_____

Date: _____

Principal (printed name and signature): _____

_____

Date: _____

Note: Retain one copy in the school, send copies to the superintendent for the school, and the agency.

EXHIBIT 11.3	Teaching Abused Students in Sensitive and Effective Ways

1. Ensure that the classroom is a safe environment.

Exercise enough control to keep the student feeling that the classroom is a safe and predictable place. Minimize chaos. You will want to directly teach positive ways to resolve conflict. Do not tolerate violence of any kind (verbal taunts, gestures, or sexual harassment).

2. Remember that abused children differ and avoid stereotypes.

Children's experiences of abuse differ widely, as do their needs. Factors like frequency, duration, and severity of abuse, as well as identity and role of the abuser (family member or camp counsellor) are influential. The child's characteristics, thoughts about the experience, and social support are all important. You should pay attention to the child in deciding what the child needs from you, and support the child's individual development, no matter the rate. Respect the child's expressed need for privacy, quiet time, or time away from noisy, busy activities.

3. Change takes time, so be patient.

Children may persist with inappropriate behaviours after the abuse has stopped. The problem behaviours may even get worse before they improve. Children who have been "spacing out" to avoid dealing with abuse will require time to drop this once-useful habit. Ask what the counsellor suggests the student do instead of "spacing out," and make the same suggestion. Consistency will be reassuring. Other once-useful responses to abuse may include running away or lying.

4. Be supportive; the child may be under greater stress than ever.

Your reporting may have caused others to punish the child. Other possible consequences include being ridiculed or called a liar. Sometimes increased violence takes place in the relationships among family members as they are required to take part in court appearances. Income may drop because a member leaves the family. Separation of the parents or incarceration of a family member are all possible as a direct consequence of the report. The child may be held responsible by the family.

5. Be compassionate, but also be firm with problematic behaviours.

The above suggestions all include concrete examples of showing the child compassion, which is very important. It is also critical to be firm and address inappropriate behaviours when they occur. The child is still responsible for his or her actions even though there has been abuse; these actions include internalized and externalized problem behaviours.

6. Teach the child, expect learning, and promote tangible skills.

Use many words of encouragement, support, and informational feedback to create positive experiences at school for the maltreated child. Experiences of maltreatment often cause children to have negative views of themselves. You can

Exhibit 11.3 *Continued*

contribute to changing these views by helping the child to be able to say, "I am the smart one who is good at math," or "I am the creative one who is good at painting." Hold high expectations for the child and provide high levels of support (and adaptive teaching if it is needed) so the child can reach these expectations. Help the child to recognize small gains, to set realistic proximal goals, and to stay on track, learning and moving toward goals.

Resources:
Horton, C. B., & Cruise, T. K. (2001). *Child abuse and neglect: The school's response.* New York: Guilford Press.
Youngblade, L. M., & Belsky, J. (1990). Social and emotional consequences of child maltreatment. In R. T. Ammerman & M. Hersen, (Eds.), *Children at-risk: An evaluation of factors contributing to child abuse and neglect* (pp. 107-146). New York, NY: Plenum Press.

SUGGESTIONS FOR FURTHER READING

Gaston, V., & Sutherland, J. (1999). *A selected, annotated bibliography of child maltreatment reporting by education professionals.* Ottawa: Health Canada. (retrieved on-line September 29, 2002 **http://www.hc-sc.gc.ca/hppb/familyviolence/**)
     A current and thorough resource on the Canadian, American, and international research on educators and child abuse.

Horton, C. B., & Cruise, T. K. (2001). *Child abuse and neglect: The school's response.* New York, NY: Guilford Press.
     This excellent resource provides relevant information for teachers about physical abuse, sexual abuse, emotional abuse, neglect, and children witnessing domestic violence. It also reports on what teachers can do to help children after the report has been submitted and the child returns to school.

Meston, J. (1993). *Child abuse and neglect programs.* Ottawa: Vanier Institute of the Family.
     A brief report, containing a summary of key information on child abuse in Canada, what it is, and how it affects children and society as well as descriptions of programs across Canada designed to prevent abuse.

Robbins, S. L. (2000). *Protecting our students: A review to identify and prevent sexual misconduct in Ontario schools.* Toronto: Queen's Printer for Ontario.
     Sexual abuse and physical abuse are different offences against children. While this case is about physical abuse, every classroom teacher needs to be aware of Robbins' important report on sexual abuse and its recommendations for ensuring the safety of students and the appropriate conduct of teachers.

WEBLINKS

http://www.hc-sc.gc.ca/hppb/familyviolence/
The National Clearinghouse on Family Violence (within Health Canada) provides information on all aspects of child abuse and neglect, including research, prevention, reporting, and continuing to work with the child and family following the report.

http://www.csica.zener.com/

The Canadian Society for the Investigation of Child Abuse provides information and training to aid in investigations of child abuse and to prepare child witnesses for court.

http://www.cfcs.gov.on.ca/cfcs/en/default.htm

Site of the Ontario Ministry of Community, Family and Children's Services. Every province has similar legislation and similar requirements for teachers' reporting when one has reasonable grounds to suspect neglect or physical or sexual abuse. In Ontario, teachers and principals are included on the list of professionals who can be charged and fined ($1000) for failing to discharge this obligation.

What Can I Do So I Can Teach Them?

Laurier Junior High is located in a poor, crime-ridden area of a Canadian city. Three decades ago the neighbourhood mostly contained well-kept homes of families with middle incomes. Today many neighbourhood homes are in poor repair with graffiti, piles of discarded possessions, and wrecked cars on the lawns. There are blocks of decaying rental units that serve as home to families who have recently come to Canada from countries all over the world. Many families are coping with unemployment. The school looks like a warehouse, built at the end of the 1940s, ignored, and falling down. The windows are covered with wire mesh to reduce the number broken, and there is spray paint everywhere on the yellow brick walls. Leslie has heard teachers at other schools say that the students at Laurier are below average in achievement, attendance, and behaviour. At her interview, the principal had told Leslie that every class contained exceptional students, some identified, some unidentified. He had said she could expect learning disabilities, emotional problems, and students at risk in every class. When Leslie asked about ethnic diversity, the principal agreed that many students spoke little English and that ESL programs served only a few of those for whom English was a second language.

At 7:45 on the first day of school, Leslie walked into the school from the parking lot. She watched little groups of black students clustering on the parking lot and knots of Asian students sitting on the school steps. She had noticed Caribbean and Asian markets in the school's neighbourhood and some other stores whose outside wares she did not recognize. The school foyer surprised Leslie. Even the "Welcome" sign was in

English only, and most of the posters and framed photographs showed white adolescents and adults. She wondered, "What was I expecting?" and answered, "It seems like the students have changed, but the school hasn't." When Leslie walked into the staff room, five teachers were already drinking coffee and discussing their vacations. What a relief Leslie felt when a teacher came over and introduced himself!

WILLIAM: Good morning. You must be Leslie, replacing Mrs. MacDonald who retired. Welcome to Laurier. I'm William Somers.

LESLIE: Right, I'm Leslie Neville. I guess you could say I'm replacing Mrs. MacDonald.

WILLIAM: [*pointing to the others, one by one*] This is Deb Wong, Phil Adams, Ron Franklin, David Johnston.

LESLIE: I'm pleased to meet you.

DEB: How did you end up at Laurier? [*All laugh and say it is not that bad.*]

LESLIE: I just graduated. I wanted an inner city school. Are there things I should know?

DEB: Well, the school has had some bad press in past years. Some people think the kids are hard to handle, but I don't think so....

DAVID: [*interrupting*] There are social problems. The things some of these kids have experienced....

LESLIE: How bad is it? You can teach the kids, can't you?

DEB: Sorry, we didn't mean to worry you. It's hard to generalize. A lot of the kids really want to learn. But so many of them barely understand English. Remember, if you ever want to talk to anyone, we're always here. We may not have all the answers, but we are always willing to listen.

Four weeks later, Leslie was standing at the overhead in front of 27 students. The students, 12 girls and 15 boys, were sitting in five parallel rows. Projected on the screen behind Leslie was a map with the names of endangered species written on countries around the world. Yesterday, Leslie had read to the class about the meaning of extinct, endangered, threatened, and vulnerable. She had led a class discussion about wildlife like the *Endangered Wildlife: Teacher's Guide* suggested. She had ended up shouting over the children, trying to convince them that wildlife meant anything not domesticated, anything that did not depend on humans for food or shelter. She had realized too late that to these children, some of whom had never left the city, it made no sense to say that humans were interacting with "wild" life, even in homes and cities, and that wildlife included all non-domesticated life forms. She wished she had invited someone from the local Naturalist Society to help her with that introductory lesson to the unit.

When they had entered the room today, the children saw four stations, one in each corner of the room. Under the Station 1 sign were a VCR and a poster that said ARKELOPE in large red letters. There was a pile of discussion guides with questions to be discussed and a space for notes to be recorded. Under the Station 2 sign were a game board and a poster that said WILDLIFE SURVIVAL GAME. At Station 3, there were a pile of copies of the same book Leslie was holding in her hand, *Endangered Wildlife,* and chart paper and markers. The poster said PANDAS. Similarly, at Station 4 there were a pile of these books, chart paper and markers, and a sign that said ORANGUTANS. At Stations 3 and 4, charts listed questions about the reading in *Endangered Wildlife*. Leslie had refused to answer their plaintive cries of "What are those? Are we having a video?" She had wanted to get into the lesson.

Leslie had reviewed yesterday's lesson wishing she had thought to put brief definitions of extinct, endangered, etc., on chart paper instead of relying on overheads. She had looked up from the projector. Today, the students seated near the front of the room appeared to be involved in the lesson. They were either looking at Leslie or writing the names of countries and animal species on an outline map of the world that Leslie had passed out. Many of the students in the back half of the room were restless and off-task. One girl was braiding the hair of a friend sitting in front of her. A quiet Asian boy yawned and put his head on the desk. Two boys, who reminded Leslie of her younger brothers, looked out the window at a pick-up truck parked in the schoolyard. A tall, black, young woman left her desk without permission and took a note to a friend on the other side of the room.

LESLIE: OK, class, look at this transparency of the world. [*Steps back and points to the screen.*] Sheila, sit down, I didn't say you could get up. [*Waiting for Sheila to sit down.*] Now which countries have we named that have endangered species? [*Points to Carla who has a hand raised.*]

CARLA: The Amazon River.

HIU: [*pointing at Carla, speaking in a mocking voice*] That's not a country! Don't you know anything?

LESLIE: [*sternly*] Hiu, put up your hand if you want to say something.

HIU: [*continuing to speak out*] She doesn't know what she is talking about!

WENDY: [*turns and glares at Hiu*] At least she has an idea! [*Wendy smiles at Carla who giggles.*]

LESLIE: OK, Wendy, settle down.

HIU: [*a bit intimidated*] I don't know which countries, but I know she's wrong. And there are a lot of countries.

FRANCOIS: Hey, what are these posters and how come there's a VCR in here? [*He points to the four stations in the corners of the room.*]

LESLIE: That's for an activity we are going to do later. Don't worry about it now. Hiu is right, there are many countries. In fact, yesterday we talked about how even Canada has endangered flowers, birds, and animals.

FRANCOIS: [*with hostility*] How can you know how many birds there are? You can't count them!

RICK: Ya, who cares!

LESLIE: [*with frustration*] Calm down. I said.... [*Leslie looks at Francois and Rick, who look like doubters.*] Here's another piece of information you probably didn't know. How many.... [*Question is drowned out by student voices from all but the students in the front. Asks Dave, who has his hand up.*]

DAVE: A few hundred. [*Only Leslie who is standing beside Dave can hear.*]

LESLIE: Good guess. Actually....

RICK: [*with disgust*] What did he say?

LESLIE: [*pauses, deciding what to do next*] Let's imagine that....

HIU: [*spontaneously*] Oh, will that be extinct? [*Points to Wanda.*]

WANDA: [*angrily*] You shut up!

LESLIE: [*moving toward Hiu*] Hey, watch it, you two! [*Hiu stares straight ahead.*] So what's going to happen eventually if we don't reverse this trend toward the extinction of species?

FRANCOIS: There won't be any birds. Or fish. Or trees. [*He laughs. Others laugh.*] Oh woe is me! [*Makes crying sounds.*]

LESLIE: [*smiling weakly*] I don't think it would be quite like that, but it would be tragic, wouldn't it? [*Some students nod their heads. Leslie walks back to the overhead projector and points to the outline map of the world.*]

LESLIE: I hope you have.... [*Looking at the back of the room.*] Some of you back there haven't done a thing all class. [*The sleeping boy lifts his head and puts it back down.*] Now what are the countries and animals we have already discussed? [*Nobody volunteers an answer.*] All right. Look at this transparency. [*Leslie puts up another one with animals and countries already named.*] Here are the five countries. Do you recognize them? [*Pointing.*] What's this one?

[*Several students speak at once each naming a different country.*]

LESLIE: One at a time. Please! I want you to remember these because next week we will be having a quiz. [*Students groan.*] Randy? [*Has seen his hand up.*]

RANDY: I'm not doin' no quiz! Last time you didn't mark it right!

BESS: You give us too much work!

LESLIE: [*with frustration*] Settle down. Be quiet!

RANDY: I do all my work!

LESLIE: Then why do I have all those zeros in my mark book?

RANDY: I know this stuff. We had it before.

FRANCOIS: Let's do something better!

SEVERAL STUDENTS: Yeah. Let's do something else!

LESLIE: [*trying to stay composed*] Now everyone settle down! This is environmental studies! We need to learn environmental studies! You need to know this for high school! [*Leslie walks over to her desk and picks up a pile of worksheets. She had copied these out of a kit in the Teacher Resource Centre, for the students who would inevitably be absent, as a way of keeping them informed about what had happened in the four stations.*] Since you seem to have trouble focusing on this activity, we are going to spend the rest of the period doing worksheets! [*There is much groaning.*] I'm sorry, but you give me no choice. We can't talk about what's in the activities [*she points to the four stations*], so we are going to answer questions instead.

RANDY: What about the posters and the VCR?

LESLIE: I'm sorry. I've had enough of this foolishness! [*Gives out sheets.*] I want all these questions answered by the time the bell rings. You better get started. Only 20 minutes. I don't think anyone can afford another failing mark.

The following morning Leslie dragged herself into the staff room, and dropped into a chair. Her colleagues asked what was wrong.

LESLIE: What a class I had yesterday! They were resisting everything. I had this great class planned on endangered species. They never let me get to the four stations with activities. I ended up giving them worksheets to shut them up.

DAVID: Sometimes they are like that. Don't be too hard on yourself. This is the inner city. The kids just behave differently. You'll get used to it. Do what you can.

David and Deb asked about the lesson. Leslie explained that the plan was to have the students work at two stations yesterday and two stations today. Then they would have discussed what they had learned, and applied these ideas to a case described in *Endangered Wildlife*. In a New Brunswick community, preventing the extinction of a riparian plant meant closing a local industry located on the river. The teacher's guide had suggested asking students to discuss the two sides of the dilemma, the long-term implications of the plant becoming extinct and the short-term implications of losing employment.

DEB: Sounds like a great way to get them to understand the concepts and implications. Do they seem interested in endangered species?

LESLIE: [*with disappointment*] I must be doing something wrong. I didn't even start the activities in the four stations. I would have had a riot on my hands.

DAVID: It is frustrating to make those plans and not be able to follow through. Are they good at working in groups?

LESLIE: They never really got into the topic. I don't know if it grabbed them. They don't seem to know how to discuss a controversial topic without putting each other down. But when I give them worksheets, they fill them in quietly and don't talk or anything. You know, I didn't become a teacher to hand out worksheets. I want to have active and stimulating classes. What can I do so I can teach them?

QUESTIONS FOR REFLECTION AND DISCUSSION

1. Identify the facts of the case briefly.
2. Describe Leslie as we know her from the case. Describe the class she is teaching in the case.
3. Use the facts and descriptions above to support your statement of the major dilemma(s). Describe the major dilemma(s).
4. Describe this class the way Randy (a student in Leslie's class) might describe it to Mr. Johnston, one of the teachers, when they meet in the hall after school.
5. What are some underlying issues that might arise from the context in which this case takes place?
6. What would you advise Leslie to do if you were one of her fellow teachers at Laurier?
7. What actions should Leslie take to resolve the dilemma(s)? Consider the consequences for Leslie, for the students, in a wider context.
8. Does this case lead us to question widely held beliefs or to recognize assumptions we might be making about some students, their teachers, and their classrooms?

EXHIBIT 12.1	Learning to Group, Grouping to Learn (One Page from an Inspirational Book)

The upshot of this disastrous day was that Deb Wong offered to mentor Leslie Neville. One day, not long after Leslie's disappointing class, Deb brought in a much-thumbed book to loan Leslie. Deb called it "Inspirational!" She said she had read and reread her favourite pages, especially after hard days. A yellow sticky note marked page 24:

Learning to Group, Grouping to Learn

Grouping young people for different activities and purposes is an integral part of classroom management, because it is directly related to classroom dynamics, but it also helps kids develop initiative, independence, and leadership. I often paired students (or let them choose partners) for brief, well-defined activities such as interviewing each other, generating lists, or responding to a single question. This five- to ten-minute exercise in working together, which I demonstrated before the pairs met, served as early preparation for more sustained small-group work. When certain students could not manage to work effectively for even a few minutes, I knew I would have to bring them to the conference table and take charge.

If too many students needed constant supervision, I devised other ways of working with them. For a while, I led the entire class in brief, well-defined activities so that everyone could practice a few simple procedures. I asked them to pair up with people sitting near them, and we repeated the procedures. I taught them quite explicitly. If students managed to accomplish one or two simple tasks, I asked them to work together again.

Some students simply could not control their behaviour, while others couldn't accomplish the simplest tasks in a group situation, so I brought these students together and worked through the process with them. A few students could not manage even when I was their leader, and I either let them sit and watch what was going on or asked them to sit outside the classroom to complete a short, manageable task alone.

If they couldn't work quietly in the hall, I sent them to the office. Then I called their parents and arranged a parent/teacher/student conference to put together a plan of action for which the student would be held accountable. In certain cases, I wrote up simple contracts that the student would read and sign in the presence of one or both of his adult family members. Although I never insisted that a parent come to class and sit with his or her son or daughter for a day or more (a management technique that can work very well), I do believe that when teachers and parents work together, students benefit.

Then, my students and I *practiced* working in pairs and small groups. We learned how to talk to each other more effectively and to accomplish more sophisticated tasks. But if a particularly disruptive student was having a bad day, I scotched my plans for small-group work and shifted into a more contained lesson. In the majority of my language arts/reading classes, students eventually learned how to work together because we took time to practice this skill throughout the school year.

Source: Reprinted by permission from *Just Teach Me, Mrs. K.: Talking, Reading, and Writing With Resistant Adolescent Learners* by Mary Mercer Krogness. Copyright © 1995 by Mary Mercer Krogness. Published by Heinemann, a division of Elsevier, Inc., Portsmouth, NH.

EXHIBIT 12.2	Principles for Establishing a Well-Managed Class

Leslie received the following principles for establishing a well-managed class at the first professional development workshop her school district held on classroom management.

1. Set rules and procedures with the students at the beginning of the year. Make no more than five rules. Keep them positive. Make streamlined procedures.
2. Teach these rules. Enforce them.
3. Organize the classroom so you can see all students at all times. You need eyes in the back of your head.
4. Plan your teaching well so it engages your students.
5. Make students aware of all tasks expected of them. Explain reasons for the way you would like things done.
6. Monitor. When someone breaks a rule deal with it quickly.

   a. Make eye contact with the misbehaving student. Use a signal to terminate the behaviour (point to where he should be, etc.). Monitor that the student begins appropriate behaviour. This does not interrupt the flow of class.
   b. If the student is not following a procedure, remind the student of the procedure.
   c. Deter inappropriate behaviour immediately. As quickly and quietly as possible, redirect student's attention to the task at hand.
   d. Enforce the rules, procedures and consequences consistently.
   e. Don't make threats you cannot carry out.

EXHIBIT 12.3	Strategies for Teachers in Classes with High Diversity

After a number of collegial chats, Leslie and Deb Wong developed a list of strategies and posted them on a Web site about teaching in culturally diverse schools.

1. Ensure that all students can see themselves in the posters, encouragements, and adornments on your classroom walls.
2. Learn about the cultures of all your students from the students and their parents. Be a good listener.
3. Incorporate your students' cultures into the learning environment.
4. Use non-threatening activities to find out how prepared your students are for the topics that you are about to teach.
5. Become aware of the language proficiencies and needs of ESL students. Talk with them individually in a quiet place to help to understand their spoken language. Consult with a language resource teacher or your principal for information.
6. Accommodate cultural diversity and ensure you make your teaching meaningful for all your students.
7. Read about antiracist education and actively look for ways to reduce the racism your students experience at school.
8. Respond quickly and firmly when you see or hear racist behaviour in the school or on the schoolyard.
9. Work at understanding how your own stereotypes might interfere with your teaching equitably in a culturally diverse school.
10. Examine your topics, materials, and teaching methods for bias.
11. Develop activities that truly engage students, and teach them by degrees how to take responsibility for their own engagement with learning. Don't assume they know how to collaborate or cooperate to learn. Teach them how.
12. Establish legitimate standards for classroom work, and make the necessary efforts to ensure that all students reach these standards; that may mean making adaptations or accommodations.
13. Help all students to relate their lives and issues to classroom learning.
14. Model the kind of caring, respectful, and community-oriented behaviour that you expect of your students.

Let your students know when they are meeting your expectations. The positive feedback is essential for enhancing appropriate behaviour and engagement with learning in the classroom.

SUGGESTIONS FOR FURTHER READING

Evertson, C., Emmer, E. T., Worsham, M. E. (2000). *Classroom management for elementary teachers* (5th ed.). Boston, MA: Allyn & Bacon.

    This practical handbook focuses on planning before the school year begins, establishing good classroom management at the beginning of the year, and then maintaining it. There is a parallel edition for secondary teachers. A classic!

Gootman, M. E. (1997). *The caring teacher's guide to discipline: Helping young students learn self-control, responsibility, and respect*. Thousand Oaks, CA: Corwin Press.

    The author suggests that she adds three more R's: respect, responsibility, and relationship. A thoughtful approach to understanding why students do what they do, and how we can respond in caring and effective ways.

Hutchinson, N. L. (1996). Creating an inclusive classroom with young adolescents in an urban school. *Exceptionality Education Canada, 6*(3&4), 51–67.

    Describes teaching students in an urban school to work collaboratively and to become better mathematical problem solvers by adopting engaging teaching methods, providing encouragement, and holding individual students accountable for what they have accomplished each day.

Krogness, M. M. (1995). *Just teach me, Mrs. K.: Talking, reading, and writing with resistant adolescent learners*. Portsmouth, NH: Heinemann.

    An inspirational teacher of Grade 7 and 8 students from a wide range of cultural and economic backgrounds describes how she was able to motivate students who had never viewed themselves as learners and teach them to work collaboratively and independently toward their own goals.

Meyers, M. (1993). *Teaching to diversity: Teaching and learning in the multi-ethnic classroom*. Toronto, ON: Irwin.

    Helpful for adapting teaching to help ESL students learning in the regular classroom. Written by an experienced classroom and ESL teacher from North York.

Obiakor, F. E. (2001). *It even happens in "good" schools: Responding to cultural diversity in today's classrooms*. Thousand Oaks, CA: Corwin Press.

    Obiakor, an American author, argues that a good school is defined by how it addresses diversity and maximizes the potential of all students. He provides many examples of the need for teachers to teach exceptional students in ways that are culturally sensitive.

WEBLINKS

http://www.teachnet.com/how-to/manage/
This site contains many ideas for handling common classroom management challenges.

http://www.lab.brown.edu/tdl/tl-strategies/crt-principles.shtml
A helpful site that lists nine principles of culturally responsive teaching and explains how to put these principles into practice in the classroom.

http://www.bctf.ca/vesta/EveryKid_Website/index.html
Teachers in the inner city of Vancouver have written a book called *Every Kid Counts* about the struggle to provide an adequate education to students in inner city schools. This Web site provides background to the book and information on obtaining copies.

case 13

Change Is So Hard!

Aaron is in Grade 8. This is his last year at Meadowlark Junior High, his neighbourhood school. Next September he will board a crosstown bus every morning to go to T. C. Douglas Senior High. Aaron hates change. He can walk to Meadowlark. His mom has volunteered in his school every Tuesday since he entered Kindergarten, first at his elementary school and then at Meadowlark. This means she understands when he comes home exasperated because Billy from his class has bullied him on the schoolyard, or the drama teacher hasn't given him a role in the school play even though it was about trains. And Aaron knows more about trains than anyone at Meadowlark. Aaron has Asperger syndrome. And trains are his special interest. Recently Aaron wrote in his journal:

> I know trains. I know all the locomotives—F units, Alco RS2s, and Morse Fairbanks C-Liners. Then there's freight cars, like pressure-differential covered hoppers, drop-bottom gondolas, and mill gondolas. I really like passenger cars, especially heavy-weight combines and the CP skyline series. I can tell you anything about trains in western Canada including the history, the lines, or how the cars are serviced. But there are too many people on the trains. When I ride the train with Dad, people always tell me to stop talking about the trains. People make noise. They don't listen. I'm just telling them about the trains.

Aaron is attending the first meeting of his transition team at Meadowlark. It is only October of Grade 8, and already Aaron's parents are insisting that Meadowlark start transition activities so Aaron will be ready for T. C. Douglas Senior High next September. Aaron's mom, Sandy, reminds the others at the meeting how she started working with the resource teacher about eight months before Aaron's transition from elementary school to Meadowlark. She knows that it took eight months for Aaron to acclimatize to the new setting. Sandy is explaining to Aaron's Grade 8 homeroom teacher, the principal, and the resource room teacher that it is necessary for the resource room teacher at the senior high to participate in the transition process. Sandy keeps repeating, "The conditions Aaron must get used to are the conditions at the high school. The teachers there know what demands he will have to meet next year. They have to inform us. Otherwise we are getting Aaron ready for a setting in which he is already thriving. And that doesn't make any sense. He loves Meadowlark; we don't have to prepare him for Meadowlark. But none of us really knows what he will face at T. C. Douglas next year. They know what he will have to do next year. That is why we need them at this table."

The principal repeats, "Your quarrel is not with me, Sandy. I'm here, my teachers are here. I invited Ms. Hammill, the senior high resource teacher, to join us. She says she begins transition in March for students with the greatest needs and in May for students with mild handicaps. I cannot make her come to these meetings."

Sandy holds her ground. She has been through these kinds of meetings a hundred times. She knows that remaining calm and persistent is likely to carry the day. So she responds, "I have an idea. Is it OK with you if Aaron and I arrange to meet with Ms. Hammill at the senior high?" She continues, "I want her to see how lost and confused Aaron is in that setting. And how much he needs orientation, not for an afternoon, or a day, but for months."

The principal smiles. "I think I see where you are going with this. You want her to see the comparison for herself."

Aaron's teacher jumps in, "So you will want to bring Ms. Hammill to observe Aaron in my classroom after he goes to the senior high. Clever!" Aaron's teacher thinks about his current schedule at Meadowlark: unlike his classmates, Aaron spends three periods each day with his homeroom teacher, and the other two with the resource room teacher. He has his most demanding classes later in the day, after he has settled in, and his resource periods (which he calls "easier") first. Aaron's teacher laughs. Then she frowns, "You are going to put Aaron in a terribly uncomfortable position, where he can't cope. And where he will probably embarrass himself. Do you think that's fair? Isn't there another way?"

Sandy looks at Aaron. She knows that Aaron will have understood the conversation even if he has not commented. She asks, "How do you feel about this?" And in a flat voice, devoid of emotion, Aaron speaks for the first time in the meeting, "Bad. Real bad." But he is smiling. His mother laughs, "Aaron, you don't look like you feel bad, you are smiling."

"Can't I stay at Meadowlark? Meadowlark is better." Then Aaron looks to his mother for help, "How does it look?" He means how does he make his face look sad. Like many children with autism and Asperger syndrome, Aaron doesn't fully understand emotions and feelings, his or those of other people. His mother frowns and Aaron looks into the pocket mirror she hands him. He frowns too, copying Sandy, sees his frown in the pocket mirror, and says, "I remember." The smile returns.

Sandy says to Aaron's teacher, "I appreciate your concern. I will talk with Ms. Hammill. And tell her about this conversation and your concern. I will ask her to join us. I know you have invited her. But as Aaron's mother, I can be more emotional than you. If she doesn't agree to join us, I will arrange to take Aaron to T. C. Douglas. Even a five-minute meeting will be enough for her to see his fear and inability to cope. I will arrange it for right after school when the noisy hordes are at their lockers."

The discussion continued with Sandy explaining that, as a parent of a child with an exceptionality like Asperger syndrome, it has been necessary for her to thrust her child into uncomfortable situations. She reminded the educators that none of them was on staff at Meadowlark when she began the transition process for Aaron from elementary school to Meadowlark. For eight months, she brought him to Meadowlark once a week, then twice a week, then more frequently. She described how he hated the crowds and the noise at first, but had learned to tolerate them by the time he started Grade 6. She reminded them that she was the only person in the room who had seen Aaron's overwhelming fear when she took him to an open house at the senior high the previous spring. She finished her reminders with, "You may not like it, but you have to admit that I know more about Aaron's struggles and successes than any of you. I have worked with 22 educators, administrators, Cub leaders, and…." She stopped, "You get the idea. I am really the first and most consistent educator in Aaron's life. And as his parent, I have to fight for what I believe is best for Aaron. I appreciate what all of you have done. But none of you has the experience with Asperger syndrome generally, or with Aaron specifically, that I have." She sighed, "Sorry, that was a long speech. But I believe that I know what has to be done. And I am asking for your help. Please."

From that point, the meeting took a different turn. The principal agreed to call Ms. Hammill again, although she expressed her view that it would not help. Sandy said she would contact Ms. Hammill to reiterate the principal's invitation. Sandy described how she would go ahead with her plan to take Aaron to meet Ms. Hammill, if necessary, at 3:05, when the senior high was at its most chaotic.

The rest of the meeting was spent mapping out a plan that would see Aaron start going to T. C. Douglas for an hour per week as soon as possible, then for two hours, with gradual increases after that. The plan included getting acquainted with his homeroom teacher and with the resource teacher who would be his main support in junior high. Actions that Aaron would need to be able to do independently before the start of school the next September included finding his way alone to both their classrooms, riding the bus without incident (perhaps with a peer), borrowing a book from the library, finding his locker, and using his combination lock. The principal suggested that they request that an older student be assigned to Aaron as a peer tutor. She had seen this system work well for a girl with physical disabilities who had made the transition to the senior high last year. Her peer tutor received a credit for tutoring, even though most of the tutoring was social rather than academic.

After Sandy and Aaron left the meeting, the educators spent a few minutes debating the merits of the actions to be taken in the upcoming week. Aaron's teacher continued to argue that it was not fair for adults to place Aaron in a situation where they knew he could not cope. She expected that, in the noise and chaos of the senior high, he would put his hands over his ears, run and hide under a table, and create a scene. The principal was more sympathetic to Sandy's argument, "Desperate times require desperate measures." The resource teacher agreed, "Transition to T. C. Douglas is tough for every student with a disability. They must have the students' needs put right under their noses, or they put it off until the last minute. Many students can benefit from a model transition program, like Aaron's, if it works. We keep hearing from the senior high that we don't have the students ready for their program. The biggest issues are always social relations with teachers and peers, and learning the routines. We keep telling them that we need their help with these things. The situation there is so different from cozy little Meadowlark."

The principal kept returning to her assessment of Sandy, "That woman has courage. I may not want all the parents of exceptional students to be that assertive, but if they were, our schools would be better for it. We would have to find the energy and resources to really do transition properly. I think that is why the new IEP procedures call for transition plans for all exceptional secondary students before leaving high school. But as she was leaving Sandy gave me a copy of an article that says the transitions *to* senior high are just as tough for the students. This article is about students with Asperger syndrome, but I bet the same could be said about students with other exceptionalities."

That night Sandy discussed her plan with Aaron. She felt badly about putting Aaron under so much stress for one afternoon, but she knew how much worse it would be if he began Grade 9 without having achieved some comfort in the senior high setting. He would feel overwhelming stress every day. She knew that the strain would cause Aaron to overreact and either fight or flee and hide, both a recipe for disaster. Aaron hugged Sandy. He tried to comfort her. Although his words were spoken a bit mechanically in a monotone voice, they sounded wonderful to Sandy. She knew that Aaron was using skills he had learned from the psychologist who had worked with him during the past year at the Child Development Centre. From this kind but firm man, Sandy had learned to be much more solid in her resolve. The psychologist kept saying that short-term pain for Aaron (and Sandy) like the short visit to T. C. Douglas could result in long-term gain if handled well. Sandy could see Aaron understanding more and showing more emotion, even if the changes were still subtle. She hugged him and told him how proud she was of him.

After Aaron was in bed, Sandy described the meeting to her husband. "I think Aaron's teacher thinks I am a monster. She doesn't want me to take Aaron to T. C. Douglas and make him look bad. She doesn't think the end justifies the means. And I know she has a point. Aaron will be really upset. And I hope the students and teachers who see him that day don't remember him."

Sandy began to cry. Her husband knew that he could not tell Sandy what to do, even if he disagreed with her "tough" approach. She was the person in the family who put hundreds of hours into Aaron's schooling and treatment. She was his mainstay, and she knew him best. So her husband listened, encouraged Sandy to talk, and asked her hard questions about the downside of the strategy she was proposing. He asked her to suggest alternative courses of action, and kept her talking until she was past her tears and back into problem-solving mode. He suggested that Sandy hold her plan for going to T. C. Douglas at 3:05 in reserve—the plan of last resort—and that she try everything else she could think of first. But he knew Sandy's commitment to Aaron. And he admitted that, if she could not get the senior high to participate willingly, she would have to shock them into it. He had to admire her.

QUESTIONS FOR REFLECTION AND DISCUSSION

1. Identify the facts of the case briefly.

2. What do we know about the student, Aaron? About his teachers? Describe his mother, Sandy.

3. Describe the situation that led to this transition meeting, first from the perspective of Aaron's teacher, and then from the perspective of Sandy, his mother. How might Ms. Hammill describe the meeting if she could have watched it, unobserved?

4. Describe the major dilemma(s) in this case?

5. What are some of the underlying issues associated with transitions for exceptional students?

6. What actions should Sandy, Aaron's mom, take to resolve the dilemma(s)? What role should the principal take?

7. Consider the consequences of these actions for Aaron's present days at Meadowlark, and for his future schooling at T. C. Douglas Senior High. Consider the consequences for other students who need transition plans for their move to junior high and from Meadowlark to senior high.

8. What can we learn from this case?

9. How does this case lead us to question widely held beliefs or to recognize assumptions we may be making about some students, their families, and their transitions?

EXHIBIT 13.1	Characteristics of Children and Adolescents with Asperger Syndrome (AS)

The characteristics described below are commonly found in children and adolescents with AS. However, it is important to remember that typical AS characteristics are manifested in ways specific to each individual, and no one person will have all of these characteristics.

Social Interaction

- show an inability to understand complex rules of social interaction
- may become tense trying to cope with the approaches and social demands of others.
- lack strategies to make friends; begin to realize that peers have friends (often at adolescence)
- may behave in socially inappropriate ways
- vulnerable to bullying and teasing

Social Communication

- may have superficial, perfect spoken language which tends to be formal, almost pedantic
- use monotone or stilted, unnatural voice
- cannot interpret the tone of voice of others (e.g., angry, bored, delighted)
- have difficulty picking up on social cues and do not understand jokes, irony, or metaphor (take things literally)
- show poor ability to initiate and sustain conversation

Social Imagination

- cannot imagine what another person is thinking (may not realize that people think)
- often have absorbing interests which are unusual for their age
- insist that certain routines be adhered to
- are limited in ability to think and play creatively

Other characteristics

- sensitivity to sensory stimuli (e.g., touch, loud noises, bright lights, etc.)
- insistence on sameness (especially in routines)
- poor concentration
- poor motor coordination
- emotional vulnerability

Resources on this topic:
Attwood, T. (1998). *Asperger's syndrome: A guide for parents and professionals*. London, UK: Jessica Kingsley Publishers.
Cumine, V., Leach, J., & Stevenson, G. (1998). *Asperger syndrome: A practical resource for teachers*. London, UK: David Fulton Publishing.
Ontario Ministry of Education. (2002). *Transition planning: A resource guide*. Toronto: Queen's Printer for Ontario.
Williams, K. (2001). Understanding the child with Asperger syndrome: Guidelines for teachers. *Intervention in school and clinic, 36*, 287-292.

EXHIBIT 13.2	Information for Teachers about Asperger Syndrome

- Unstructured times of the day, when the rules are not clear, are the most difficult for students with AS and their teachers.
- Learning the social skills necessary for the classroom and playground is very demanding and stressful for these students. They may not have much energy left for dealing with academic tasks.
- The routine or extremely familiar may reduce stress.
- It is usually necessary to teach listening, turn-taking in conversation, etc.
- The child's or adolescent's language level may not represent his or her communication level; check for understanding.
- The student with AS may not be able to read your intentions from your behaviour.
- The child will need to learn that other people have feelings, thoughts, beliefs, and attitudes.
- The child may not recognize that he or she has feelings, thoughts, beliefs, and attitudes.

What Teachers Can Do to Teach Students with AS

- Provide a predictable and safe environment; offer consistency in routines; prevent bullying.
- Plan well for transitions and expose the student to the new situation gradually, long before the transition takes place.
- Educate classmates in a sensitive way about the disability, especially the social problems, and about the child's strengths.
- Use a classmate as a buddy for checking comprehension and giving task reminders.
- Do not allow the student with AS to perseveratively discuss or ask questions about isolated interests; limit this to a specific time of the day, perhaps as a reward after some assigned work has been completed.
- Develop a highly structured approach for the student, with assignments broken into small units with frequent feedback and redirection.
- If necessary, lessen the amount of classwork and homework; arrange for use of a computer for completing assignments if necessary.
- Arrange for resource room time during which the student can have questions answered and can work on assignments, homework, etc., and mandate the resource room as a "safe haven" for the student with AS.
- Work out a nonverbal signal with the student (e.g., a gentle pat on the shoulder) for times when he or she is not listening.

| EXHIBIT 13.3 | Easing Transitions for Students with Asperger Syndrome |

Changes That Make Junior High and Senior High School Challenging for Students with AS

- All change (even minor change)
- New building, classrooms, and support person (educational assistant or resource teacher)
- Bigger school and more teachers
- Different expectations and classroom rules every period
- Increase in noise in the corridors
- Expectations for more independent learning, behaviour, and problem solving
- Competition used to motivate students
- More reading from abstract textbooks and more homework
- More rigorous grading policies
- More complex peer relationships, organized by adolescents, not by teachers or parents

Transition Strategies for Students with AS

- Expect to provide significantly increased support for each transition.
- Begin planning at least six months, and preferably 12 months, prior to the move taking place.
- Involve a teacher (and administrator) from the receiving school as well as the sending school, and the student and a parent.
- Begin with a school tour; use the student's experience during the tour and the demands of the receiving school as the basis for the transition activities and supports.
- Develop transition activities and supports to meet each of the academic, social/emotional, and physical needs; take advantage of strengths (academic, social/emotional, and physical).
- Enable the student to spend gradually increasing amounts of time in the receiving school, participating more over time.
- Foster the development of a supportive relationship between the transition student and an older buddy. (Try to find a buddy who is considered "cool" by other students.)
- Have all supports in place before school begins.
- Extend the transition support for months until the student with AS is accustomed to the demands of the new setting.
- Remember that the resources put into the transition will reduce the demands on resources later.

Resources on this topic:
Adreon, D., & Stella, J. (2001). Transition to middle and high school: Increasing the success of students with Asperger syndrome. *Intervention in school and clinic, 36,* 266-271.
Cumine, V., Leach, J., & Stevenson, G. (1998). *Asperger syndrome: A practical resource for teachers.* London, UK: David Fulton Publishing.

SUGGESTIONS FOR FURTHER READING

Adreon, D., & Stella, J. (2001). Transition to middle and high school: Increasing the success of students with Asperger syndrome. *Intervention in school and clinic, 36*, 266-271.
  One of the best resources available on the specific challenges and strategies associated with transitions for adolescents with Asperger syndrome.

Attwood, T. (1998). *Asperger's syndrome: A guide for parents and professionals*. London, UK: Jessica Kingsley Publishers.
  A highly respected source for non-researchers written by a prominent researcher.

Cumine, V., Leach, J., & Stevenson, G. (1998). *Asperger syndrome: A practical resource for teachers*. London, UK: David Fulton Publishing.
  This book provides teachers with a clear sense of what it is like to have AS in a world designed for people who can follow discussions, participate in conversations, and understand unwritten rules of social interaction.

Ontario Ministry of Education. (2002). *Transition planning: A resource guide.* Toronto: Queen's Printer for Ontario.
  This current guide to the requirements for transition planning in Ontario describes a thorough set of procedures that would benefit all exceptional students and their families, especially with the transition from secondary school but also with other transitions.

Stewart, K. (2002). *Helping a child with nonverbal learning disorder or Asperger's syndrome: A parent's guide*. Oakland, CA: New Harbinger Publications.
  This new resource for parents provides many examples in brief vignettes. Recommended by a parent who has found it helpful.

Williams, K. (2001). Understanding the child with Asperger syndrome: Guidelines for teachers. *Intervention in school and clinic, 36*, 287-292.
  A brief, straightforward article that focuses on characteristics of students with AS and on ways in which teachers can adapt their teaching in response to these characteristics.

WEBLINKS

http://www.users.dircon.co.uk./~cns/
University Students with Autism and Asperger's Syndrome: A British site devoted to helping post-secondary students that contains research on the experiences of students with AS including first-person accounts and resources.

http://www.genevacentre.com/
The Geneva Centre has provided support and information about autism and related disorders to Canadian families and professionals since 1974–they have an outstanding library from which families and teachers can borrow.

http://www.udel.edu/bkirby/asperger/
O.A.S.I.S. stands for Online Asperger Syndrome Information and Support. Click on the Education link for a host of useful ideas (and overlook the information about American legislation).

A Report To My Teachers

Maria Cerini's last English class of the morning was just finishing. While she was collecting her teaching notes and ensuring that all members of her Grade 12 class had received the handout on the play to be discussed next day, Heather Johnson slowly rolled her wheelchair through the door from the hall. For the past three months, Heather, who was in Grade 11 at Dominion High, had sought Maria as a mentor. Maria sometimes wondered why Heather had chosen her.

Maria had taught Heather Grade 9 English and now was her teacher again, this time for the Grade 11 drama course. Heather was born with spina bifida and has always used a wheelchair. When Heather was in Grade 9, Maria had suggested that she write a report for her teachers about herself and her spina bifida. This had given Heather a sense of control and a feeling of a greater role in her own education. Maria's brother used a wheelchair, so she understood how individuals with physical disabilities could feel powerless in their own lives. As Maria looked at Heather, she realized that powerless was exactly how Heather looked at this moment. When she greeted Heather warmly, Heather said, "We have to talk. Big trouble. I always knew it was too good to be true." And she broke into tears.

While Maria comforted Heather and let the tears run their course, she thought about what could have caused this downturn in Heather's spirits. "It must be serious," she said to herself. "I have not seen her in a state like this since Grade 9." When Heather first came to Dominion, she had been quiet, almost timid, and definitely afraid to challenge the system. But Maria had known that if Heather was to be successful, she would need to challenge the system. Maria's brother did not learn until halfway through university that he had to insist on his rights, accommodations, and equitable treatment. And, as he had learned to say, "Equitable does not mean equal. You can walk up those stairs, but it will only be equitable for me when there is an elevator to carry me to the second floor."

Dominion High was a sprawling one-storey secondary school built in the expansion heyday of the 1960s. Although a shiny building when it was new, Dominion had tarnished quickly. The suburban neighbourhood had once been solidly middle class, but as developers put up large, prestigious homes in the fields beyond Dominion, families who could afford it moved out of the neighbourhood. Dominion became a magnet school for special programs in the 1980s—probably because it was wheelchair accessible and because forward-looking administrators saw programs for gifted students and students with learning disabilities as a means of keeping the Dominion enrolment from dropping drastically. Even with the onset of inclusive policies in the school district, exceptional students were over-represented at Dominion. Heather's family had joined the exodus to the outer suburbs, but Dominion was the only high school where Heather could access every classroom. Also, the teachers were accustomed to working with students with disabilities and students who were gifted.

In Grade 9 all students at Dominion participated in a self-awareness unit in the required Teacher Advisor Groups with their homeroom teacher. It was as an assignment for this course that Heather had prepared her report about herself and her physical condition. Most of the teachers had been impressed by Heather's frank report and her articulate way of speaking about her disability. Each term, Heather gave a copy of the report to each of her teachers. She had twice updated the report, so it was current and accurate. Maria thought this suggestion of hers was the reason Heather had chosen Maria as her mentor. During Grade 10, Maria had seen little of Heather. She knew Heather was taking one less course each term than her peers, attending learning assistance in the period when she had no class, and expected to graduate one year later than the students with whom she had started high school. But through Grade 10, Maria had been almost out of touch with Heather.

Then at the start of Grade 11, Heather had asked to be placed in Maria's drama class. Maria was pleased. She had always found Heather thoughtful and eager to learn. The first week of school, Heather had sought Maria's support for a "new idea." Heather wanted to ask for a monthly meeting with all her teachers so she could hear how she was doing, make suggestions, and help her teachers learn from each other. Maria supported Heather, but she had suggested Heather approach first the principal and the head of Guidance, and then each of her teachers. Some teachers had come to discuss the plan with Maria, thinking that this, too, had originated with her. Maria had explained that this was Heather's idea. Eventually all Heather's fall semester teachers had agreed to a three-month trial period.

Maria thought that they had agreed because Heather had given each of them a copy of her report and suggested they ask her former teachers if it had been helpful to them. Most of Heather's teachers would have agreed that they found her frank report helpful. She explained a bit about her condition, expressed her pleasure in having girlfriends and her concern that no boys would overlook her wheelchair to take her on a date. She described a few of her frustrations in a world largely inaccessible to wheelchairs. Mostly, Heather gave teaching tips for her teachers.

A Report to My Teachers by Heather Johnson

Spina bifida:

It is a birth defect of the spinal column in which the bones of the spine fail to close around the column of nerves it protects. The extent of the disability resulting from this condition can vary with respect to paralysis, sensation in the legs, and various degrees of bowel and bladder incontinence.

Heather Johnson:

I am an adolescent who was born with spina bifida, which was surgically corrected shortly after birth.

My interests are similar to other girls my age. I like high school, belong to the photography club, and have many girlfriends. Boys talk to me in school and seem friendly enough, but none of them seem to want to go out with me. I think it is because they aren't sure how to help me in and out of the car with my wheelchair. I like going to the mall with my friends, but that presents problems. Although the signs say the stores are wheelchair accessible, some have a step or two not noticeable to people walking. These can be a major obstacle to people in wheelchairs. Often, the dressing rooms are too small for my chair. The rest rooms are like the ones at school. They say they are accessible, but they are really too narrow for turning a wheelchair around. None of the sinks is low enough, and some have a cabinet underneath, so it is hard to get close. I have the same problem with drinking fountains.

I do quite well in my classes and am thinking about what my future holds—careers, going to college, independence? I love my courses in English,

drama, history, and computer studies. I find math and science challenging. The teachers at Dominion High have accommodated my needs and helped me keep up with the academic program. Students and teachers in the school treat me like the age I am. I am really quite like everyone else.

Teaching Tips for My Teachers:

- Modify the classroom for my needs (e.g., wider aisles for my wheelchair, a low shelf for storage).
- Avoid overprotection; provide opportunities for many activities so I can discover my strengths and weaknesses.
- Become familiar with my special equipment (my wheelchair and computer).
- Arrange and adjust my seating and my working area.
- Allow extra time for assignments, moving around the school, etc.
- Be sensitive to my self-care needs and social needs.
- Collaborate with physical therapists, counsellors, and other consultants.
- Be prepared for absence for hospital treatment and home care.
- Design classroom procedures for emergency situations; assign students to help me in an emergency.
- Contact the Physical Disabilities Association.
- Talk to me about anything that you need to know about spina bifida, me, and about how to teach me.

Maria knew from reading Heather's file that there were many details Heather had omitted from her report to her teachers. Heather's fine motor control was weak and using a pencil tired her hands and arms. Heather was embarrassed about her incontinence and needed to attend to herself in private in a restroom on a rigid schedule. Urinary infections and pressure sores (caused by something so small as a wrinkle in Heather's clothes that she could not feel) kept Heather away from school at some point every semester. Heather's mother, a registered nurse, had taught Heather to take a mature, coping attitude toward her disability and to refuse to allow it to keep her from living life to the fullest. Extensive reading about adolescents with disabilities had informed Maria that Heather was unusually determined and successful in dealing with her disability. "If only my colleagues understood how amazing Heather's response to her disability is," Maria thought, "and if only I knew how to help them understand."

Maria returned to the present. She knew some teachers loved the idea of the monthly meeting, and some said Heather was taking self-advocacy too far. Could this be the source of Heather's despondency? "Heather, what is wrong? I can't help until you tell me what is going on."

"Ms. Cerini...Mr. Hobbes says he won't come to any more team meetings to hear about how I want my classes 'watered down.' But I never asked him to make it easier for me. I know I find math difficult. I just asked him for more time on the big unit test. I thought he said *yes* in the last meeting. But today in class he told me that he has changed his mind. I have to have the same amount of time for the test as everyone else. He says he feels pressured in the meetings because everyone else caves in to me. He says that it is his decision about how much time he gives me to write my tests, not the decision of the team of all my teachers. He thinks he's losing his freedom to make teaching decisions. Can you talk with him for me, please? I don't think he will listen to me."

"Heather, let's think about why you wanted to have meetings of the team. What did you hope to accomplish? Wasn't it to advocate for yourself? Wasn't this practice for you for the kind of advocating you will have to do in college and in the workplace? What will it do to the whole effort if I go to Mr. Hobbes?"

Heather replied, "But I don't know if I can do it. He is so critical of me. Maybe you can come with me. Just stand beside me. That will make me feel stronger. I will do the talking. Please."

"Heather, you have been very successful so far. Even if Mr. Hobbes leaves, don't you think the others will continue to attend the meetings? You are breaking new ground, remember. None of these teachers has ever been part of organized self-advocacy by a student. In the last meeting, everyone but Mr. Hobbes told of a successful adaptation they had worked out with you. Maybe you will have to settle for four out of five this term. The other four have agreed to meet this Wednesday at noon. Now I want to hear what you think you should do next and why. You will need a plan and a calm way to act on this plan. What should be done to resolve this problem and who should do it?"

QUESTIONS FOR REFLECTION AND DISCUSSION

1. What are the key facts/elements of this case?
2. What do we know about Heather? About her teacher and mentor, Maria Cerini?

3. Describe the main dilemma(s) in this case.

4. What underlying issues contribute to the dilemma(s)?

5. What issues are most important to Heather? What issues are most important from Ms. Cerini's point of view? From Mr. Hobbes' point of view?

6. How should Heather and Ms. Cerini resolve the dilemma(s)?

7. Consider the consequences of such a resolution for Heather, Mr. Hobbes, Ms. Cerini.

8. What can we learn from Heather's experiences in this case? Ms. Cerini's experiences?

9. Does this case lead us to question any long-held beliefs or to recognize assumptions we might be making about students, teachers, and self-advocacy?

EXHIBIT 14.1	**Request for Adapted Assessment**

In her reading about self-advocacy, Maria had come across a formal system that students could use to help them advocate for the test modifications they needed. Maria thought that looking at the steps of the formal system might remind Heather of how to lead the discussion in the next meeting of her teachers and remind her of how well she was doing in self-advocacy.

Name _____ Subject _____

Date test scheduled _____ Period _____

Teacher _____ Modification on IEP? Yes __ No __

Modifications

1. Revised format
   - ___ oral response, rather than written response
   - ___ Braille format
   - ___ large-print format
   - ___ reduced number of items (specify _____)
   - ___ point-form response, rather than written response
   - ___ web-of-ideas response, rather than written response
   - ___ peer assistance (specify _____)
   - ___ other (specify _____)

2. Revised directions
   - ___ oral directions, rather than written directions
   - ___ directions reread for each page

Exhibit 14.1 *Continued*

___ simplified language in written directions

___ additional examples provided

___ each question read orally

___ other (specify _____)

3. Flexible scheduling or setting

___ extended time (specify _____)

___ separate location (specify _____)

___ adaptive furniture

___ removal of distractions

4. Use of assistive devices

___ visual magnification

___ auditory amplification

___ computer

___ calculator

___ scribe

___ spelling provided upon request

___ notes previously prepared by the student

___ other (specify _____)

5. Other

___ _____

___ _____

For more information on adapted assessment consult:
Hutchinson, N. L. (2002). *Inclusion of exceptional learners in Canadian schools: A practical handbook for teachers.*
Toronto, ON: Prentice Hall.
Weimer, B. B., Cappotelli, M., & Dicamillo, J. (1994). Self-advocacy: A working proposal for adolescents with special needs. *Intervention in school and clinic, 30*(1), 49-50.

EXHIBIT 14.2	How Can Report Card Grades Be Adapted for Exceptional Students?

Maria located a handout she had received at a conference on changing assessment practices. She made copies for all the teachers who attended Heather's next self-advocacy meeting. This handout helped the teachers to remember that adapting assessment is a new and dilemma-laden endeavour.

Issues in Grading Adaptations

Report card grading is perhaps the most prevalent and controversial evaluation option used in schools. The practice began early this century when great faith was placed in educational measures to assess student learning accurately and predict future levels of learning. High grades were intended to spur students on, while low grades were intended to encourage them to join the workforce.

In recent years laws have been passed to ensure the right of all students to an education, not just those who succeed with minimal intervention. Further, our ability to compete in the emerging global economy will depend on better educational outcomes for all our citizens, not just a privileged few. These changes have led to new demands that go beyond the relatively simple matter of identifying "good" and "poor" students. For example, how can evaluations be modified to ensure that they do not discriminate against students with disabilities? How can they be used to motivate students to stay in school, to communicate educational competence and progress to parents and students, and to guide our teaching as we move to meet the needs of an increasingly diverse student body? Although answers to these questions are beginning to emerge, in large part we continue to use a grading system that was intended to fulfil a purpose much narrower in scope.

The use of traditional letter and number grades has caused problems for teachers who must communicate with many audiences, including parents, students, administrators, and potential employers. These audiences are often looking for information that is not readily communicated using a single number or letter. For example, students may be interested in how much progress they have made, whereas their parents want to know how their children compare to their classmates as well as to children nationwide. Schools, on the other hand, may need to provide university admissions offices with indicators of student potential to do university work. Teachers are also increasingly left with conflicting concerns about grading, including upholding the school's standards, maintaining integrity with other teachers, being honest with students, justifying grades with other students, motivating students for better future performance, communicating accurately to the students' next teacher, and avoiding the reputation of being an "easy" teacher.

Increased inclusion has made specific challenges to grading systems. Teachers can adapt grading systems to ensure they are fair to all students. As summarized below, grades can be adapted by changing grading criteria, making changes to letter and number grades, and using alternatives to number and letter grades.

Exhibit 14.2 *Continued*

Examples of Grading Adaptations

Change Grading Criteria	**Change to Letter and Number Grades**	**Use Alternatives to Letter and Number Grades**
Vary grading weights.	Add written comments.	Use pass-fail grades.
Change to letter and number grades.	Add student activity logs.	Use competency checklists.
Modify curricular expectations.	Add information from portfolios and/or performance-based assessments.	
Grade on the basis of improvement.		
Use contracts and modified course syllabi.		

Source: Text based on, and chart reprinted from, *Including Exceptional Students: A Practical Guide for Classroom Teachers* (Canadian edition) by M. Friend, W. Bursuck, and N. Hutchinson, 1998, p. 359. Copyright © 1998 Allyn & Bacon, Toronto, ON. Reprinted with permission of Pearson Education Canada, Inc.

EXHIBIT 14.3	Postscript to Parents

Parents of children with disabilities come to realize that their children learn much of their attitude toward their disability from the model set by the parents. However, adjusting to the birth of a child with a disability is not easy for most parents. Parents of children with disabilities also learn that they can provide understanding, support, and advocacy for one another. In a wonderful book from the heart, parents have written letters to their children with disabilities and some have written postscripts for other parents. Shirley Crozier of Calgary, Alberta wrote the following frank words within a letter to her son, Cam, who has cerebral palsy:

> You, my dear, have tested my patience, intelligence, courage and integrity more than anyone else in this world. I know it was good for me but I'd be hard pressed to say thank you. You also asked the hardest questions I've ever had to answer. Questions like: Why do I have cerebral palsy? Will I get married?...I wish I had a penny for every philosophical, moral, and ethical discussion we've had. Thank you for not holding me to all my answers or asking me to repeat them word for word.

In a "Postscript to Parents" she included the following:

> I hope you have derived a feeling of optimism from my letter to Cam. His life is not what I had dreamed it would be but I rejoice in his wholeness, his spirit, and his *joie de vivre*....

> I wish my belief that Cam's disability is neither good nor bad, but simply is, had been quicker in coming. For, until I reached that level of understanding, I was not able to stop dreaming of him as being someone different than he really is. I am now aware that until I felt this way it was impossible for me to nurture and support his quest for identity, self-esteem, and wholeness.

> Here are three rules I think worthy of passing on....

> • Look after yourself. You really can't give away happiness if you are worn out, and your life is not balanced. Swallow your pride and ask for help from family, friends, and professionals.

> • Don't try and predict the future for your child....

> • Don't allow anyone to patronize you. Neither you nor your child deserve to be treated in a condescending manner. What you do need is support, education, and appropriate resources so you can be in control of your lives.

> How would I feel at this stage of the game if a miracle were to take place? What if Cam suddenly became average in every way? I think one part of me would be ecstatic and the other part of me would be profoundly sad, for I have enormous respect for this young man, whose unique personality has evolved because of his difficulties.

> Take care and celebrate the good days.

SUGGESTIONS FOR FURTHER READING

Badry, D. E., McDonald, J. R., LeBlond, J. (Eds.). (1993). *Letters to our children.* Calgary, AB: University of Calgary Press.
   This book is about the dreams of parents for their children with disabilities, and about the realization that every life is to be treasured; powerful messages for all of us who work with children and adolescents with disabilities, about advocacy, courage, and respect.

Kaufman, M. (1995). *Easy for you to say: Q & As for teens living with chronic illness or disability.* Toronto, ON: Key Porter Books.
   A doctor in a clinic for adolescents at a large hospital provides honest and candid answers to questions she has been asked by her young clients; questions about sexuality, friendship, and school.

Test, D. W., Karvonen, M., Wood, W. M., Browder, D., & Algozzine, B. (2000). Choosing a self-determination curriculum. *Teaching Exceptional Children, 33*(2), 48-54.
   Self-determination goes beyond self-advocacy in that it describes students taking an active role in all decisions that affect their future; this review of programs helps teachers to choose a program that systematically enhances self-determination of exceptional students.

Van Reusen, A. K., & Bos, C. S. (1990, Summer). I PLAN: Helping students communicate in planning conferences. *Teaching Exceptional Children,* 30–32.
   Describes a practical and effective strategy to enhance the participation of adolescents with disabilities in their IEP meetings; such a strategy can help exceptional youth to engage in self-advocacy both in the school and in the workplace.

Wolff Heller, K., Alberto, P. A., Forney, P. E., & Schwartzman, M. N. (1996). *Understanding physical, sensory, and health impairments.* Pacific Grove, CA: Brooks/Cole.
   A readable textbook on physical disability that can help teachers, on a need-to-know basis, when they find themselves teaching a student with a physical disability or a chronic illness.

WEBLINKS

http://www.selfadvocatenet.com/
A community self-advocacy group that describes itself as "...a strong voice for people with intellectual disabilities during the good times and the difficult times. We like to let people know what is possible if they speak up and stand up for their rights."

http://www.teennetproject.org/index.html
An innovative site intended to engage adolescents in health promotion using information technology; includes information on self-determination for adolescents (co-ordinated by the Department of Public Health Sciences at the University of Toronto).

http://www.sbhac.ca/index.php?page=main
Spina Bifida and Hydrocephalus Association of Canada: a community advocacy and support group for people with spina bifida and their families. Includes information on research, scholarships, and links.

Sorry, I Got the Wrong Day, Again!

Setting: Two teachers overheard in the staff room at Loon Lake High School, in October.

FIRST TEACHER: "I think you teach Len, a quiet guy, a bit serious, Grade 10."

SECOND TEACHER: "Yes. I just saw his mid-term report. He failed everything. What's going on? He comes to every class."

FIRST TEACHER: "Did he hand anything in? I didn't get a single one of the three independent assignments."

SECOND TEACHER: "You might be right. I don't think he did. OK, let's get Vicki on the case."

Len was referred to Vicki Kruger, a guidance counsellor and resource room teacher. The first thing Vicki did was talk with and listen to each of Len's teachers. The teachers also made a few written comments for Vicki about Len in their classes. Then, Vicki talked with and listened to Len. They sat in her office where no one could overhear. Len seemed relieved to be telling someone his difficulties. He told Vicki that he went to his classes. "But I'm sometimes late, because I get mixed up about what day it is, or which floor the room is on. Sometimes I go to the wrong class." Vicki asked about the assignments. Len replied, "I worked on them all, but I never got them done. So I didn't hand them in. How could I? They weren't finished."

Vicki encouraged Len's fall semester teachers to talk with and listen to him so they could hear about his difficulties firsthand. She knew she would repeat this process with the winter semester teachers. Vicki read Len's file carefully. His file showed Vicki that in the past his teachers had often said "needs improvement" or "could work harder." The most common comment was "Len is disorganized." His current teachers agreed. When Vicki met with them, she learned that he rarely turned in assignments and rarely contributed to class discussions. When he did speak, he had good ideas. His test scores were low; he didn't finish the tests. He was somewhat better at completing hands-on work in class.

Vicki invited Len's parents to meet her at the school. Time was going by, and Vicki wanted to plan a program for Len for second semester, so he would have some chance of succeeding. Vicki was telling the other teachers about the interview. "Len's mother came, but she wasn't happy about it. She said she's tired of being on his case. Len had a tutor last year; I guess that's why he didn't show up on the all-failures list in Grade 9. Len's mother also said she thought he was bright, but school had always been difficult for him. Apparently, Len had been talking at home about taking courses in an applied stream. His mother said she was willing to go along with it because he seemed so overwhelmed this year."

Vicki suspected that Len might have a learning disability. She was reluctant to recommend that students who seemed to have average ability drop into an applied stream, because usually with a few accommodations they could succeed in the academic stream. In her experience, these students often grew bored in applied stream classes and either caused disruptions or gradually stopped attending. If Vicki referred Len for formal assessment, it would take months to get the testing done. If she did not refer him, she would be running on her own professional judgment and that of her fellow teachers. She had to make some decisions before second semester. With formal test results and a report from a school psychologist, teachers would have more incentive to follow the recommendations in the report. Without them, Vicki would have to convince the teachers, by herself, to try adapting Len's program. Vicki knew the teachers usually worked with her because most of the time her suggestions helped the students (and did not cause the teachers excessive work). Recently, the school district had been easing its demands for formal testing. The alternative was for Vicki to conduct observations and informal assessments and record these in Len's file. What should she do?

Vicki and Len decided he would try applied stream classes in the winter semester, even though Vicki wasn't convinced that was the whole answer. It would take the pressure off until she could find time to work with Len, and to get his teachers involved in some curriculum adaptations.

Vicki set about to observe Len in all his winter semester courses. Early in the winter semester, Vicki sat at the back of one of Len's classes, Applied Science. She had arrived about ten minutes after the class started. She observed that the students sat in groups of four with their desks pushed together. Len was looking in his desk for his notebook while everyone else was writing their data from the lab experiment in their books. Finally, he started writing and asked to see what a member of his group had recorded. Ms. Lever, the teacher, encouraged the other boy in the group to help Len catch up. When Ms. Lever asked the students to read the rest of the chapter to be ready for tomorrow's class, Len breezed through the 10 pages and looked around.

Vicki thought, "He couldn't have read that fast. I'd better find out how well he can read." She also decided to ask each teacher to complete a questionnaire on "assessing the demands of the course." Before she could suggest adaptations to teaching, Vicki would need to know the match (or mismatch) between classroom demands and what Len could do.

When the students left, Vicki spoke to Ms. Lever, Len's science teacher. "Oh, he hasn't handed anything in. Len's a nice kid, but his marks are going to be low if I don't get any work from him. They have a few minutes of homework every night—finishing some reading, or watching for environmental issues in magazines and on the television news, or something. Also, he has one project related to environmental science, and there will be two tests, one for each unit this semester." Vicki asked Ms. Lever to fill in the questionnaire on classroom demands (Exhibit 15.1).

Vicki arrived before the beginning of Len's art class later that day. She wanted to see Len at the start of class. The students were working on a design project in groups. Vicki thought this would appeal to Len. The teacher, Mr. Penn, told her Len often arrived late, worked hard in class and had good ideas, but had failed to hand in his drawings. Len came bursting in. "Sorry. I got the wrong day, again. Went to the cooking lab. Oh, I gotta go to my locker. Forgot my drawings." From Mr. Penn's smile, Vicki figured this happened every day. Vicki wondered, again, whether Len really needed less academically demanding classes. He certainly needed some organizational strategies.

Vicki made a plan and gradually found time to carry it out. She told Len's teachers she wanted to assess Len with informal measures, in addition to her observations, but not request formal testing at this time. Vicki wasn't confident she was doing the right thing, but she thought she and her colleagues could help Len, and she knew she could always submit her reports to show what they had done in pre-referral actions. Vicki asked his teachers to complete the assessment of their classroom's demands on Len. She gave each teacher a copy to read of her observations of Len and her one-page report. Then she asked each teacher to suggest two classroom adaptations they could use from the list they had received in a professional development workshop, "Adapting Your Teaching" (Exhibit 15.1).

When Vicki met with Len, he said, "I'm bored in these applied-stream classes. I really miss the ideas in Literature and the discussions in the other classes." Vicki asked him to describe his organizational strategies for dealing with the demands of his classes. He said he wasn't sure what she meant, but he didn't think he had any. He certainly had many of the characteristics of adolescents with learning disabilities, especially his lack of organization and his poor reading comprehension. Vicki thought she should check out his skills in written expression, too. She asked herself whether she should suggest oral instead of written assessment to his teachers. How to decide?

Vicki and Len met in the resource room whenever they could—during noon hour, after school, or during his spare. She even took him from classes a couple of times. Vicki explained that she wanted Len to focus on organizational strategies, and showed him how to use an agenda book to keep track of the days, the classes, the assignments. She told Len, "Mark off the days as they pass, write the classes and rooms in the daybook for each day, write the assignments in a master list with the dates, and write them on the day in the calendar when they are due. Look in the book at the end of each class, to figure out what comes next and where it is. Try to bring everything you need, so you don't have to return to your locker."

Vicki suggested that Len use coloured highlighters to keep assignments, classes and rooms straight: pick a colour for each class and then highlight all list entries (assignments) and daybook and calendar entries (for classes, rooms, and due dates) with that colour. With a different colour for each class, Len could see at a glance which books he needed at home and at school.

Next, Vicki showed him how to break an assignment into parts, and set a date when each part would be done. Once Len began to try the system, Vicki and Len showed the system to his teachers. Ms. Lever said she loved it, and Mr. Penn smiled. But both agreed to work with Len, helping him use the system in their classes. Len also listened to Vicki and considered the idea of submitting incomplete assignments. He even took her advice, talked to other kids about it, and found out that they sometimes submitted partially completed assignments. He finally agreed with Vicki that teachers could mark what he had done only if he handed it in, and that a part assignment was better (to most teachers) than no assignment at all. Vicki set out long-term and short-term goals for Len in the area of organization. In her plan and Len's agenda book, she wrote the following lists.

Long-term goals:
1. Len takes responsibility for organizing himself.
2. Len submits work consistent with his potential.

Short-term goals:
1. Len uses a daybook or agenda.
2. Len uses a highlighter.
3. Len makes and carries out plans to complete assignments.
4. Len submits something for every assignment.

Vicki also followed up on his reading. Len's reading comprehension right after he read was close to grade level. But he skipped over what he didn't understand. He remembered little of what he had read and could not answer interpretive questions. He usually listened in the discussions "for a while, and then I think about something else." Len was a passive reader. He ran his eyes over the words. But he didn't stop to ask himself whether or not he understood. Vicki taught him the RAP strategy. Len practised with Vicki until he could use the strategy independently. Len wrote the strategy in his agenda book.

"RAP": Take one paragraph at a time:

Read
Ask yourself questions
Paraphrase

Some of Len's teachers explained RAP to the whole class and put a poster with the strategy up on the wall. They let the whole class practise RAP with some in-class reading. Len figured that was mostly for him, but the teachers said it was for everyone in the class, to ensure they were getting the meaning of what they were reading.

Each teacher chose a few adaptations to make in their teaching. The trick was to accommodate Len without disadvantaging others, and to choose adaptations that were feasible with their workload. By the end of the year, Len's teachers were pretty much accustomed to making adaptations, and to thinking proactively so that they worked out the adaptations when they did their planning. All term, Len met each teacher to get organized after each assignment was handed out. He still met with Vicki every week to monitor his keeping up, even though Vicki said, "I don't do anything, and Len and the teachers do it all." Len was meeting his goal of handing in all his assignments on time (or close). He was passing all his courses. He was talking about getting back into the academic stream. Len seemed to be feeling pretty good about himself and what he was learning.

Vicki thought the whole team had really pulled together. Should she refer him to be tested to confirm whether or not he had a learning disability? It was already May. Central Services had suggested there would be a four-month wait for assessment. Vicki decided to suggest a meeting between Len, his parents, all his second semester teachers, and herself to discuss stream and course selections for next year, and to discuss the decision to refer Len for assessment.

QUESTIONS FOR REFLECTION AND DISCUSSION

1. What are the key facts of the case?
2. What do we know about Len? About Vicki Kruger?
3. Describe the major dilemma(s) in the case.
4. Describe how Len might tell his best friend about the events of the year. Describe the winter semester from his mother's perspective, from Ms. Lever's perspective.
5. What solutions do you recommend to resolve the major dilemma(s) in the case?
6. Why are these courses of action appropriate? Consider the consequences for Len, Vicki, Len's teachers and parents.
7. What have we learned from this case?
8. In what ways has this case raised questions for us and caused us to challenge our beliefs and assumptions?

EXHIBIT 15.1	Assessing the Demands of Your Course and Making Adaptations

(To be completed by the teacher)

Teacher _____ Course _____ Student _____

1. For what percentage of class time do students typically listen to lectures or instructions?
2. How many pages of in-class reading do you assign to be done in a typical class?
3. How many pages of out-of-class reading do you assign to be done in a typical evening?
4. List typical classroom activities (e.g., lectures, demonstrations, labs, cooperative learning, independent work, discussion, pairs, videos, etc.).
5. How many hours of homework do you typically assign in a week?
6. Describe the typical assignment and the number of days from assignment given to assignment due.
7. Do you assign projects or long-term assignments? (If so, how much structure or guidance is given?)
8. Do you give a final test at the end of each unit?
9. How are grades assigned?
10. What are your expectations for student behaviour in class?

After answering these 10 questions, please star up to three where you perceive a mismatch between the strengths of the named student and the demands of your course.

Turn this page to find a list of adaptations based on the *Study Skills Handbook*. Choose two (or more) that you could implement in this course that might reduce the mismatch between the named student's strengths and the course demands.

Let me know what I can do to help implement the adaptations you choose.

Thanks,

Vicki Kruger

Adaptations

The classroom adaptations in this list were introduced in the District Workshop based on *The Study Skills Handbook* by Judith Dodge. Choose two (or more) that make sense to try in your course that you assessed on the preceding page. Choose adaptations that will be helpful for many students. You may decide to excuse students who may be bored or who may not benefit from these adaptations (and perhaps provide a stimulating alternative at their level). Think about ways in which I could assist you to implement these adaptations.

Thanks,

Vicki Kruger

_____ 1. **RAP (read, ask questions, paraphrase) strategy.** Use with reading paragraph by paragraph. Posters in my office.

_____ 2. **Study Buddies.** Encourage students to study in pairs. Ask them to plan and carry out three study sessions using the best "active" study techniques and complete the Study Buddies form. Forms in my office.

_____ 3. **Test-Prep Kit.** Give students a form to complete that gets them prepared for the content and format of the test. Forms in my office. [See Exhibit 15.3.]

_____ 4. **Open-Notebook Tests.** Tell students in advance, and then occasionally use open-notebook tests to encourage students to take good notes. These tests are usually easy for students who have thorough and accurate notes, so they provide encouragement for some students, but more important they help students value good notes. May be worth the trade-off if used occasionally, especially early in the course.

_____ 5. **K-W-L.** Use this strategy at the beginning of a unit to help students activate prior knowledge. **K:** students jot what they already **K**now about the topic. **W:** students jot a list of questions about what they **W**ant to know about the topic. (If students say they don't **W**ant to know, ask what they **N**eed to know.) **L:** after the unit, students write what they have **L**earned in the unit (usually guided by their answers to the questions they jotted under **W** at the beginning of the unit). Forms in my office.

_____ 6. **Text Learning Strategy (Paired Reading Strategy).** Partners A and B read the opening passage silently and turn it over. A summarizes, identifying main ideas. B adds anything omitted or corrects any inaccuracies. A and B work together to learn the summarized information by making a drawing, chart, or anything that works. They switch roles for the next passage, and cooperate to learn together, switching roles for successive passages. Copies of the strategy in my office. [See Exhibit 15.3.]

_____ 7. **Web of Topics and Subtopics.** Model the strategy with familiar topics like "Recycling" and kinds of materials than can be recycled (aluminum cans, paper, juice boxes, etc.). Ask students to put the topic in a circle in the centre of the page and write the subtopics on spokes coming out in all directions from the circle for a topic on which they are preparing a report. Web forms in my office.

Note: All these adaptations for enhancing students' study strategies are described in detail in _The Study Skills Handbook: More Than 75 Strategies for Better Learning_, Judith Dodge, Scholastic Professional Books, 1994.

EXHIBIT 15.2	What Are Children and Adolescents with Learning Disabilities Like?

This is a hard question. They are all different. No list of characteristics would describe every student with learning disabilities. Frequently, they puzzle us because they strike us as bright kids, but on closer inspection, they have real strengths and real weaknesses. Often they are overwhelmed by the volume of work they must do in the classroom, and are always behind. They can feel frustrated by these things. They do have average or better ability, but achievement lags behind ability.

Let's think about how students with learning disabilities learn. Definitions suggest they have a disorder in one or more of the basic psychological processes involved in understanding or using language. "Language" refers to symbols of communication—spoken, written, or even behavioural. "Basic psychological processes" refers to taking in information (listening, reading, observing), making sense of information (relating, remembering, evaluating), and showing (speaking, writing, calculating). Students with learning disabilities seem to be less active as learners, to do less meaning-making, to be less strategic.

Psychological Processes

1. PERCEPTION: organizing, interpreting what we experience; has greatest impact when perception is critical to learning during the early years in school; may confuse letters more often when learning to read, and these confusions may persist longer.

2. ATTENTION: refers to focusing on information; coming to, and maintaining, attention; some students identified as having attention deficit disorder (ADD) or attention deficit disorder with hyperactivity (ADHD); "in her/his own world"; distracted, in constant motion.

3. MEMORY: arranging what they have perceived and attended to; many processes; e.g., problems in working memory (storing and retrieving information); too much information may mean they only take in part of it (e.g., note-taking during a lecture); may not make connections.

4. METACOGNITION: monitoring, regulating, and evaluating own learning; identifying most effective way to learn; critical to learning from experience, generalizing, and applying; without it, may act impulsively, not plan.

5. ORGANIZATION: may come without pencil; lose papers; have difficulty getting good ideas into an essay or assignment; lose track of goal, especially if it is long-term.

What We Can Do

WE CAN: segment pieces of information that are perceptually confusing; avoid presenting them together until at least one is learned well; highlight important characteristics of information.

WE CAN: break task into smaller segments; gradually build up; give cues which can bring attention to key words in explanations; use meaning-check after giving instructions; help student to learn to identify the important, independently.

WE CAN: help develop strategies for remembering (e.g., minute hand is longer than hour hand, minute is longer word); provide more practice; remind to find relationships; make it meaningful; teach strategies.

WE CAN: teach self-monitoring; model thinking out loud; ask student to give reasons; give cues, give feedback, encourage, be clear when we teach; teach strategies.

WE CAN: teach routines; put checklist on desk or notebook; break task into steps; put agenda on board; warn about major changes; ask questions to keep putting the onus on the student.

EXHIBIT 15.3	Two Strategies: Test-Prep Kit and Text Learning Strategy

Test-Prep Kit

Day/Date of test: _____

Topic of the test: _____

Five main ideas about the topic (important concepts, key ideas, causes, results, important events or people):

1.   4.

2.   5.

3.

Ten important terms (vocabulary words) related to the topic:

1.   6.

2.   7.

3.   8.

4.   9.

5.   10.

On the back of this page, write 15 questions you think the teacher will ask on the test.

Ask your teacher about the test, and check off which of the following you should include in your review:

_____ class notes   _____ teacher review sheets

_____ text readings   _____ past quizzes and tests

_____ handouts/dittos/worksheets   _____ other: _____

What format will the test follow:

_____ short answer (true–false, multiple choice, fill-in, matching, and so on)

_____ essay

_____ labelling a picture (a map, parts of a plant, the water cycle, and so on)

Check off how many study sessions you will set aside to prepare for the exam:

_____ 2 sessions _____ 3 sessions

Write which days you will study: _____ _____

_____

Exhibit 15.3 *Continued*

Check off which "active" study strategies you plan to use in preparation for the test:

_____ reciting the main ideas

_____ making a study review card

_____ making and using a set of
flashcards

_____ drawing a map, sketch, or other
diagram

_____ creating a "semantic map"

_____ creating a mnemonic device

_____ drawing a time line

_____ other: _____

Text Learning Strategy (Paired Reading Strategy)

Cooperative Learning Script

1. Flip a coin to determine who will be Partner A and who will be Partner B. (If there is a trio, one becomes Partner A and two become Partners B.)
2. Both partners read Passage I of any reading or Section I of any text.
3. When both are finished, they put the passage out of sight.
4. Partner A orally summarizes the contents of Passage I. He or she discusses key points and identifies main ideas.
5. Partner B detects and corrects any errors in Partner A's summary and points out any important ideas his or her partner left out. Partner B's focus should be on the content.
6. Both partners work together to develop images, diagrams, semantic maps, lists, charts, mnemonic devices, and so on, to help make the summarized information memorable. They ask themselves, "How can we learn and remember this information?" The focus is on the process of learning.
7. Both partners read Passage II.
8. Partners reverse roles and repeat steps 3–6.

[Adapted from: Donald Dansereau, *Journal of Reading*, April 1987.]

SUGGESTIONS FOR FURTHER READING

Dodge, J. (1994). *The study skills handbook: More than 75 strategies for better learning.* Toronto, ON: Scholastic Professional Books.

Dodge provides clear descriptions of many effective strategies and inviting forms to copy and use in the classroom. These strategies and forms provide structure and guidance for students with learning disabilities and for others who may have difficulty comprehending textbooks, writing notes from a lecture, taking initiative to study for tests, etc.

Markel, G., & Greenbaum, J. (1996). *Performance breakthroughs for adolescents with learning disabilities or ADD: How to help students succeed in the regular education classroom.* Champaign, IL: Research Press.

Theory-based but very practical, this book describes what teachers can do to foster breakthroughs. Includes many excellent checklists that teachers, students, and parents can use together to enable adolescents with learning disabilities to be more metacognitive and self-regulating.

Swanson, H. L., Hoskyn, M., & Lee, C. (1999). *Interventions for students with learning disabilities: A meta-analysis of treatment outcomes.* New York, NY: Guilford Press.

A scholarly and comprehensive review of a large body of research which shows that explicit instruction with high structure and metacognitive components is effective for students with learning disabilities. An impressive book.

Swanson, P. N., & De La Paz, S. (1998). Teaching effective comprehension strategies to students with learning and reading disabilities. *Intervention in School and Clinic, 33*(4), 209–218.

This brief, easy-to-read paper provides clear guidelines for teaching strategies to improve reading comprehension in the classroom. The rationale and strategies show teachers *how* to teach students with learning and reading disabilities to comprehend the material they read.

Weinstein, C. E., & Hume, L. M. (1998). *Study strategies for lifelong learning.* Washington, DC: American Psychological Association.

Occasionally, the American Psychological Association invites a prominent researcher to write a book for practitioners on an important topic, conveying the results of research in a highly readable form. Check this one out.

WEBLINKS

http://highschoolhub.org/hub/study.cfm
This Web site provides a list of study skills for high school students, as well as links to study strategies for tests and exams in areas like math and science.

http://www.cec.sped.org
The Web site of the Council for Exceptional Children provides access to journals, and resources for teachers and parents. Important site to know about.

http://www.coun.uvic.ca/learn/index.html
This site offers access to fine resources prepared by the University of Victoria to help students take charge of their own learning. Handouts available for printing online. Many universities and colleges offer similar services.

Having Someone Explain
Things To You Is Important

"I really thought I was doing a good thing here, enriching my history class for all these highly able kids. But look at the feedback they gave me this week about the fall semester. I'm not certain that I should keep going with this. What do you think? I want to do the best thing for the students, and I want to keep my workload reasonable." Danny Vachon is meeting with his history department head and his vice-principal to review an enrichment program that Danny tried out in the fall term.

For the first three years that he taught at Streeter District High, Danny worked hard to teach to the middle of his classes. There is little streaming in Danny's province and especially in his subject. But Danny is convinced that, even if there were streaming in history courses, there would still be an enormous range of ability and interest in the students that make up every class. At Streeter, students come from many backgrounds, ranging from students who are homeless and live in an abandoned warehouse to students who drive sports cars to school. About one-third of the students in this bedroom community have immigrated to Canada recently with their families, one-third have moved from the nearby city bringing their urban experiences and outlooks, while one-third come from families that live on the farms and acreages surrounding the town. Seven years ago, the citizens of Streeter elected an ambitious mayor and council who have attracted three small industries to the town. Streeter has learned that what can boom can bust. One industry has closed and one has laid off about half its workforce after four years. While the economy is improving and the people of Streeter are generally returning to work, Danny is convinced that it is increasingly important to adapt his teaching to accommodate a wide range of students preparing for an unpredictable future.

In the past year, Danny has been thinking a great deal about how to teach to more than the middle group in the class. He has come up with some approaches that seem to work for the students who need more time with the complex ideas and who need textbooks with lower reading levels. He has introduced some choice in assignments and texts and has worked with the school librarian to purchase videotaped materials. But Danny has been less satisfied with his efforts to challenge the most capable students in his classes.

Danny explained to his head of department and vice-principal, "They are probably gifted in the social sciences and need more from my classes in order to be challenged and also to be prepared for the independence expected in university courses. Each term I have a few students in my Grade 11 and 12 history classes who are superior in the subject and who find my class boring. As you know, I set out to change my teaching and the experience of these students in my class. Last summer I read a lot of the literature in this area. Then in the fall I invited eight students to take part in a program I saw as designed for students 'above average academically, university bound, mature, responsible, and potentially capable of self-directed learning.' My goal was to organize my teaching to suit these students without a crushing workload for myself and without ignoring the others in the class. I also wanted to know how the students would react to this program."

Danny reviewed what he had done: "I invited eight students to take part. At a meeting outside class time, I explained what I had in mind, told the students I would make changes as we went, and asked the students to write a letter saying they wanted to take part. All eight did. The next meeting, at noon, focused on investigating personal career options, and the next on reports of career research."

The vice-principal interrupted, "Why focus on careers? I would think gifted students need that less than all the other students."

Treading carefully, Danny explained, "Yep, I was surprised, too. Last summer when I read about the needs of gifted students, one thing I learned was that they often find it hard to focus because they have so many talents. That is certainly true of Allyson who was in the group of eight. She is a talented musician and a top student in almost every curriculum subject. She told the group that she changes her mind about what she should do as often as she changes her clothes. She said that after a cello lesson she knows she wants to be a musician, and after an exciting English class she wants to be a teacher. She has applied to go on an archaeological dig next summer...." Danny paused. "I was also surprised to learn that most of these eight students didn't have much knowledge about careers. In that way, I think they are like all other adolescents."

The vice-principal looked at his watch, "Talk faster, Danny. I have a meeting at the district office coming up."

"Next, I encouraged the students to work ahead on the topic the class was studying. They could request permission to go to the library to work independently on a unit on changes in Canadian society that are apparent when examining the last two sets of Canadian census data. Each student or pair of students had selected one or two aspects of Canadian society that interested them and proposed to me which data available on the StatsCan database would help them answer their questions. This is a topic not usually taught in the course. I think this was a form of enrichment.

"At the end of three months I interviewed the students individually. I asked what their impressions were of the enrichment experience. Look at the answers." Danny gave a copy of the students' responses to the department head and the vice-principal.

- I didn't know what to think. I didn't know if I wanted to be in it or not...but I decided it would be good because...I get to do things that I want to do, like things that interest me. (Miriam)

- I was eager because I find that in my classes all the symptoms [are there] like what you explained, how like you're sitting in the class and you're bored and you wanted to do stuff on your own. (Phil)

- At first, I felt like, well, I might have missed something important. But after I left [class] a few times I began to realize that I really didn't miss anything. (Brendan)

- I find that since I've started this, I feel that I have to do more work in my other classes, and it helped me realize how much of myself I actually have to put into it. (Allyson)

- If there was an explanation in the book you'd have to kind of make up your own, I don't know, cartoons in your head, in order to understand things better [when there was no teacher to lay it out for you]. I don't memorize as much any more. (Sophia)

- I thought it would be more structured than it was. I thought that there'd be more involvement between the teacher and the student. (Marcel)

- I guess probably meeting more often would be better. You can share the work you've done and your ideas. (Lyndon)

- Yes, I like the career stuff, or I'd be going into university like not having a clue what I was going to do. But after this, I have more of an idea. I don't think education should be all solely on independent studying...because I feel that having someone to explain things to you is very important. (Christine)

Danny pointed to the three student comments he had placed at the end of the list: "They really didn't like it, those three—Marcel, Christine, and Lyndon. They are saying I abandoned them. I don't know if I should go ahead with this in the winter. I thought they really liked it."

The head of the history department seemed surprised at Danny's interpretation. "But Danny, five gave only positive comments, one gave a positive and a negative comment, and two gave only negative comments. If you are counting, count them all. If they had been voting, there are more *yes*es than *no*es."

The vice-principal added, "You know I was a doubter. I said show me. And you just did. I want to know what you think the last three students were trying to tell you. And then I want to know what you could do about the message they were giving you. Just as important, I want to know what these students learned and showed you in their independent project reports, as well as how they fared in their work assigned in the course compared to the rest of the students. Finally, I want to hear how you can juggle the demands these students place on you and keep up the good work you have been doing with the rest of the class. What I don't want to see is you giving up on your ideas after one term, one pretty successful term at that. Of course, it is your decision, and I respect that. But...how do you answer my questions?"

Danny tried. He described how all the students but one—Christine—had completed projects that were good enough to be entered in the Social Studies Fair the next spring, with only minor changes in response to Danny's feedback. Christine could not work independently and had turned in a half-completed project. The students' marks were similar to their usual marks on tests and exams, at the top of the class. But the hard part, Danny explained, was, "How do I meet the students' demands for more attention without detracting from the program for the rest of the class? And how do I ensure that everyone succeeds? How important is it if some of the students don't like the enrichment? What changes would I have to make to use this approach in Grade 12 as well as in Grade 11? If I made a mistake in selecting the Grade 12s, this could really penalize them, and make them much less ready for university than my usual classes. It could even result in lower grades that could prevent someone from getting into university or college."

The vice-principal and department head smiled and both started to talk at the same time. The department head said, "After you," (what choice did she have?) and then she echoed the comments of the vice-principal: "This is amazing work you are doing, genuinely adapting your program, and collecting student input, and using the data from the first cycle to plan the next cycle. You can't quit now."

The vice-principal was more restrained, "You are asking all the right questions. Work out the answers and...." He stopped. "It's your call. You tell me what you want to do in the winter and, after you write a brief report on the fall term, you have my support—whichever way you decide to go. Good luck with your decision. I only wish my meeting at the school district office was going to be half as interesting as this discussion about your enrichment project."

QUESTIONS FOR REFLECTION AND DISCUSSION

1. Identify the facts of the case briefly.

2. What do we know about the teacher in this case, Danny? About the students who took part in the enrichment project?

3. Describe the situation as seen by the student who did not finish her enrichment project (Christine), the student who referred to making up cartoons in her head and memorizing less (Sophia), and a student who was not selected to take part in the enrichment.

4. Describe the major dilemma(s) in the case?

5. What are some underlying issues that might arise from the context in which the case takes place?

6. What actions should Danny take to resolve the dilemma(s)?

7. Consider the consequences of these actions for Danny, his colleagues, the enrichment students, the rest of the class. Does the grade level (11 or 12) make a difference in your considerations of the consequences?

8. Does this case lead us to question any long-held beliefs or to recognize assumptions we might be making about teachers, gifted students, curriculum?

EXHIBIT 16.1	Creating a Range of Options for Gifted Adolescents

After reading a paper by Dona Matthews, a researcher at the University of Toronto, Danny prepared the following summary to put into his report for the vice-principal.

Why and How to Provide Enrichment in Individual Subjects

Many researchers in gifted education, including Dona Matthews, suggest that gift-edness be viewed as advanced development in specific domains like history or mathematics. This view suggests that gifted students require adapted instruction in specific subjects. Matthews recommends that what works best is what stays close to students' interests and competencies. She suggests that a range of enrichment options allows students some choice and makes it more likely that good matches can be found for more students. This range could include the opportunity to accelerate to a higher level course in the same subject after demonstrating knowledge of all that would be taught in the course at the student's grade level. Other options include compacting the curriculum so one student or a group meets the same learning outcomes as the rest of the class, only at a much faster pace. Compacting can be combined with project-based learning in which students develop meaningful projects, with assistance, in some depth, over a period of time. Curriculum compacting may serve as a prerequisite to a number of other options, but it is always important for the teacher to work out a balance between guidance and autonomy in relationships with the students involved in curriculum compacting.

There are many options available outside the school that could follow curriculum compacting. These include apprenticeship programs in the community, work experience, and mentorship programs. Matthews suggests that all of these can provide intensive and meaningful high-level experiences that teachers may not be able to make available within schools.

No matter what options are chosen, it is important to consider the needs of gifted adolescents: to discover and develop their interests and talents, to grow in autonomy, to feel accepted, and to experience challenges that match their learning needs. These may be good guidelines for teaching all adolescents, not simply those who are gifted.

Source: Written after reading "Giftedness at Adolescence: Diverse Educational Options Required" by D. Matthews, 1996, *Exceptionality Education Canada, 6*(3&4), 25-49.

EXHIBIT 16.2	Compacting the Curriculum
	Prepared by Danny Vachon of
	Streeter District High

After many questions about what he was doing, Danny wrote the following brief synopsis for his colleagues about compacting the curriculum.

What Is It?

- Compacting the curriculum is intended to reduce the amount of time students spend on the regular curriculum in subjects in which they are advanced.
- The students show what they know and complete their assignments in areas of the curriculum where they need work.
- Then the students can work on projects, enrichment activities, or extensions of the curriculum content that challenge them.

How Do You Do It?

- Decide which students will not be challenged by your course.
- Decide what students need to know in the area(s) of the curriculum you are planning to compact.
- Assess the knowledge of the advanced students in those areas (use tests, observations of performances; keep records).
- Provide assignments or experiences so students can determine what they don't know.
- Work with the students to develop individual learning plans.

Tips

- Meet with the students regularly so they feel supported and so they can ask questions about what they don't understand.
- Encourage collaboration among students to enhance feelings of support and belonging and to enhance learning.
- Create opportunities for student input during the process as well as at the end. Pay attention to what the students tell you.

EXHIBIT 16.3	Example of an IEP for a Gifted Student

Name: Christine Comolli **Grade:** 11   **School:** Streeter District High

Date: September 28, 2001 **Subject:** Social Studies **Teacher:** Daniel Vachon

DESCRIPTION OF STUDENT

Learning Strengths: Broad general knowledge; reads widely; learns quickly; has many ideas; especially advanced in social studies, English, and music

Student Interests: Other cultures, travel, music and literature

Special Abilities: Verbal, speaking, dramatic performance (Concern: getting ideas on paper; bores quickly when material is repeated)

Summary of Needs: Challenging exchanges of ideas with peers; opportunities to use her verbal and reasoning skills; support in organizing her ideas and communicating in writing at a level comparable to her oral presentations

Recommendations: Compacting and enrichment with peers in English, social studies, and music

PLAN

Curriculum Differentiation: Enrichment in social studies through extension of classroom topics, following compacting of curriculum

Processes and Products: Analysis and synthesis of ideas, analysis of statistical data to support hypotheses; communicate findings in independently prepared project to be entered in Social Studies Fair; keep daily learning log

Criteria to Evaluate Outcomes: Assessment by self, peers, teacher, and Social Studies Fair judges; the first three to evaluate according to criteria set with the student, including: planning, research skills, quality of hypotheses, appropriateness of analyses of data and conclusions drawn, organization, clarity and appearance of final product

Review Date: February 28, 2002

Source: The IEP format for gifted students was adapted from the format used in *Gifted Education: A Resource Guide for Teachers* by the British Columbia Ministry of Education, 1995. Victoria, BC: Queen's Printer for British Columbia.

SUGGESTIONS FOR FURTHER READING

British Columbia Ministry of Education. (1995). *Gifted education: A resource guide for teachers.* Victoria, BC: Queen's Printer for British Columbia.

   A classroom guide to understanding what makes giftedness and how you can recognize it in the classroom. A great deal of information packed into 60 pages.

Hutchinson, N. L., & Freeman, J. G. (1994). *Pathways: Knowing about yourself, knowing about careers.* Scarborough, ON: Nelson Canada.

   A Canadian career development program; these activities can be completed in a relatively short period of time, and their implications can be discussed with gifted adolescents while these students are engaged in work experience, mentorships, or cooperative education.

Matthews, D. J. (1996). Giftedness at adolescence: Diverse educational options required. *Exceptionality Education Canada, 6*(3&4), 25–49.

   Matthews provides a readable account of the issues that need to be considered when developing educational options for students who are academically advanced, or gifted, in a particular curriculum area.

Reis, S., Burns, D., & Renzulli, J. (1992). *Curriculum compacting: The complete guide to modifying the regular curriculum for high ability students.* Mansfield Center, CT: Creative Learning Press.

   The book provides a thorough presentation of compacting with detailed and well-developed examples, common problems, suggestions for remedying these, and answers to frequently asked questions.

Renzulli, J. S., Leppien, J. H., & Hays, T. S. (2000). *The multiple menu model: A practical guide for developing differentiated curriculum.* Mansfield Center, CT: Creative Learning Press.

   Six practical menus to guide curriculum developers, with step-by-step planning guides and a list of how-to resources.

WEBLINKS

http://ccdf.ca/home_e.html
Canadian Career Development Foundation: links to career tips, books, on-line resources, labour market information, and research.

http://www3.bc.sympatico.ca/giftedcanada/
Gifted Canada: Canadian information (about teaching, resources, research, and provincial organizations) concerning bright and gifted children and adolescents.

http://www.gifted.uconn.edu/resource.html
The National Research Center on the Gifted and Talented (University of Connecticut) with links to monographs, brochures, and online resources for teachers, researchers, parents.

case 17

Kids in the Hall

Malcolm Buterra had hall duty again. He rushed out of his math room, telling the students waiting outside the door, "No noon-hour chat today. Sorry, I have hall duty. It is Thursday, isn't it?"

The students laughed and teased him, "Sir, calendars, a great mathematical invention, you should get one."

Malcolm knew it was something he would say to a student who had forgotten to bring an assignment and tried to claim ignorance of the due date. Malcolm particularly liked when students made connections between the mathematics he taught and the life they lived in the early 21st century. He smiled to himself, and then he remembered why he couldn't spend the noon hour challenging students with brain-teasing problems, or regaling them with stories of how mathematical inventions had changed the course of history. Malcolm had found math and history a particularly invigorating combination to study when he was in university and still loved both disciplines passionately. He had once been afraid that his cerebral approach to teaching might put students off, but he had learned in 20 years of teaching how to share his passions so students caught them. But he had never learned to appreciate the custodial aspects of teaching—like hall duty. "Why is it always Thursday?" he muttered to himself. "This is a waste of time."

"What'd you say, Sir?" Malcolm saw that the question had come from Tom, a student in his only Grade 9 class this term. Since he had become department head, Malcolm rarely taught Grade 9. Tom was sitting on the steps leading to the math and sciences wing of the school. Knowing that Tom was falling further behind every day in his math class and having heard in a recent staff meeting that other teachers were frustrated by Tom, too, Malcolm sat down beside Tom on the stairs.

MALCOLM: [*gently*] Hi, Tom. How is it going?

TOM: [*hesitantly*] I know I'm really screwing up in math, but believe me, things are going good in art and technology! I like those two, I can do them.

MALCOLM: [*more like a question*] I've noticed that you're not handing in the activities for the math-around-us unit in our class?

TOM: [*unconcerned*] I didn't think it mattered. Mine aren't very good and I never thought we had to.

MALCOLM: But I explained on the first day, they go into your portfolio, and you can choose the best ones to have graded. They go towards your mark.

TOM: I guess I wasn't listening. I find high school pretty hard. And people are always picking on me. I want to have some guys to hang around with, but I don't know any.

MALCOLM: Is that why you seem to be finding the time long at noon hour?

TOM: I don't get it...umm...I didn't say I'm finding it too long.

MALCOLM: Do you know what it means to find time long? I can see that you think this is an odd expression. I find time long when I'm sitting in traffic, and I just want to get to the Muskies hockey game to watch my son play goal. Or when I'm waiting for my daughter to finish her swim practice, and I've forgotten my book. What do you think it means to find time long?

TOM: I get it, to be bored or have nothin' to do.

MALCOLM: Bingo! You got it! And when people are bored, they often get into trouble. One day when I was waiting for my daughter, I was so bored I agreed to become the assistant swim coach. And I can barely swim. I really got myself into trouble, because then I had to get out of it, and I thought I was going to have to lie. But I finally thought to show the coach what a terrible swimmer I was, and he told me he didn't want me. But being bored can really get us into trouble.

TOM: Lunch hour is boring. I don't know many people. But I am not getting into trouble. I don't do anything. They pick on me.

MALCOLM: But two teachers told me they saw you harassing other students in the basement corridor and in the art room at noon. Other students who saw these incidents also reported you were the aggressor—taunting, tripping, and teasing. And I heard that you accused the other students involved. Are you sure you don't find time long at noon?

TOM: Well, if you don't have anyone to eat lunch with, an hour is a long time. My friends all went across town to Baldwin High. I guess you could say I find the time long. But I still think that's an odd thing to say.

MALCOLM: You know, I find the time long, too, at noon hour. So most days some students from my classes come to eat their lunch in my room, and we talk about mathematics in history and we try brain puzzlers. Usually they are puzzles with numbers in them, but sometimes they are optical illusions or word puzzles, anything we think is odd, that challenges us. You are welcome to join us. Do you know Maddy, oops, Madeleine, in our math class? She is the only Grade 9 student who has found out about us this term, until you. You see, people have to find out about us before they can join.

TOM: I'm afraid I'm not very good at math. Never have been. You see, I have a learning disability.

MALCOLM: I read about it in your file. But I didn't really understand. I thought learning disabilities usually affected people's reading and writing, not their math.

TOM: Well, I got behind. In reading, math, almost everything. My math is awful. I never really got what we did in decimals and stuff like that in Grade 5 and around there. So I think math is as much of a problem as reading for me. But not for everyone. Most people are like you said, mostly reading and spelling and writing.

MALCOLM: So what are you good at, Tom?

TOM: Actually, my photographs win prizes at the Notwood Fall Fair, at least they have the last three years. And I sing in the choir at my church, even though I'm not very good at reading music. I have a darkroom now, paid for with money I earned last summer. I set up a booth at the Riverside Water Slide Park. People paid me and I took photographs of them with my instant camera, and put the pictures in frames I had made at home and brought to the park with me.

MALCOLM: Tom, what help are you getting here at Pearson Collegiate, given that you have a learning disability?

TOM: Well, I get tutoring. I think they call it learning assistance. But they only do it in reading and writing, not in math. So I am getting frustrated in math.

MALCOLM: Well, I don't know that much about learning disabilities. But I think Mr. Rippler does. Do you know him? He's one of the counsellors. Maybe you and Mr. Rippler and I could talk about some ways to stop other kids from picking on you, or to stop you from picking on them—whichever it is that is happening. I think you would like Mr. Rippler. Sometimes he has lunch in my room with me and the students who come by, and we talk. He sometimes helps teachers and students make plans for how to have more success in high school. I think he could help us to figure out what we should be doing in math, so you can learn in spite of your learning disability.

TOM: I already go to the learning assistance centre for reading and writing. Why can't they just help me with math, too? Why can't you? You're my teacher. Now you want me to see some counsellor, too. And eat lunch with a bunch of people I don't even know. I don't want to do all this extra stuff. I shouldn't have to. In high school, teachers always tell you to go see somebody else. They should just help you themselves. Like they did at my old school—Victoria Public School. Everyone says how great it is to go to high school. But I don't think it is so great. People pick on me, and then I get blamed. No one wants to eat lunch with me. And the teachers all pass you on to somebody else. As if they don't care. Just teach me the stuff I don't know, like decimals. Instead of teaching me algebra that I don't get. That's what would help me. Can't you do that?

MALCOLM: I'm not sure I can do that. But I know I want to help. What about after school? Can you meet me then, for a few days, and I will review decimals and fractions and other topics that might help.

TOM: Yeah, but I go to the camera club on Tuesday and Thursday after school. And I may have choir practice on Mondays. But I might be able to come on Wednesdays. I'll see.

With that Tom walked away.

Three weeks later Malcolm Buterra was talking with his friend, Hal Rippler, in the staff room. It was Wednesday afternoon, about an hour after the end of the school day.

HAL: Well, did Tom show up today?

MALCOLM: No. I've reminded him in class. That is, when he comes. He misses once or twice a week for no apparent reason. And I've sought him out in the hall, when I'm on hall duty. And he always says, "I might do that, I might come, I might hand in that assignment," but he doesn't. I think I want him to learn more than he wants to learn. I am putting a lot of energy and worry into this. And he doesn't seem to be putting anything into it. And I can't learn it for him. I can do a lot to ensure that he learns what I am teaching this year, even if he misses a few classes, but how can I help him to understand decimals and important concepts that underlie most of later mathematics if he won't meet with me for individual help? It's like he doesn't want to learn these things that he has already failed at, and if he doesn't want to learn, what can I do? I can't reteach decimals to the whole class, can I...or can I?

HAL: Well, Malcolm, I've dealt with lots of students who act in ways that appear to be self-destructive. I usually find that what they are doing makes sense from their point of view; for example, maybe it is all they can handle. I am quite sure he isn't doing this simply to annoy you. To him, somehow, this behaviour meets his needs, or maybe it is all he can deal with. Let's arrange to meet with Nicole, who runs the resource room, and find out what he does there and how she reaches him. Maybe she can do the tutoring in math, if she already has his confidence. I'll put it in my daybook, so I bring it up when I have my weekly meeting with her tomorrow. Give me some times when you could meet....

QUESTIONS FOR REFLECTION AND DISCUSSION

1. Identify the facts of the case briefly.
2. Describe Malcolm Buterra, the math teacher. What do we know about the student, Tom?
3. Describe the situation as seen by Tom, the student who does not respond to his math teacher's offer of help. As seen by Malcolm Buterra. By Hal Rippler.
4. State the major dilemma(s) in the case.
5. What are some underlying issues that might be important to consider in coming to an understanding of this case?

6. What actions should Malcolm Buterra take to resolve the dilemma(s)?

7. Consider the consequences of taking these actions (and not taking these actions) for Malcolm, Tom, the other teachers mentioned in the case, and other people you think could be affected.

8. What assumptions does the case cause us to question, and what beliefs does the case help us to identify, about exceptional adolescents and their teachers in secondary schools?

| EXHIBIT 17.1 | Learning Disabilities in Mathematics |

During the past 20 years, researchers like Byron Rourke at the University of Windsor and Linda Siegel of the University of British Columbia have investigated the diversity and heterogeneity found among children and adolescents with learning disabilities. While reading disability is dominant in these children and adolescents, it is not the only kind of disability. Both researchers have found students with reading disability who have concomitant disability in mathematics. The older the student, the more likely reading disability will be accompanied by learning problems in mathematics.

These learning problems in mathematics are shown in a wide range of errors. These include problems with spatial organization, aligning numbers in columns, and difficulties with visual details, like reading mathematical signs. Procedural errors in the steps in mathematical operations are common. They also tend to experience difficulties with the logic and reasoning that go into understanding mathematical problems and into generalizing from what is known to new problems or problems that appear different.

Rourke and his associates have also shown that there is a group of students with learning disabilities whose problems in mathematics are primarily centred on poor memory. They fail to remember the multiplication tables and the steps in computation. They also are likely to avoid math problems that demand reading.

Recent research suggests different connections between mathematics and memory. Studies by Lee Swanson of the University of California, Riverside report that mathematical computation is better predicted by verbal working memory than by visual-spatial working memory. Perhaps disabilities in mathematics are influenced by difficulties with both mathematics-specific memory and difficulties with general working memory.

There are many students with learning disabilities in mathematics. However, there is much more research on learning problems in reading and there is much more learning assistance for reading disabilities than for mathematics disabilities.

To read more about students with learning disabilities in mathematics, consult any of the following research sources:

Hutchinson, N. L. (1993). Effects of cognitive strategy instruction on algebra problem solving of adolescents with learning disabilities. *Learning Disability Quarterly, 16*(1), 34–63.

Rourke, B. P. (1989). *Nonverbal learning disabilities: The syndrome and the model.* New York, NY: Guilford Press.

Shafrir, U., & Siegel, L. S. (1994). Subtypes of learning disabilities in adolescents and adults. *Journal of Learning Disabilities, 27*, 123–134.

Wilson, K. M., & Swanson, H. L. (2001). Are mathematics disabilities due to a domain-general or a domain-specific working memory deficit? *Journal of Learning Disabilities, 34*, 237–248.

Wong, B. Y. L. (1996). Chapter 8: Arithmetic and mathematics and students with learning disabilities (pp. 169–194) in *The ABCs of learning disabilities.* Toronto, ON: Academic Press.

EXHIBIT 17.2	Helping Students Understand Their Thoughts and Feelings

Often students don't recognize how their negative thoughts about themselves may influence their moods, feelings, motivation, and sense of power or agency over their own learning. If a student thinks, "School is so hard. Especially math, I just can't do this. That teacher makes me feel bad when he says I need help," the student is likely to feel hurt, disappointed, and angry. On the other hand, if the student chooses to think, "It would be nice if I didn't need help in math, but it's not that big a deal. That teacher is offering to teach me what I don't know. I guess I better make sure I fit this in, and he's an OK guy, really," his feelings can be a lot different.

Students can learn that their interpretations are just that—their interpretations—something they can control. Often feeling negative about themselves or insecure in the classroom causes students to misbehave, avoid opportunities to learn (which they see only as opportunities to look bad), or to act in other self-destructive ways. In their book, *Motivating Hard to Reach Students,* Barbara McCombs and James Pope suggest that teachers can help students to understand these thoughts. For example, a student who appears unwilling to engage in math tutoring with his teacher may think, "I am a stupid troublemaker." His thoughts can lead to hostility, resentment, and/or frustration. Acting on these feelings, the student may show rude, avoiding behaviour, fighting or refusing to cooperate. The result could be that the teacher gives up trying to reach the student. That is likely to reinforce the student's original view that the teacher thinks poorly of him. McCombs and Pope suggest that:

- teachers talk with their classes about this cycle of feelings and describe how it works;
- teachers and students generate examples together, preferably examples that have nothing to do with the interactions between the teacher and the individuals in the particular class;
- students identify negative thoughts they have in certain situations, in relation to home, friends, and school, and consider the cycle of consequences for each one;
- teachers and students work together to understand thoughts and feelings and avoid attributing negative views to the other.

Sources to consult:
Bos, C. S., & Vaughn, S. (1994). *Strategies for teaching students with learning and behavior problems* (3rd ed.). Toronto, ON: Allyn & Bacon.
McCombs, B. L., & Pope, J. (1994). *Motivating hard to reach students.* Washington, DC: American Psychological Association.

EXHIBIT 17.3	Checklist for Homework Easily Completed (CHEC): 15 Steps to Success

Mr. Buterra created and distributed a 15-step checklist to help students like Tom CHEC to ensure their homework was completed. He used the checklist in class to help students develop the habit of CHEC-ing.

Before You Leave School:

___ 1. List your assignments (with due dates).

___ 2. Attempt at least one question of each assignment.

___ 3. Ask your teachers about anything you do not understand and need to know to do your assignments.

___ 4. Locate any textbooks or materials needed to do homework.

___ 5. Put it all in your backpack.

At Home:

___ 6. Read the assignments; make a homework list and plan for the day; set goals.

___ 7. Re-read the first assignment on the list and complete it.

___ 8. Recognize your efforts; compliment yourself, and check off the first assignment on your list.

___ 9. Take a brief break and complete second assignment, and so on.

___ 10. Check work for accuracy, decide when homework is done, and return completed assignments to your backpack.

When You Return To School:

___ 11. Bring backpack, homework, and textbooks to school; show homework or submit homework to teacher(s).

___ 12. Revise and correct your homework based on feedback from your teacher(s).

___ 13. Review your progress and record whether you reached the goals you set for last night's homework.

___ 14. Ask questions about anything you do not understand.

___ 15. Begin the CHEC-ing process again at #1.

For younger students, you may want to involve parents in monitoring homework completion.

To read more about helping students manage the homework completion process, consult:
Callahan, K., Rademacher, J. A., & Hildreth, B. L. (1998). The effect of parent participation in strategies to improve the homework completion of students who are at risk. *Remedial and Special Education, 19,* 131-141.
Markel, G., & Greenbaum, J. (1996). *Performance breakthroughs for adolescents with learning disabilities or ADD.* Champaign, IL: Research Press.

EXHIBIT 17.4	Example of an IEP for a Student with Learning Disabilities

Student Name: Tom Deziel

Grade: 8

Date of birth: September 1, 1987

Date of IEP: November 2000

School: Victoria Public/transition to Pearson Collegiate

Background information:
Tom's ability is in the high average range, with higher scores on non-verbal than verbal subtests. His achievement test scores in reading, spelling, and written expression remain about three to four years below grade level. On the last reassessment of achievement, his math scores dropped to about four years below grade level. In classroom performance, Tom refuses to read aloud, even what he has composed. He writes reluctantly, and benefits greatly from assistance with editing. Tom keyboards well and has been encouraged to complete his high school assignments on computer. The decrease in mathematics performance is of concern. Tom expresses frustration with questions involving decimals, fractions, word problems, area, and volume. He has been taught to use a calculator but needs frequent reviews. Tom is reluctant about leaving Victoria to attend Pearson Collegiate. A transition plan and open communication between the two resource room teachers are recommended. Tom is generally reluctant to talk about his learning disabilities. Counselling and advocacy training are recommended.

Strengths:	**Weaknesses:**
photography	written language: expressive, receptive
design	lack of understanding of math concepts
drawing, painting	shy, easily discouraged
entrepreneurial initiative	lack of self-control when provoked

Goals for Grade 8, November 2000 to May 2001:

Tom will improve organization of written assignments.

Tom will learn strategies to edit his writing.

Tom will continue to improve his keyboarding skills.

Tom will increase his motivation to complete longer assignments.

Tom will continue to use calculator for calculations in math.

Tom will visit Pearson Collegiate to meet Nicole Walker, resource teacher.

Note: Tom will be tutored outside of school (at parents' suggestion) in mathematics.

Exhibit 17.4 *Continued*

Adaptations and Resources:

30 minutes daily with resource teacher (in small group): writing, editing strategies, keyboarding

gradual increase in expected length of journal entries in classroom; self-charting of length

calculator for math daily work and tests

give choice of assignment format, allowing posters, photographs, etc., prepared by Tom

Year end review, transition plans:
School-based team will meet to review progress and plan transition meeting with resource staff of Pearson Collegiate.

SUGGESTIONS FOR FURTHER READING

Markel, G., & Greenbaum, J. (1996). *Performance breakthroughs for adolescents with learning disabilities or ADD: Helping students to succeed in the regular classroom.* Champaign, IL: Research Press.

A practical book with many suggestions for ways classroom teachers can help students who lack organizational skills and study skills. The authors include many checklists that are long and thorough.

McCombs, B. L., & Pope, J. E. (1994). *Motivating hard to reach students.* Washington, DC: American Psychological Association.

In this publication for the American Psychological Association, the authors tackle one of the most difficult and debated issues in education—motivation. They put the onus squarely on teachers to understand what might be going on in the heads and hearts of their resistant students and to act to "motivate" these students.

Rief, S. (1998). *The ADD/ADHD checklist: An easy reference for parents and teachers.* Paramus, NJ: Prentice Hall.

Written in a simple checklist format, packed with information on characteristics, strategies, and interventions for students with ADD and learning disabilities. For parents, teachers, and adolescents.

Wong, B. Y. L., & Donohue, M. (Eds.). (2002). *The social dimensions of learning disabilities.* Mahwah, NJ: Erlbaum.

A book of readings containing reviews of current research on many social implications of learning disabilities, including loneliness, friendship, and classroom participation.

WEBLINKS

http://www.dldcec.org/
Homepage for TeachingLD, a service of the Division for Learning Disabilities in the Council for Exceptional Children (CEC). Its purpose is to provide trustworthy and current resources about teaching students with LD. Great site!

http://snow.utoronto.ca/best/accommodate/org.html
This page of the SNOW (Special Needs Opportunity Windows) provides practical information on how to help students get and stay organized. SNOW is a valuable Canadian resource.

http://www.schoolnet.ca/degrassi/
SchoolNet's Degrassi Homework Helper is a Canadian site designed to help students complete their homework. Claims to link to over 5000 teacher-approved online resources. Check it out.

case 18

Where Do I Draw the Line Between My Responsibility and Her Privacy?

"Oh, oh! Excuse me, class, I will be right back. Turn to the end of the chapter and answer the first three questions on organic compounds. Work in your usual groups and remember that everyone in the group must be able to answer these three questions tomorrow. Any questions about that? None. Good!" With that Gary Kowalski ran out of his classroom and down the hall of Red River Collegiate. He was looking for Clara Macdonald. He asked himself, "What did I do? I don't get it."

Gary had been teaching his Grade 12 chemistry class a particularly complex lesson on organic compounds. He liked to use a quiet voice in class and force the students to pay close attention to what he said. Today Gary had to keep raising his voice, louder and louder, to be heard over Clara's constant coughing. Finally he had stopped, and asked her if she would like to leave the room. Clara had grabbed the books off her desk and stormed out. Gary was looking for her. He knew from experience that it was extremely embarrassing for serious students like Clara to return to class after running out.

When Clara had entered his class in September, she had told Gary to be certain to look at her file. This was unnecessary because he had already read the details and knew that Clara had cystic fibrosis. The file was full of detailed information and Gary had taken a page of notes to keep in his classroom. Between September and January, Clara had changed. While he looked for her in all the likely places, he thought about how challenging it must be for an adolescent to cope with a condition like cystic fibrosis along with all the other growing pains of adolescence.

Red River was a comprehensive high school that served the students from three towns along the river and all the rural areas between the towns. There were 400 students in the school every fall and by June about 350 remained. Although unemployment was high in the area, students dropped out every year. The most common reasons they gave were to seek employment, to have a child, and to get away from the demands of school and of teachers who didn't care about them.

Gary Kowalski knew that he was not one of the teachers that Red River students accused of being uncaring. Although he had completed a master's degree in chemistry at the largest university in the province and could have continued into a doctoral program, he had opted for teaching. And in the past nine years, he had never regretted his decision. Five years ago he had moved from a city school to Red River High, bought an acreage, and embraced the rural lifestyle. What Gary missed, teaching in a rural school, was the extensive professional development that had been available in the city and was so difficult to come by in the country. He regretted not knowing how to prevent blow-ups like the one that had just occurred. And he knew there would never be a conflict resolution workshop offered on any PD day in the near future. He wondered sometimes how much the adolescents liked life in the country. For example, Gary knew that for every appointment with her doctors Clara had to travel into the city, 60 minutes each way when the traffic was light.

Gary showed he cared by keeping up with changes in the field of teaching through professional reading and information available at good Internet sites. His students appreciated the way he varied his teaching notes and approaches. For example, in Clara's class he was using collaborative group activities that allowed students to work together on challenging problem sets until everyone in the group could do the problems. He offered help after school to individual students, and coached the badminton team each year. But he wasn't always sure how to handle the confidences that students shared with him and, although there were few conflicts in his classes, he hated these "messy situations."

Clara was becoming a particularly challenging student for Gary. She seemed moody recently and had not been dropping by after school to chat about the challenges of organic chemistry. Whatever Gary said seemed to annoy Clara, and whatever he did seemed to alienate her even further. Gary knew she had a boyfriend, probably her first, and a new gang of friends, a small, popular clique in the school. He had seen Clara laughing and smiling with her friends in the corridors, and, on the other hand, scowling and muttering in class. But always, recently, she had been coughing. Before he turned the corner and saw Clara, Gary heard her.

There she was, sitting alone on the floor beside her boyfriend's locker, coughing and looking defiant. Her oversized jeans and her long checked shirt seemed to swallow her up. Clara looked smaller than ever in these huge clothes that were fashionable these days. Gary put aside his feelings of sympathy. He knew they wouldn't sit well with Clara. "Don't try to help me. Don't feel sorry for me. Leave me alone. Just go back to class, please, Mr. Kowalski. I don't want to talk about it."

Gary decided quickly to try to strike a deal. "Sure, Clara, I'll go back to class. I need to do that anyway. But let's meet after school." He knew she would want to hang out with her friends, especially her boyfriend, as soon as the bell rang. So he lied, just a little. "I have a meeting at 2:30. So I can't see you until 3:10 anyway. Can you meet me around then? I will put on my coffee pot, and let's have a cup of coffee. If we don't talk today, then it will be tough for both of us to be comfortable when you come back to class. You can't afford to miss any classes this week. You are soon going into hospital for tests, aren't you?"

"Don't remind me! OK, I'll come, but you don't have to call my parents about this, do you? They are hassling me enough about going out with Jed. They treat me like a baby. I'm almost 18." Clara's anger was fierce.

Gary knew he and Clara would be able to talk when she came to his room after school. They were already starting to talk. But he thought he might be out of his depth. "Can I ask Shirley Tennant to join us? Are you comfortable with that?"

Clara's response was dull this time, rather than angry. "Sure, I don't care. Ask her. I'll be there after Jed gets his bus, OK? We'll have to finish by the time the late bus goes. I can't ask my Mom to pick me up again."

Gary knocked on Shirley Tennant's door on the route back to his class. "I'm in a hurry. My class is alone. I gotta get back. Can you come to my room right after school? Blow-up with Clara Macdonald. Something's up." Shirley was the career education teacher and guidance counsellor for Red River High. Gary wondered how she handled all the demands from teachers, students, and cooperative education employers, but she did. And she usually kept smiling. Gary knew that Clara liked Shirley. "Thank goodness she does," he thought.

No real problems had developed in Gary's absence, just some strange graffiti on the blackboard. He knew he should have notified someone that he was leaving the room. "An experienced teacher like me knows these things, but I had to act fast. And I thought I'd only be gone a minute," he rationalized to himself. It looked as though all the groups had been working on the tough questions Gary had assigned. One group was even at the board drawing the compounds and arguing about the reactions. Gary got through the rest of his class, but his concentration was poor. He was thinking more about the upcoming meeting than about the ideas he was trying to explain.

Gary dismissed the class and told them that he couldn't answer any questions today after school because he had a meeting. He quickly put on a pot of coffee before Shirley arrived. While the coffee ran through, Shirley and Gary talked about the changes in Clara over the past few months. They had both noticed that Clara was coughing more, and getting thinner. Gary told Shirley that Clara was rarely asking to leave chemistry class to go to the health room to do her breathing exercises. Because Clara's class with Gary was late in the afternoon, she had often left class in the early fall on a signal she had arranged with Gary during the first week of school. Now she stayed in class and coughed. Gary told Shirley how today Clara's coughing had caused him to raise his voice and to ask her if she wanted to leave the class.

Shirley suspected that Clara was rebelling against having cystic fibrosis. She suggested to Gary that she thought Clara was not leaving class to do the breathing exercises that cleared her lungs, not taking enzymes every time she ate to enable her to digest her food, and not eating as much or as often as she should, all for the same reason. "I think she wants to be a person who doesn't have cystic fibrosis. She has a boyfriend and is in with a new gang of friends who are cool and who don't know much about her condition. I think she is trying to make her condition invisible—by not doing the things that make her different. But these are the very things that she needs to do to stay well."

Gary asked if Shirley thought his question to Clara about leaving the class was offensive to her because it drew attention to her and how she was different. Shirley nodded. Then she thought out loud: "The important thing right now is to handle this meeting with Clara well. I think another reason she is suffering is because she is making the transition from the children's CF team at City Hospital to the adult's CF team. The children's CF team—these are the people who have got her through every crisis. But the adult team are all new to Clara. They called me to say they want to start on vocational counselling and Clara won't attend.

She doesn't want to make another trip into the city every week, and who can blame her? They asked if she could join a vocational counselling group here. But I don't think she will. She has to be hospitalized and undergo some tests so they can decide what to do about her failure to gain weight. There is a lot going on. Where should we start today?"

Gary thought he should open the conversation because he had provoked the conflict, even if he had not meant to. "Let me begin. I want to apologize for drawing attention to Clara. Then I would like to ask her to tell me what she is thinking and feeling about my chemistry class and her upcoming absence. Let's start with specifics that she and I need to talk about anyway. She is a strong science student, in spite of her absences. At one time she was thinking of studying sciences in university or community college. I might ask her what she is thinking about, on these issues, these days. Maybe by talking about her future, we can focus her on what she has to do to ensure she has a future. Let's see where she takes the discussion. I don't want to pry, even if her lungs and her life are at stake. I have difficulty drawing the line between where my responsibility ends and a student's privacy begins. I cannot force her to make good choices and healthy choices. I am her chemistry teacher. You, at least, are her counsellor. But one thing I did tell Clara was that I wouldn't tell her parents about her blow-up in class today. So if you think you need to call her parents or her CF team, you will have to negotiate that with Clara yourself."

Shirley nodded. "I don't think that telling is an effective way to teach adolescents, or to guide their behaviour. Clara is a smart girl. We can reason with her; we can ask questions that help her to see the contradictions and potential dangers in what she is doing. But we can't make her do what we think, as adults, is the best thing for her health. We can especially listen and support Clara, so she doesn't give up on adults and try to get all her support from her friends who don't know what is at stake with her condition. Also, I suspect that all adolescents with conditions like CF go through this kind of trauma about being different, on top of trying to figure out what to do with their life, what they need and want in a partner, and what will make them happy."

Clara Macdonald knocked on the door frame as Gary Kowalski poured three cups of coffee. "I'm here!"

QUESTIONS FOR REFLECTION AND DISCUSSION

1. What are the facts/key elements in this case?
2. What do we know about Clara? About Gary Kowalski?
3. Describe the circumstances that led to the after-school meeting, first from the perspective of Clara, then from Gary Kowalski's perspective.
4. Describe the major dilemma(s) in this case.
5. What actions should Gary Kowalski take to resolve the dilemma(s)? What role should Clara's guidance counsellor, Shirley Tennant, take in resolving the dilemma(s)?
6. Consider the consequences of these actions for Clara's social life, academic life, and health. Consider the consequences for Shirley Tennant, and for Gary Kowalski.
7. What can we learn from this case?
8. Does this case lead us to question any assumptions or to recognize any beliefs we may have about students with physical disabilities, their education, other issues?

EXHIBIT 18.1	What Is Cystic Fibrosis?

Cystic Fibrosis (CF) is an inherited condition affecting approximately one in every 2000 children born in Canada. The effects of CF primarily involve the function of the exocrine glands. The exocrine glands secrete their products outside the body and on the surface of internal organs via ducts. Tears, mucus, sweat, and digestive juices are all examples of substances emitted by exocrine glands. CF causes these glands to produce abnormally thick and sticky secretions. This causes problems in the respiratory and digestive systems. The extent to which each system is involved varies from person to person. Thus, the symptoms experienced by each individual will also vary.

You may have heard of endocrine glands. Endocrine glands secrete hormones that are responsible for growth, sexual maturation, etc. CF does not affect these glands directly, but malnutrition may affect growth and rate of sexual maturation.

Source: From *CF and You: A Guide for Adolescents* (2nd ed.) by Y. G. Korneluk, N. E. MacDonald, M. Cappelli, P. McGrath, & C. E. Heick, 1996, McGill-Queen's Press, p. 3. Reprinted by permission.

Questions and Answers for Teachers of Children and Adolescents with CF

Q: *What do children and adolescents with CF do about the mucus that stays in their lungs and blocks their breathing passages?*

A: They take drugs and use airway clearance techniques. Students may need to carry out special breathing techniques or receive physiotherapy at school. They will need a private location and the full support of the teachers and administration to leave classes without undue attention. Also, coughing is a natural way of helping to clear the lungs of excess mucus and germs.

Q: *What happens if they stop doing physiotherapy or their breathing techniques?*

A: Mucus builds up in the lungs, which can lead to infections, inflammation, and eventually to irreparable damage. At first, these consequences may not be apparent to the individual or may be denied.

Q: *What do children and adolescents with CF do so the secretions do not prevent them from digesting their food?*

A: They usually take enzymes each time before they eat, with the dosage depending on the amount of enzymes they naturally produce. About 15 percent of adolescents with CF do not need any enzyme replacement.

Q: *What happens if they don't take the enzymes and they need them?*

A: They will probably experience cramps, bloating, and unusual stools, initially. However, over time they can lose weight and become malnourished. The intestines could become obstructed, which is painful and may be dangerous.

Q: *Why do they need to eat frequently, and why do they eat so much food high in calories and fat?*

A: They are helped to plan balanced diets, but they need a diet high in fats and calories to ensure that they maintain their weight or gain weight.

Q: *If they do not follow this diet or it does not maintain their weight, what are the alternatives?*

A: They can be fed through a tube that is placed in the nose and threaded into the stomach, or through a tube surgically placed directly into the stomach or directly into the small bowel. The latter two options require surgery and do sometimes cause social discomfort, although most people who take this route experience increased growth and energy and are pleased with the results.

Q: *Why are children and adolescents with CF hospitalized more often than their peers?*

A: There are a number of reasons, including serious infection or intestinal obstruction. The cause could be a change in health, like weight loss or decrease in lung function, which needs to be investigated.

Source: Developed after reading *CF and You: A Guide for Adolescents* (2nd ed.) by Y. G. Korneluk, N. E. MacDonald, M. Cappelli, P. McGrath, & C. E. Heick, 1996, McGill-Queen's Press.

EXHIBIT 18.2	What Characterizes a School Where Students Feel They Belong?

Students
- Students enjoy school.
- Students report a feeling of belonging to a group.
- Students say they have friends at school.
- Students participate in their classes.
- Students have choices and feel autonomous.
- Students' efforts are recognized by their teachers.

Teachers
- Teachers listen, help, and supervise co-curricular activities.
- Teachers know their students by name.
- Teachers' efforts are recognized by the school administration.
- Teachers have high expectations for students academically and provide high support to help students meet these expectations.
- Teachers share good news with parents.
- Teachers listen when students have problems.
- Teachers show students that they do not condone bullying and harassment.

Principals
- Principals report less bullying, swearing, and fighting.
- Principals provide leadership for positive programs of student involvement (e.g., peacemakers, community service, etc.).
- Principals provide leadership for school-wide discipline approaches.

Parents
- Parents feel comfortable in entering the school and communicating with faculty and administration.
- Parents participate in decision making about the school program and about their children's programs.

Community
- The school is a vital and integral part of the community.

Resources on this topic:
Newton, E., & Newton, P. (1992). *Voices, vision and vitality: Redesigning small schools.* Calgary, AB: Detselig.
Osterman, K. F. (2000). Students' need for belonging in the school community. *Review of educational research, 70,* 323-367.

EXHIBIT 18.3	Defining the Teacher's Role as a Counsellor

Counselling means helping students solve problems that involve feelings. Most secondary schools employ counsellors who handle personal and emotional crises. However, teachers are frequently called on to assume a role as a counsellor. What teachers need to fill this role is a "counselling attitude." This means they listen more than they talk and pay more attention to feelings than facts. When students sense that their teachers feel empathy for them and understand their problems, they are more likely to accept the suggestions their teachers make.

Six counselling roles have been described that secondary teachers can expect to be thrust into without warning:

1. **Listener-Advisor:** Because they spend so much time with their students, day after day, teachers get to know them quite well. Teachers who have trusting relationships with their students are likely to be aware of problems in students' lives.

2. **Referral and Receiving Agent:** Teachers refer students to school counsellors and then support students during and after counselling. Sometimes teachers must persist in encouraging adolescents to take advantage of the help that is available to them.

3. **Discoverer of Human Potential:** Teachers may recognize the talents of individual students; for example, the student who shows others in the classroom how to connect a video camera to a classroom computer. Teachers may direct students to counsellors or simply affirm that students are talented. Christopher Pratt, the Canadian painter, tells a story about one of his teachers who was the first adult to acknowledge and encourage his talent as a visual artist.

4. **Career Educator:** Teachers can incorporate discussions about careers within their discipline into classroom lessons, and also model positive attitudes towards the work involved in attaining qualifications to fulfill one's aspirations.

5. **Human Relations Facilitator:** Teachers can create classroom environments in which students feel safe and willing to take the risks involved in embracing challenges.

6. **Counselling Program Supporter:** Teachers influence students' views of the counselling services in the school. Being knowledgeable about, and supportive of, these services is part of a teacher's role. Teachers should know when and how to encourage students to seek the help they need.

Source: Developed after reading *The Reflective Roles of the Classroom Teacher* (Chapter 6, "The Counsellor Role"), by D. J. McIntyre & M. J. O'Hair, 1996, Wadsworth (ITP), Toronto, ON.

SUGGESTIONS FOR FURTHER READING

Hargreaves, A., Earl, L., & Ryan, J. (1996). *Schooling for change*. Bristol, PA: Falmer Press.
  In Chapter 5, "Care and Support," these Canadian authors make the case for secondary schools to care, as well as teach curriculum. They describe a number of organizational approaches that could be used, including mentors, teacher-advisors, and homerooms.

Korneluk, Y. G., MacDonald, N. E., Cappelli, M., McGrath, P., & Heick, C. E. (1996). *CF and you: A guide for adolescents* (2nd ed.). Montreal, QC: McGill-Queen's Press.
  Straightforward, written so adolescents can understand their own condition, and containing much valuable information for teachers, including helpful reminders about the extensive individual differences among children and adolescents with cystic fibrosis.

McIntyre, D. J., & O'Hair, M. J. (1996). *The reflective roles of the classroom teacher*. Toronto, ON: Wadsworth (Nelson Canada).
  In Chapter 6, the authors elaborate on the counsellor role of the classroom teacher; their goal is to help teachers develop a "counselling attitude," that is, to listen more than to tell, to pay more attention to feelings than to facts, and to be caring.

Newton, E., & Newton, P. (1992). *Voices, vision and vitality: Redesigning small schools*. Calgary, AB: Detselig.
  Describes the issues that face small schools, and the approaches that have been tried with some success to take advantage of the characteristics of small schools to make them vital places to learn and teach. Based on experiences in small, rural schools in western Canada.

Noddings, N. (2002). *Educating moral people: A caring alternative to character education*. New York, NY: Teachers College Press.
  A fitting follow-up to Noddings' influential 1992 book, *The Challenge to Care in Schools: An Alternative Approach to Education*.

WEBLINKS

http://www.ssta.sk.ca/research/small_schools/95-09.htm
Small Schools Network: Created by the Saskatchewan School Trustees Association, this site allows representatives of small schools to share ideas and best practices.

http://www.ael.org/eric/rural.htm
The Web site of ERIC (Educational Resources Information Center) Clearinghouse on Rural Education and Small Schools contains links to many resources including ERIC Digests, which are clear, brief summaries of the implications of recent research for educators, schools, and students.

http://www.cysticfibrosis.ca/home.asp
Home page of the Canadian Cystic Fibrosis Foundation with information for persons with CF, parents and caregivers, and partners and friends. Valuable information for teachers about what it means to live with CF.

Don't Ruin Good Books for the Students Who Deserve Them!

Wayne Monson raised his head, pulled back his shoulders, and told himself, "I can do this. I want to be a teacher." With these uplifting gestures, an almost-novice supply teacher walked through the ancient, graffitied doors of Central High School once again. This time he smashed his fist into the door frame as hard as he could. That felt better! He had just had the first argument of his career with a colleague. And he had no idea what to do. Arguing in the parking lot at 7:30 in the morning, two of the keenest people in the building! No one would believe him.

Wayne Monson had graduated the previous spring from a faculty of education, with a shiny, new teaching certificate, into a cold, unhiring reality. With cutbacks and budget reductions rampant in education, supply teaching for a couple of years was the best Wayne and his peers could expect. After two months of volunteering in schools all over the town of Clear River, Wayne had been called to Central High. Wayne thought back to how differently he had been feeling two weeks ago, when he had walked through these doors at Central for the first time.

He knew that first morning that Central had once been the only high school in town. Inside its doors stood cabinets packed with trophies and plaques attesting to a long and proud history. But Wayne also noticed that first morning how the building looked worn and the cups were tarnished. And it smelled like a high school. Although it was only 7:45 AM, the halls were filled with jostling, shrieking adolescents. Wayne saw hair of every colour and students from many racial backgrounds. He had never taught or volunteered at Central, not during his student teaching in Clear River last year nor during his volunteering this fall. But Wayne thought this was part of the excitement—his first long-term substitution position was in a completely unfamiliar school.

The secretary in the office had pointed to a green door across the hall and told Wayne that Mr. Chan, the head of the Special Education Department, was waiting for him. The sign on the door said "Teachers Only." Wayne smiled to himself. "I'm a teacher."

From there, things happened fast. Wayne remembered a blur of faces, introductions, and facts—"your mail" (in Ms. Burdett's box—"Open everything that does not say 'personal'"); "your desk" in the departmental workroom; "your classroom"; "your class lists"; and the long-term plans left by Pam Burdett.

When Mr. Chan had called Wayne on Sunday afternoon to offer him the long-term substitution position, he had provided few details. Pam Burdett had been called away to a family emergency. She expected to be away for two or three weeks. Pam had left long-term plans on her desk. Wayne would have the help and support of the other members of the Special Education Department at this inner city school. But he would make the day-to-day teaching decisions and would be a member of the department for as long as Pam was away. Mr. Chan wanted one supply teacher to replace Pam for the entire time. "These students don't do well with change. It would be best for them if one teacher could be with them consistently. They like Pam and will really miss her." Wayne had agreed to complete the long-term substitution. When he had asked why Mr. Chan chose him, he learned that it had been Pam's idea. Pam and Wayne had met at a workshop hosted by the local learning disabilities association the previous spring. They had chatted at the coffee break.

Wayne knew he would be teaching three classes each day in the stream called, "Preparation for the World of Work." The classes were Grade 12 communications, Grade 10 communications, and Grade 10 mathematics. In his fourth teaching period, he would supervise a peer tutoring program, and in the fifth period, he was supposed to prepare for the other four. The catch was that all 12 students in the Grade 10 communications class had been identified as having behavioural problems. Wayne had worked in the summers for five years in a program for youth with behavioural difficulties. This was probably what Pam Burdett had remembered from her chat with him and was probably why he had just put in one of the toughest days of his life.

At the end of the first day, Wayne sat at "his" desk in the classroom and wrote in his journal:

> I cannot believe how little they do in a one-hour class. Is it because they don't try? I know they have to be here, by law. But don't they want to learn anything? The hardest class is Communications 10. Only 7 of the 12 showed. And there are no scores to show me their reading levels, even though it is October. I bet most of them can't read above Grade 4. And what an assignment—two paragraphs to read and six worksheets of exercises. I can't do that with them for three weeks. We'll all go mad together.

What bothered Wayne most was that some students ignored the paragraphs and went straight to the questions below. When he asked why, Anwar piped up, "We done so many. We know how they go. Reading it don't help." When Wayne asked the students what they would like to do in communications class, they said things like, "watch films" and "have debates." Anwar, always ready with an answer, suggested, "Maybe read books like other classes."

After the second day of worksheets and discussion with communications 10, Wayne wrote in his journal:

> I was too harsh yesterday. I think they want to learn. But they know that they can't learn from these worksheets. I want to do a real unit with them. Three weeks should be long enough. Even if Pam comes back after two weeks, she can finish it if we aren't finished.

That night, Wayne looked back at his notes from his courses at the faculty of education, particularly at the list of easy novels with high interest for adolescents, and at the list of Central High English Department Resources he had found in the department workroom. He re-read some chapters of Nancie Atwell's *In the Middle: Writing, Reading, and Learning with Adolescents*. And suddenly the answer jumped off the pages—*The Outsiders* by S. E. Hinton. It was on the resources list and on the list of low-reading, high-interest novels. There was a film of it around, too.

Later, in summarizing the events of two weeks with the Grade 10 communications classes, Wayne wrote in his journal:

> I knew many of the students in the class had difficulty reading, so I began by reading the novel aloud to the class, with them reading along silently with me. The first day I managed to read for about 10 to 12 minutes. Then they worked on their worksheets and other things for the rest of the period. Then next day I read for a few minutes longer and then they worked on other things for the rest of the period. The third day I read for 20 minutes and then I had the students read on their own for 5 minutes. By the fourth day, I read for 10 minutes and had the students read for 10. Not all of them read happily or easily. But most made the effort for at least a short period of time. My idea was to slowly try to get the students to read on their own and, at the same time, have them do some activities associated with the novel. I did have some success. By the end of my second week there, three students were taking the book home to read so they could find out what was going to happen next. I also held a carrot in front of them, promising to show the movie the next week.

Wayne's next journal entry was written at 7:45 the following morning. He knew that Jim Boychuk arrived at 7:30 every day. Jim was a keen member of the English department who was known for his imaginative units and for teaching well in the academic streams of the English program. Jim always said he did not have enough patience and loved literature too much to teach communications courses in the applied and preparation for work streams. Wayne had hoped to meet Jim in the staff room, not on the parking lot. But both had arrived at the same time. So, in the grey mist, they had stopped to talk. Wayne started, "I heard yesterday that you wanted the class set of *The Outsiders*. I only need 13 of them, and I expect to finish in a few days. I wondered if you had any really good suggestions for pulling the whole unit together. I remember when you talked to our class at the university, and you said a good wrap-up of a novel study can stay with students for a lifetime."

Jim's response was short and bitter. "I don't want the novel now. You've ruined it for my class for this year. When they find out that the 'low stream' did *The Outsiders,* it will be 'baby stuff.' That class you're teaching can't handle novels. But now you've ruined the book for my students. That's why we got those paragraph studies. Didn't Pam leave them for you? Those are for the non-readers." With that, he stalked into the school.

Wayne had been controlled and polite with Jim in the parking lot. He had smiled and said that he did not believe the novels were spoiled for Jim's class. And that if they were, they shouldn't be. When he arrived at his classroom, he wrote what he really felt in his journal:

> He basically told me that students who are not in the academic classes shouldn't ruin good novels for better students who deserve them. And that students in the work stream deserve boring paragraph worksheets that teach them nothing. No wonder these students in Communications 10 don't know much! He thinks they don't deserve to know much! How can he say that? I respected him!

Wayne chuckled to himself and continued to write in his journal:

> Lucky for me that he didn't want to teach Macbeth! What would he say if he knew I was using the Global Series Macbeth with my Grade 12 Communications class? I suppose he might find out—I am recording all this in my journal, and leaving notes for Pam.

With the Grade 12 class, Wayne had been uncertain about what to teach. For the first few days, he had followed the plans left by Pam Burdett and conducted discussions based on recent events in the community and around the country that students heard on the news or read about in the newspaper. Pam had arranged for copies of the local paper, the *Courier,* and of the *Globe and Mail* to be delivered to the classroom daily. The students had become engaged in a lively discussion about the occult and witches, and the stereotype of witches as the personification of evil in fairy tales. Wayne had asked them if they knew the name of the most famous play in which witches played a major role. He suggested that although this play had been written a long time ago, people still debated whether the playwright meant readers to think of the witches as real or as the product of an evil man's thoughts. The students had surprised Wayne. A number said that he must be talking about *Macbeth.* They asked Wayne to tell them the story. He decided that he would bring in his copy of Lamb's *Tales from Shakespeare* the next day and read them the tale of "the Scottish Play." Before he left for the day, Wayne checked the Department Office. It was his lucky day—a new class set of *Macbeth,* in the Global Shakespeare Series prepared by high school teachers from Canada, the United States, and Australia. These were brilliant! They were illustrated, with clear liner notes, in an attractive paperback format, and accompanied by related readings. It was here that Wayne found *Macbeth and the Witches* by Richard Armour. Because it read almost like jazz and was full of puns, Wayne knew he would have many opportunities to engage the students in "word play," one of his favourite parts of teaching English. For example, Armour described the end of the first scene of the play this way:

The witches hear some dear friends[1] calling and depart. "Fair is foul, and foul is fair," they comment philosophically as they leave. This must have been pretty upsetting to any moralists, semanticists, or baseball umpires who chanced to overhear them.

For three days, Wayne and the students had played with the language, made puns, and talked intensely while they sorted out the events of "the Scottish Play." All this time, Wayne had tantalized the students by refusing to call the play by its given name. Finally on the third day, he read from the Global Series *Macbeth* Norrie Epstein's essay, "The Curse of 'the Scottish Play,'" about the bad luck and fear of retribution associated with the play.

In the next few days, the students read three poems from the same book, "At the Fire and Cauldron Health-Food Restaurant," Stuart Dischell's poem about the power of Macbeth's imagination, and Mel Glenn's poem that ends, "You got any books that deal with real life?" The first provoked a range of disgusting recipes and menus that could only come from adolescent imaginations. The latter two poems stimulated heated debate about whether or not the witches were an evil product of the mind of an evil man, and about the many ways in which "the Scottish Play" was about real life and how people in all times throughout history could be tempted to make the ends justify the means.

The students wrote letters that might have been carried by the characters who delivered messages, like the letter Lady Macbeth received from Macbeth after his first meeting with the witches. They also wrote reports of battles and accounts of banquets that might have appeared in a newspaper of the time. Wayne relished these discussions and the written work. He recalled the laughter and intensity that had accompanied the readings that he and the Grade 12 communications classes had done of some of the key scenes "from the real play," to quote one student. The students had certainly thought, talked, and written about how people can and do externalize evil and rationalize their actions.

Wayne also remembered how, in the staff room, when he said he'd had a good day with communications 10 and communications 12, one teacher had responded, "You mean, no fights broke out?" And everyone laughed. Wayne thought about the piles of untouched photocopied exercises that Pam had left for him to teach. And the lack of information about student reading levels. He wrote:

> I don't think anyone expects them to learn. I think that is why they don't learn. It is a case of low expectations fulfilled. Teachers don't just use different means to get to the same goals, or modify the goals for these kids, the way they should. They throw away the goals! Now what should I do? I'm just a supply teacher trying to get a job. Should I show Pam my journal and the students' assignments? Who should I talk to? Should I pretend my blow-up on the parking lot never happened?

[1] Armour added in a footnote that the friends were a cat and a toad, with the cryptic comment that witches have to take friendship where they can get it.

QUESTIONS FOR REFLECTION AND DISCUSSION

1. Identify the facts of the case briefly.

2. What do we know about Wayne Monson, the substitute teacher? About the two classes described in the case?

3. Use the facts to support your statement of the major dilemma(s) facing Wayne.

4. Describe the classes taught by Wayne Monson the way Anwar (in Grade 10 communications) and Jang-Li (in Grade 12 communications) might describe them to Pam Burdett when she returns. How might Wayne respond when Pam asks him how the teaching went?

5. What are some underlying issues that might arise from the context in which the case took place?

6. What would you advise Wayne to do in the remaining time he teaches at Central High, if he were to ask your advice?

7. What actions should Wayne take to resolve the major dilemma(s)? Consider the consequences for Wayne, for the students, for Pam Burdett when she returns, for other students in the school.

8. What beliefs or assumptions does this case cause us to question about students in urban schools, beginning teachers, curriculum?

EXHIBIT 19.1	Teaching for Understanding: A Four-Part Framework

In the approach called teaching for understanding, teachers focus on helping students to be able to carry out a variety of thought-demanding actions with a topic, such as finding new examples, making applications, and engaging in other performances that show understanding. Teachers and researchers have developed a framework that provides a language for planning such teaching. This framework highlights four concepts:

- generative topics, that is, topics that are central to a discipline, accessible to students, and connected to many topics both in the discipline and outside the discipline;

- understanding goals, that is, goals that stress understanding and appreciation and that can focus teaching (e.g., students will understand that playwrights use subtle and complex imagery to affect the reader's imagination and emotions, including the use of the unnatural, sickness, blood, and animals to evoke images of evil for readers of *Macbeth*);

- understanding performances, that is, performances that support the understanding goals and that demonstrate understanding all through the unit, not just at its culmination; these present students with progressively more subtle, but still accessible, challenges (e.g., creating recipes and menus in the spirit of the witches' brew in the cauldron early in the study of *Macbeth*; writing letters to be carried by messengers, and preparing newspaper accounts of the main events of the play, or obituaries of the main characters);

- ongoing assessment, that is, public criteria and opportunities for reflection and feedback from self, peers, and the teacher throughout the unit; such assessment enables learners to sharpen the focus of their efforts.

For many examples of teaching for understanding in action, consult the thematic issue of *Educational Leadership* on "Teaching for Understanding," 1994, volume 51, issue 5.

EXHIBIT 19.2	Principles of Cognitive Approaches to Teaching Advanced Skills to Disadvantaged Students

Taking a New Attitude toward Disadvantaged Learners

- Appreciate intellectual accomplishments all young learners bring to school.
- Emphasize building on strengths rather than just remediating deficits.
- Learn about children's cultures to avoid mistaking differences for deficits.

Reshaping the Curriculum

- Focus on complex, meaningful problems.
- Embed instruction on basic skills in context of more global tasks.
- Make connections with students' out-of-school experience and culture.

Applying New Instructional Strategies

- Model powerful thinking strategies.
- Encourage multiple approaches.
- Provide scaffolding to enable students to accomplish complex tasks.
- Make dialogue central medium for teaching and learning.

Source: From *Teaching Advanced Skills to At-Risk Students* by B. Means, C. Chelemer, and M. S. Knapp (Eds.), Copyright © 1991, Jossey-Bass. Reprinted by permission of Jossey-Bass, a subsidiary of John Wiley & Sons.

EXHIBIT 19.3	Books and Articles for Preparing Communications Classes

Aagesen, C., & Blumberg, M. (1999). *Shakespeare for kids: His life and times, 21 activities.* Chicago, IL: Chicago Review Press.

Atwell, N. (1987). *In the middle: Writing, reading, and learning with adolescents.* Portsmouth, NH: Boynton/Cook Publishers.

Burdett, L. (1996). *Macbeth for kids.* Windsor, ON: Black Moss Press.

Hinton, S. E. (1967). *The outsiders.* New York, NY: Dell Publishing.

Hull, G. A. (1989). Research on writing: Building a cognitive and social understanding of composing. In L. B. Resnick & L. E. Klopfer (Eds.), *Toward the thinking curriculum: Current cognitive research* (pp. 104-128). ASCD Yearbook.

Lamb, C., & Lamb, M. (1994, first issued 1807). *Tales from Shakespeare.* London, UK: Puffin Books.

The outsiders: A study guide (Novel Ties Series). (1992). New Hyde Park, NY: Learning Links.

Salini, D., Ferguson, C., & Scott, T. (Eds.). (1997). *The tragedy of Macbeth with related readings (The Global Shakespeare Series).* Toronto, ON: International Thomson Publishing (Nelson Canada).

EXHIBIT 19.4	Self-Assessment for Teachers of Diverse Classrooms

Questions for teachers to ask themselves as they strive to teach equitably in diverse classrooms:

- Do I question in a way that fosters complex thinking by all students, regardless of racial background or gender?
- Do I encourage critical thinking, even when it reflects values different from my own?
- Do I encourage students' racial and cultural pride?
- Do I avoid feeling defensive when students describe their experiences of racism in Canadian society?
- Do I encourage my students to take risks in their use of English, especially those for whom it is not the first language?
- Have I created a positive climate in my classroom in which students feel confident enough to take risks as learners?
- Have I been patient, supportive, and responsive to the language of students who speak a dialect or speak with an accent?
- Have I affirmed the cultures of all the students in my class?
- Have I enabled all students to see their experiences in my teaching?
- Do I encourage my students to examine whether the racial differences in the class facilitate or hinder class discussion?

Sources on this topic:
Fleras, A., & Leonard Elliot, J. (2002). *Engaging diversity: Multiculturalism in Canada* (2nd ed.). Toronto, ON: Nelson (Thomson Learning).
Lee, E. (1985). *Letters to Marcia: A teacher's guide to antiracist education*. Toronto, ON: Cross-Cultural Communication Centre.

SUGGESTIONS FOR FURTHER READING

Burdett, L. (2001). *Macbeth for kids*. Toronto, ON: Firefly Press.

> Burdett, a Grade 2 teacher, has rewritten the play in rhyming couplets comprehensible to children (with teaching); the book is illustrated with children's drawings and letters that demonstrate they understand the key speeches and the plot of the play. Great teaching resource.

Canadian School Boards Association. (1997). *Students in poverty: Toward awareness, action, and wider knowledge*. Ottawa, ON: Canadian School Boards Association.

> Canadian school boards have recognized and begun to develop resources to help schools deal with the challenges of students who live in poverty. This is one of their resources on this important topic.

Knapp, M. S., and associates. (1998). *Teaching for meaning in high-poverty classrooms*. New York, NY: Teachers College Press.

> This book contains many examples of teachers using an integrated management style to create an orderly and enabling classroom environment that stressed challenge and was not too restrictive. The authors advise emphasizing understanding rather than drill and exercises in high-poverty schools.

Newton, D. P. (2000). *Teaching for understanding: What it is and how to do it*. New York, NY: Routledge/Falmer.

> Describes understanding, teaching for understanding, how to motivate and engage students, and how to help students regulate their own learning.

WEBLINKS

http://www.cfc-efc.ca/docs/ccsd/00000323.htm
The Canadian Fact Book on Poverty: offers a broad introduction to poverty in Canada, including measures of poverty, misconceptions of poverty, and the impact of poverty on children.

http://www.temple.edu/lss/htmlpublications/publications/pubs97-4.htm
A 1997 paper by Wang, Haertel, and Walberg titled "Fostering educational resilience in inner-city schools" reprinted from *Children and Youth* (vol. 7). Reviews the research and makes recommendations for educational practices that promote resilience.

http://www.newhorizons.org/
A Web site that serves as an interactive clearinghouse and resource locator about effective teaching. Take a look.

Don't Push Me! I Can't Take It!

"Don't push me! I can't take it! I shouldn't be in here anyway. I'm not like them!" Suddenly the shouting stopped, the heavy classroom door slammed, and the room was absolutely silent. Billy Preston was gone. It took Greg Smith a moment to regain his composure. In his three years of teaching he had never had a student storm out of a class before. He flipped on the intercom on the wall and notified the office of Billy's departure. Keeping the tone light, Greg opened with "Man overboard."

The senior secretary responded, "We have him. Storm brewing. Heavy seas ahead."

Greg Smith continued to teach his Grade 9 applied science class. After, he wondered how he had remained so calm. At the time, he kept telling himself, "Keep control of your response, old man. Don't let him control you. He just wanted to get a rise out of you." Greg knew, rationally, that Billy Preston was not particularly out to get him. Billy had made dozens of trips to the office this year for relatively minor but persistent and annoying classroom disruptions. Billy was convinced that he was the target of a racist campaign to get him out of Sandford Secondary.

Billy's file showed that he, his mother, and his two brothers had immigrated to Canada four years ago. Billy told Greg the three boys had been born within about five years, all to the same mother, but each had a different father. The boys were well known because they were all outstanding athletes. Billy, the middle boy, was probably the best athlete, but of the three boys he had probably had the most severe emotional problems since last May.

Although Billy and Greg enjoyed a pretty good student-teacher relationship, Billy had never told Greg about the day that had changed his life last May. Greg had learned the details from the resource teacher at Billy's elementary school, Pat Nalen. This made it difficult, because Greg did not want to let on to Billy that he knew. One day last May, Billy had been the first of the three boys to arrive home after school, because he had decided to skip a track-and-field practice. He had not had a full night's sleep since. Billy had entered an unusually quiet house to find that his mother had committed suicide. He told his confidante, the resource teacher in his elementary school, that he knew the reason. After coming to Canada, his mother had finally found a partner who did not threaten her, abuse her, or leave her. She had been happier than ever before in her tough life. And, without warning, after two wonderful years, her partner had been killed in a road accident. Billy told Ms. Nalen that his mother had cried most of the lonely two months between the first disaster and the second. He had been worried about her, but he did not know how to help her. He had gone so far as to ask Ms. Nalen if she would speak to his mother and remind her how much her sons needed her.

Since the opening of school in September, Billy had alternated between sullen silences and uncontrollable outbursts. Every small conflict had turned into a conflagration. Because of his low academic achievement in elementary school, his history of oppositional behaviour, and his recent emotional setback, the elementary school and Sandford Secondary had advised Billy's foster family to place him in applied classes, rather than in the academic program. Greg wondered whether Billy might be right, that if he had not been black, the schools might have come to a different placement recommendation. Some days Greg thought that on top of being depressed and lonely, Billy was bored with the lack of challenge in his classes.

Sandford Secondary had changed, reluctantly, over the past 20 years as the neighbourhood around it had changed. Once Sandford had been the home of the provincial debating champions for four years in a row. In the past couple of years, one debating coach had retired and the other had acknowledged that debating was not a high priority for the students and their families who now made up the community around Sandford Secondary. Every year, the number of black students in the school had increased, although most of the teachers were white and middle-aged. Greg wondered how long it would take the school district to begin actively seeking minority teachers and developing a program to help black students take pride in their heritage and in being black.

As a relatively young teacher, Greg often felt that the veterans didn't take his ideas seriously. Greg had recommended that the school needed a consistent approach to standards of behaviour, so that no matter where Billy lost control, he would be met with similar expectations and responses. This would improve the predictability of the school for all students and for all teachers, not just for Billy Preston. Greg had also suggested that the high school counsellors seek a grief counselling specialist for Billy and his older brother. Greg had lost his sister at a young age and had made little progress in dealing with her death until his parents had recognized and accepted that they could not help him, that he needed someone who specialized in helping young people grieve. After six months of weekly counselling, Greg had stopped blaming himself for his sister's death and started to live again.

All of these thoughts were bouncing around in Greg's head as he walked toward the office after school. He wondered how many years of teaching it would take before he stopped feeling like a bad student every time he walked into the office to discuss an incident with a student. The senior secretary told Greg that Billy had gone home, suspended for a day. "But I didn't want him suspended!" Greg's temper flared. "Why suspend him after an incident in my class? I have never sent him to the office all year; I have always handled our disagreements myself. I didn't want him suspended. I want us to get him some help." Greg stopped. "Sorry, I know it wasn't your decision. I had better talk with Erica. Where is our illustrious vice-principal?"

Greg did not get to talk with Erica Best, the vice-principal, until the following morning because she spent the evening in a community meeting for parents, teachers, and administrators on the other side of the city. By then, Greg had cooled down and Erica had been considering some of the staff's suggestions for a unified approach to helping Billy Preston.

Greg had sat in the office after school reading all the files relevant to Billy Preston's case. He learned that the incident cards were 13 x 18 cm file cards, written up by whomever happened to receive Billy when he reached the office. Some bore great detail, others merely Billy's name, the date, and the class from which he had been ejected. With so little information and such inconsistent information, it was difficult to discern a pattern showing whether the situation was deteriorating or simply eroding the patience of those who had to deal with Billy. Greg could find no clear policy on how many referrals to the office resulted in a suspension. He knew Billy had been threatened with suspension a month ago, but could find no reason for the suspension taking place today, rather than some other day.

Greg wondered what usually happened when Billy was sent to the office. The secretary suggested that that, too, depended on who was there to receive Billy. She tended to talk with him and remind him that if he continued in this way, Ms. Best would be forced to suspend him. Ms. Best, apparently, preferred to make him "sit and think about his sins." One of the counsellors had mentioned to Greg that he thought Billy should be required to complete a form on which he would respond to a series of questions about what he had done; specifically, what classroom rules his behaviour violated, what negative impact his behaviour had on others, how he could prevent such behaviour from happening in the future, and so on. This counsellor had seen this system work effectively in another secondary school. Greg could see the possible effects of the emphasis on consequences and on Billy having to consider the perspectives of others. But Greg remained convinced that Billy needed more than structure to help curb his inappropriate and disruptive behaviours. Greg remained convinced that Billy needed help to deal with the emotional upheaval and overwhelming loss that he had experienced only six months ago.

When Greg met with Erica Best before school the following morning, she surprised him. She said, "I phoned in for my messages during a break in the meeting last night and the senior secretary had put the entire story on my voice mail. So, I phoned Billy Preston's home. I spoke with him and then with his foster father. I asked Billy if there was a teacher or counsellor that he thought could help him turn things around. And, brace yourself, he named you."

"Me?" Greg sputtered, "He stormed out of my class. And I can't even think of a reason. I have reviewed our class and all I can think of as a trigger for his outburst is boredom. I like the boy. I think I know what he is going through. I have never told anyone around here, because I never know how people will take it, but I went to a psychiatrist for six months after my sister died. I was about Billy's age. I don't think I would have ever got over it without that help. I blamed myself. I felt like I didn't want to live some days, other days I was deliriously happy for no reason. My life was a roller coaster, and I had no control over my feelings."

"Well, there you are," Erica answered. "Billy says that you are the only one at school who understands. I guess he is right. He doesn't know why you understand. Do you think you could tell him? He told me last night that he needs help. I think he had been discussing it with his foster parents, because he used almost the same words as his foster father did when he got on the phone. Did you know that his foster dad is a social worker? He never handled Billy's case professionally; he is with Workers' Compensation. But I guess the foster family was chosen because the man is a social worker and the woman is a nurse. I would say that social services must have been pretty worried about Billy. I am wondering why no one told us how worried they were. You knew about Billy finding his mother, didn't you? He told me that he thought you knew, but that he had not told you. His foster family asked us not to tell the teachers because Billy felt he could not handle people's false sympathy. Who told you?"

"Ms. Nalen—Pat Nalen—the resource teacher at the elementary school phoned me. I guess Billy goes back to talk with her, and he told her about my class and me. So she phoned me, but asked me to be discreet. I think we have to call a meeting of all Billy's teachers and get our act together; yesterday was a wake-up call. I think this boy needs our help. He may need firmer discipline and consistency, but he also needs psychological and emotional support. More than his teachers can give. Now, tell me what you meant, a few minutes ago, when you said you and Billy thought I could help him turn things around."

Ms. Best explained to Greg that she wanted someone to become the lead teacher on the team of Billy's teachers—a role model, a confidante, and a liaison with the psychiatrist or whomever the family chose to work with Billy. "I have been meaning to talk with you and encourage you to think about starting to work on additional qualifications that would allow you to work as a counsellor in the school. This has just tipped my hand. You know, I worked with exceptional kids for years before going into administration. Students like Billy need to trust the people who are responsible for their individualized program. That's why I asked him whom he would like. What do you think? Can you lead on this one? It means you will finally get us to listen to your suggestions. Haven't you been saying we need to get a plan for some time? This is your chance."

QUESTIONS FOR REFLECTION AND DISCUSSION

1. What are the facts/key elements in the case?
2. What do we know about Billy Preston? About his teacher, Greg Smith?
3. Describe the situation of the past six months and of the past day as seen by Billy Preston, by Greg Smith, by another student in the same class.
4. Describe the major dilemma(s) in this case.
5. What actions should Greg Smith take to resolve the major dilemma(s)? What role should the vice-principal, Erica Best, take in resolving the dilemma(s)?
6. Consider the consequences of these actions for Billy's social/emotional well-being, academic life, and future. Consider the consequences for Greg Smith, Erica Best, other students at Sandford Secondary.
7. What do we learn from this case?
8. Does this case lead us to question our assumptions or recognize our beliefs?

EXHIBIT 20.1	Components of a Schoolwide Student Management Plan

Many educational writers and researchers have argued that schoolwide student management plans are essential to well-managed classrooms. Such plans provide students with clarity and consistency of expectations for appropriate behaviour and for the consequences that follow inappropriate behaviour. This means both teachers and students can enjoy a fair and predictable climate. The following list itemizes the components of a schoolwide student management plan.

- A philosophy statement
- School rules and procedures that are effectively taught and re-taught when problems occur
- A statement of student behaviours that can lead to a direct office referral
- A focus on specific teacher interventions that will be used prior to an office referral
- A requirement that all teachers teach students (and provide the administration with) their classroom management procedures
- Classroom consequences that are educational and treat students with dignity
- Clear, sequential responses by the school administration to office referrals
- Consequences for office referrals that are educational and treat students with dignity
- A clear procedure for teachers to seek assistance when they have continued problems
- Forms for communicating effectively about student behaviour among staff, administration, and students
- A process for developing a personalized plan for all students receiving a specified number of office referrals in a designated time frame
- Data collection to determine where referrals occur and to assess the results of interventions

Sources on this topic:
Jones, V. F., & Jones, L. S. (1995). *Comprehensive Classroom Management: Creating Positive Learning Environments for All Students.* Toronto, ON: Allyn & Bacon.
Marr, M. B., Audette, B., White, R., Ellis, E., & Algozzine, B. (2002). School-wide discipline and classroom ecology. *Special services in the schools, 18*(1), 55-73.

EXHIBIT 20.2	How Schools and Teachers Use Proactive Approaches to Prevent the Development of Behavioural and Emotional Disabilities in At-Risk Students

1. Inclusive schools try to increase the staff's sense of ownership of the well-being of all students.
2. Teachers and administrators emphasize proactive teaching of expected behaviours rather than punishment for inappropriate behaviours.
3. They develop individual behaviour change plans for students who display chronic problematic behaviours.
4. School-based teams work effectively to make decisions and to support teachers.
5. Teachers receive assistance as soon as they are confronted with challenging behaviours.
6. Assistance for teachers and students continues as long as it is needed and is evaluated throughout the process.
7. Teachers remain involved, rather than handing over students and problem classroom behaviours to someone else.
8. Psychologists and psychiatrists provide deeper interventions for serious emotional problems that arise from experiences like child abuse, neglect, divorce, or death of family members.
9. Administrators show their support and commitment for all components of the proactive approach.
10. Strong leadership by faculty and administration characterizes schools that succeed in preventing the development of behavioural and emotional disabilities in at-risk students.

Relevant sources:
Cooper, P., Smith, C. J., & Upton, C. (1994). *Emotional and behavioural difficulties: Theory to practice.* New York, NY: Routledge.
Marr, M. B., Audette, B., White, R., Ellis, E., & Algozzine, B. (2002). School-wide discipline and classroom ecology. *Special services in the schools, 18*(1), 55-73.

| EXHIBIT 20.3 | Program Teaches Students to Overcome |

It's past noon, the lads are hungry, but teacher Jamil Kalim won't let them quit. Not yet. He can almost taste victory in this fast-paced game of handball.

"Come on man, just one more game," Mr. Kalim enjoins his students. "This is our literacy and numeracy lesson."

They laughingly oblige, dismissing their teacher-mentor's version of the score. That they are even here, at school, on a balmy spring day is a victory of sorts.

But then they've never had a teacher quite like 30-year-old Mr. Kalim.

Like his students, Mr. Kalim is black. And like his students, he has been affected by racism in the school system. He can relate—but he won't let them quit.

From art class in the morning to choir practice after the handball game to a rigorous pre-exam review of this semester's lessons on African civilizations, Mr. Kalim never stops teaching, never stops challenging.

He left another high school teaching job in February to head the Nighana program, an alternative "Afrocentric" program that operates out of Toronto's Eastdale Collegiate Institute. His two dozen students have been bounced around, alienated, neglected or rejected by the mainstream education system. Nighana offers them a chance to gain academic confidence and reintegrate.

Youth worker Jerome Trevena helps with any outside issues that might be hampering school performance. "I just want to make sure these guys have a choice [about their futures]," he says.

Mr. Kalim says his students are "intensely brilliant." But most have not, until now, enjoyed much success at school. Each one of his students has encountered racism at some point in his or her schooling.

Indeed, a recent three-year study, led by University of Toronto sociology professor George Dei, concludes that "systemic racism" is still prevalent in the Canadian school system of the late 1990's, placing black students at greater risk of tuning out or dropping out.

...Black parents complain that white teachers have lower expectations of black students who are overrepresented in non-university-track courses in high school.

...Mr. Kalim says it burns him up when students tell him they have never before been encouraged by a teacher to work harder, do better.

...Mr. Kalim wants his students to develop the confidence to thrive in the mainstream school system and "express themselves to the dominant culture." They're getting there. Last night, Nighana students staged an exhibition of their music and art at a downtown Toronto gallery.

Source: Reprinted with permission from the *Globe and Mail.*

SUGGESTIONS FOR FURTHER READING

Bullock, L. M., Gable, R. A., & Rutherford, R. B. (Eds.). (1998). *Preparation of teachers of students with emotional/behavioral disorders*. Reston, VA: Council for Children with Behavioral Disorders.
Although the title suggests that this publication by the Council for Exceptional Children might be focused on teachers of special classes, there are chapters on full inclusion, comprehensive classroom programs, and the needs of inner city students.

Colvin, G., Kameenui, E. J., & Sugai, G. (1994). Reconceptualizing behaviour management and school-wide discipline in general education. *Education and treatment of children, 16,* 361–381.
An application of proactive, behaviour management systems in inclusive schools that focuses specifically on the implications for students who demonstrate problem behaviours but have not yet developed behaviour disorders.

Cooper, P. (Ed.). (1999). *Understanding and supporting children with emotional and behavioural difficulties*. London, UK: Jessica Kingsley Publishers.
Cooper has written a number of excellent resources on how teachers can make a difference in the lives of students with behavioural and emotional difficulties and on how schools can act preventively. Another fine resource.

Jones, V. F., & Jones, L. S. (2000). *Comprehensive classroom management: Creating communities of support and solving problems* (6th ed.). Boston, MA: Pearson Education (Allyn & Bacon).
In this thorough text, the authors emphasize strategies for working with individual challenging students and the development of consistent, schoolwide approaches to management.

Palmer H. (Ed.). (1997). *"...but where are you really from?" Stories of identity and assimilation in Canada*. Toronto, ON: Sister Vision.
In this anthology, women of colour discuss what identity is, where it comes from, assimilation, and what immigrants lose in making cultural adjustments; they describe their frustration at not feeling a sense of belonging in Canada because they do not feel fully accepted as Canadians.

White, R., Marr, M. B., Ellis, E., Audette, B., & Algozzine, B. (2001). Effects of a model of school-wide discipline on office referrals. *Journal of At-Risk Issues, 7*(2), 4-12.
These researchers found that a schoolwide discipline model improved classroom behaviour and reduced the extent to which all students, especially those with emotional and behavioural problems, were involved in disciplinary actions.

WEBLINKS

http://www.leagueofpeacefulschools.ns.ca/
The League of Peaceful Schools, which began in Nova Scotia, provides support and recognition to schools that have declared a commitment to creating a safe and peaceful environment for their students. It advocates schoolwide discipline approaches. An application form is available on the Web site.

http://www.nsnet.org/start/emotional.pdf
This short, Canadian paper is titled "Meeting the Needs of Students with Emotional/Behavioural Difficulties," and discusses characteristics of these students, technology-related strategies, and general strategies. (Site requires Acrobat Reader.)

http://www.edu.gov.nf.ca/discipline/introduction.htm
The Newfoundland policies and related documents on schoolwide discipline are available from this Web site.

What a Puzzle!

My name is Mika Matsuda. I love to write—poetry, long letters to my friends and family, and reflective journals. This account is based on entries in my reflective journal kept during my eighth year of teaching. I am 33 years old. My first teaching position was in a small school in a small city. After two years of teaching, I moved to a big city to settle in to a life of teaching, writing, and training for marathons.

I teach history at A. L. Peterson Secondary School—a suburban school on the fringe of a large Canadian city. One of my classes this semester is Grade 11 history, and one of the students in this class is most unusual. His name is Adam. For the first few days of the term, I observed Adam reading a science fiction book in my class. When I asked him a question to draw him in, I could not understand anything he said. I asked him to stay after school to talk with me about his history project for the term. My original purpose in asking him to stay behind was to learn to understand him by listening to him talk about the parts of the project. He would be using familiar words, and I hoped that would help me become accustomed to his unusual speech and language. At our first after-school chat, I noticed that Adam began every sentence three or four times. He left out important words, and often forgot the point he was trying to make by the time he got to the end of the sentence. But Adam always had a point when he started to speak, and the ideas he was trying to communicate were usually the most interesting of any in the class.

Soon, I found myself translating Adam's ideas for the class. I would say, "Did everyone hear what Adam said?" And then I would interpret Adam's incomplete, incoherent sentences that I knew no one else had understood. I scared myself when Adam's bizarre sentences made so much sense to me. But I found that the other students listened carefully to what I interpreted, and then they paid attention to Adam. Sometimes they even asked him questions. The questions meant more interpreting for me, this time, of Adam's answers to his peers' questions. However, this system quickly became an integral part of my teaching approach with the Grade 11 history class.

I always talk with the students individually as they enter the classroom. I like to think it serves as a reward to those who arrive early, and it certainly helps me to know my students and to gain their respect. I ask them about their hockey games and about their challenges editing the Grade 11 page of the school newspaper, and they ask me about my marathons and my poetry-writing group. One day before class, I happened to ask Adam what he was learning in his other classes. He drawled, "Nothin'." He described how instead of participating, he read his science fiction novel and fantasized about the computer games he would play when he went home. In my class, however, Adam continued to contribute thoughtful, thought-provoking ideas with the help of my translations.

When I spoke with Adam's other teachers, I learned that mine was the only class in which he participated in discussion. His teachers worried about this at length at our first meeting called by the resource teacher, Bert. Bert described the peer tutoring system he had arranged for Adam in the resource room. Upper level students received credits in Career and Life Management for tutoring Adam individually and helping him complete his assignments. Bert argued that Adam was only able to focus and learn in one-to-one situations. I invited Bert to observe Adam in my class. I insisted that Adam was focusing and learning, although I had to admit that his written work in my course was short, conceptually inadequate, and illegible. I finally agreed to a peer tutor helping Adam edit his history assignments. I continued to try to administer Adam's tests orally whenever I could, and encouraged other teachers to do the same. But they claimed they couldn't understand him well enough to figure out his responses. What do you do when a student's disability severely limits his capacity to express his ideas both orally and in writing? This is the problem we faced with Adam. Because of the efforts of his peer tutors, helping Adam to edit assignments and study for tests, he will probably receive some credits this term, in addition to History 11.

For some time now, I have wanted to pair Adam with Stew, a quiet, socially competent young man in my class, who is kind and tolerant. I think he could help Adam to stay on task and maybe help him learn to be a friend. The other teachers on the team, including Bert, think I am asking too much of a student who is not academically strong himself and who is, in the words of one teacher, "probably afraid of Adam because he is strange." I think Adam is harmless and needs a friend. My colleagues think I am being unfair to Stew, and that other students may dislike him if he befriends someone as strange and unpopular as Adam. How can Adam learn social skills if no one ever socializes with him, except students who help him in order to earn a credit? What can I do as a teacher? He doesn't need to become comfortable with adults; that is his relative strength. He needs to learn how to communicate with his peers, how to be a friend, and how to have a friend. Now that I know how much my colleagues disapprove of my idea, I'm not sure what to do.

Adam is a 17-year-old Grade 11 student. When I was in Grade 11, I had a best friend and a circle of friends I talked with on the telephone every night. School was as much about seeing my friends as about studying history, my favourite subject. I often see Adam wandering the halls of ALPSS during lunch and the mid-morning break, and he is always alone. He looks like he is trying to find someone to talk to in all the social buzz that fills the halls of Peterson High. Adam has severe learning disabilities and attention deficit hyperactivity disorder (ADHD).[1] His psychoeducational report says his strengths are short-term memory and mathematical reasoning. "Adam has difficulties with oral communication," the report says in that understated way that psychologists have of delivering bad news. His sentences are characterized by strings of false starts, thought fillers ("umm" is his favourite), and incoherence. If I had been writing the report, I would have added, "All of this makes it challenging for any listener to know what he is talking about, ever."

Adam finds it difficult to focus his attention. The reports in his file suggest that he has been on and off medication (Ritalin, the most common medication prescribed to persons with ADD) for about eight years, and that Adam and his parents have decided recently that he will no longer receive medication. While Adam has fascinating ideas, he is almost unable to commit his ideas to paper, and it is more than challenging to read his handwriting. Quoting again from the understated report, "He is a reluctant writer whose work contains many spelling errors." I would add that Adam does not shine in sports activities or social activities. He reads novels, almost always science fiction, and describes the plots to me in great detail. I have never seen him read his history text; he simply places his novel in front of his history book and reads on, in spite of all my efforts to involve him in reading the text in class and for homework.

In one of our units early in the semester, the students were preparing to interview an "elder" in the community about local history. One day I asked them to practise their interviewing skills in pairs in class and complete a short assignment based on their partner's answers to the interview questions. I assigned myself to be Adam's interview partner because I thought he would frustrate any student who had to untangle his garbled sentences for an assignment. This also provided me with an opportunity to get to know him better. I was confident he would cooperate with me, while I feared he would snub a peer and read his science fiction book instead of taking part. I asked Adam what high school memories he would carry with him. He could think of no memorable experiences. When I asked him who his friends had been in high school, he said "I float around to...you know...sort of known...I'm well known...all the crowds." I asked Adam to name one good friend, and he told me about a classmate who had moved from the school over a year ago, and whom he had not seen since then. When I asked how far away the friend had moved, Adam named Community High, another local high school. He told me that he had no close ties with anyone at ALPSS.

Adam has brown shoulder-length hair. The day I interviewed him his hair was dyed black with patches of brown showing through. When I asked him to describe himself, he

---

[1]There seem to be considerable differences in the local definitions of attention deficit disorder (ADD) and attention deficit hyperactivity disorder (ADHD). These terms are used differently from one book to another as well. The key difference is that individuals with ADHD show all the characteristics of those with ADD (primarily inattention) and, in addition, show impulsivity and overactivity. (For recent theoretical and applied advances in the field, consult Barkley, R. A. (1995). *Taking charge of ADHD: The complete, authoritative guide for parents.* New York, NY: Guilford Press.)

told me that he was "more of a freak than anyone else" at the school in both appearance and behaviour. He reported, almost with pride, that some people were afraid of him because he looked different and acted different, "by my own rules." Other students in my class commented frequently on Adam's dirty fingernails, dirty hair, and dirty clothes. Adam didn't seem to register their suggestions that he clean up. I have met his parents. They are both professionals, tidy themselves, and yet tolerant of Adam's choice to remain unkempt.

During class conversations, Adam has vocalized his fantasies, made faces, gnawed on his sleeve, and stared straight ahead as if he were in a trance. He frequently expresses his desire to be an individual and boasts of being different, but he also has told me that "If you're different, it is easy for people to dislike you." Adam's only passionate interests in life are computer games and the Internet. Adam occasionally talks with Stew, the one patient student in the class who will engage him in conversation, until he has bored Stew completely. They talk about computers. Stew is interested in computers, but he doesn't play Adam's favourite computer game. Adam steers the conversation to his favourite game; Stew changes the topic to general computer applications on the Internet; and Adam steers back to computer games. Stew listens and asks a couple of questions, and when there is a break, changes the topic again. After a few minutes, Stew walks away. When I once asked Adam if he knew why Stew had walked away, he answered, "I don't know what's wrong with him." Adam has no sense of reciprocity, no notion that he would need to listen to what Stew was interested in as well as talk about his own interests in order to keep a conversation going.

Adam has repeatedly said in class that school is boring and that he is alienated from everyone. "I get really bored here. Really, really bored. I know lots of...I don't know how to...I don't relate to...to a lot of the people, anymore." School is an ordeal to be endured, with no highlights. When I asked Adam what might cause his lack of friends, he attributed his social failures to external causes. He said his fellow students were inconsiderate or they were prejudiced against him because of stereotyping. He has never taken any responsibility or expressed any awareness of his need to mature.

When I raised my concerns at the team meetings, I was almost as isolated as Adam wandering the halls of A. L. Peterson Secondary School. I was the only person present who felt that, as Adam's teachers, we had a responsibility for his social development as well as his academic development. The resource room teachers and educational assistants suggested that as soon as we have figured out how to teach Adam successfully, we should turn our attention to his social development. But I think that Adam is as hampered by his attention deficit disorder and communication difficulties in social situations as he is in learning situations. So much of learning and showing what you know *is* communicating—listening, talking, reading, writing. And Adam is in Grade 11. We are running out of time. I doubt we will figure out how to teach him successfully before he wanders away or stops coming or finishes the endurance test that high school has become.

My training partners for marathons have banned all discussions about "my student." They say they are not running a therapy group. By the time I get around to asking the right questions about Adam, the semester will be over. And I still won't have any answers. What do we do to help a student like Adam realize his considerable potential? Is the regular high school program a productive place for him to pass his time? What alternatives do we have? What a puzzle!

QUESTIONS FOR REFLECTION AND DISCUSSION

1. What are the facts/key elements of the case?

2. What do we know about Adam? About Mika Matsuda?

3. Describe the entries that Adam might dictate for his reflective journal during the same period that Mika has described. Describe the entries Stew might make about this period if he kept a journal.

4. Describe the major dilemma(s) in this case.

5. What actions should Mika Matsuda take to resolve the major dilemma(s)? What role should Adam's resource teacher, Bert, take in resolving the major dilemma(s)?

6. Consider the consequences of these actions for Adam's social life, academic life, and future. Consider the consequences for Bert and for Mika Matsuda.

7. What can we learn from this case?

8. What assumptions and beliefs are called into question by this case?

EXHIBIT 21.1	Characteristics of Effective Teams

Shared goals: All members of the team understand and agree to a common mission or primary goal.

Communication: Interactions of the team are characterized by open and honest dialogue.

Trust: Team members trust one another and know no one will deliberately take advantage of another team member.

Support: Members feel the support of one another, and know that the solutions come from the group; no one member has to have all the answers.

Managed differences: Differences among members are understood and used for creative problem solving.

Managed time: Meetings are well organized, but not rushed; they are focused, and respectful of the time of all members.

Team leadership: Successful teams usually have effective leaders who empower others to lead.

Sources:
Briggs, M. H. (1993). Team talk: Communication skills for early intervention teams. *Journal of Communication Disorders, 15*(1), 33-40.
Friend, M., Bursuck, W., & Hutchinson, N. L. (1998). *Including exceptional students: A practical guide for classroom teachers.* Toronto, ON: Prentice Hall Canada.
Ogletree, B., Bull, J., Drew, R., & Lunnen, K. Y. (2001). Team-based service delivery for students with disabilities: Practice options and guidelines for success. *Intervention in School and Clinic, 36*(3), 138-145.

EXHIBIT 21.2	Secondary School Students with ADD and ADHD: A Puzzling Group

How Can I Identify Them?

- Usually they have been identified while children, but not always.
- Many of their behaviours and attitudes are characteristic of all adolescents, making identification even more difficult in adolescents than in children.
- Distractibility: while this is an issue for most adolescents, watch for persistent and extreme distractibility that means they accomplish almost nothing during an entire class.
- Disorganization: most students suffer disorganization at the start of high school, and then develop strategies for keeping track of books, papers, schedules, assignments, etc. These students don't.
- Daydreaming: like their peers, they gaze into space; only for students with an attention disorder, it gets in the way of getting on with everything else.
- Poor motivation: most adolescents would rather pursue what interests them, but students with ADD/ADHD are more likely to resist doing anything that does not interest them, or refuse outright.
- Impulsivity: adolescents tend to be impulsive, but watch for excesses that seem out of control.
- Overactivity: watch for adolescents who seem to have "ants in their pants" or are in "overdrive" all or much of the time.
- Remember that teachers do not make formal identifications, but share their concerns with an in-school team, and are expected to make adjustments in their teaching whether or not students have been formally identified.

What Kinds of Teachers Are Best for Adolescents with ADD/ADHD?

- Highly organized teachers who plan ahead, communicate expectations clearly, and teach in a structured, interesting manner usually provide the sort of structure that benefits adolescents with attention disorders.
- Enthusiastic teachers who engage students in learning are usually able to keep these students motivated and keep boredom from setting in.
- Flexible teachers who can see the merit of alternate forms of assessment, like oral or video reports, and who use various forms of communication when they realize that a student has not understood, are likely to be successful with students with ADD/ADHD.

Exhibit 21.2 *Continued*

- Teachers who are aware of ADD and continue to learn about such exceptionalities will be cognizant of student needs and understanding of their strengths and weaknesses.

- Respectful and sensitive teachers who attempt to understand how the student sees the world and then endeavour to communicate their perspective to the student are more likely to be successful in winning the student's respect and best effort. They are also less likely to misinterpret the student's impulsive actions and words.

- Maintaining a sense of humour can make the work with adolescents with ADD and ADHD less stressful and more rewarding.

Sources to consult:
Guyer, B. P. (Ed.). (2000). *ADHD: Achieving success in school and in life.* Boston, MA: Allyn & Bacon.
Nadeau, K. G., Dixon, E. B., & Biggs, S. H. (1993). *School strategies for ADD teens.* Annandale, VA: Chesapeake Psychological Publications.

EXHIBIT 21.3	Questions for Teachers and Parents to Ask about Medication

The most commonly prescribed medications for children and adolescents with ADD are Ritalin (methylphenidate) and Dexedrine (dextroamphetamine). Parents and teachers should be well informed about these medications.

- What is the medication? What information can I read about it?
- Why is this medication prescribed for this adolescent? What changes should we expect to see at home? At school?
- What behavioural program or behavioural therapy is being implemented in conjunction with this drug therapy?
- How long will this medication be prescribed for this adolescent?
- What are the side effects in the short-term? In the long-term?
- What is the dosage? What is the schedule on which the medication will be taken?
- How often will the adolescent be seen by the prescribing physician for re-evaluation?
- Should the medication be stopped for a short period of time to see if it is still required? When?
- Are there foods, beverages, or other substances that should not be consumed when one is taking this medication?
- What kind of communication is necessary among home, school, and the adolescent to evaluate whether the medication is having the desired effect?
- What procedures should be followed if the adolescent accidentally ingests an overdose?
- Who explains all of this to the adolescent and what should the adolescent be told?

Resources to consult on this topic:
Barkley, R. A. (1995). *Taking charge of ADHD: The authoritative guide for parents.* New York, NY: Guilford Press.
Sweeney, D. P., Forness, S. R., Kavale, K. A., & Levitt, J. G. (1997). An update on psychopharmacologic medication: What teachers, clinicians, and parents need to know. *Intervention in School and Clinic, 33*(1), 4-21, 25.
Ziegler Dendy, C. A. (1995). *Teenagers with ADD: A parents' guide.* Bethesda, MD: Woodbine House.

SUGGESTIONS FOR FURTHER READING

Barkley, R. A. (1995). *Taking charge of ADHD: The complete, authoritative guide for parents.* New York, NY: Guilford Press.

    A prominent researcher writes for parents with compassion and clarity. Reading Barkley's guide should help parents to be better informed and more confident in their dealings with teachers, doctors, and psychologists.

Guyer, B. P. (Ed.). (2000). *ADHD: Achieving success in school and in life.* Boston, MA: Allyn & Bacon.

    An edited book with chapters written by practitioners who know the field well and provide straightforward information on a range of topics, including controversial approaches to meeting the needs of individuals with ADHD.

Levesque, N. L. (1996). Peer relations of adolescents with learning disabilities: A review of the literature. *Exceptionality Education Canada, 6*(3&4), 87–103.

    In this short paper, the author suggests that it is important to listen to the accounts of adolescents with learning disabilities and with attention deficit disorder in order to learn from them about their peer relations.

Nadeau, K. G., Dixon, E. B., & Biggs, S. H. (1993). *School strategies for ADD teens.* Annandale, VA: Chesapeake Psychological Publications.

    In 45 pages, this booklet provides readable, practical information for adolescents, parents, and teachers. It would be a good place to start in acquiring information on a topic that can be complex and confusing.

Quinn, P. O. (1995). *Adolescents and ADD: Gaining the advantage.* Washington, DC: American Psychological Association.

    This book is written for young adolescents. It is easy to read and has small sections written in the voices of young adolescents with ADD that provide encouragement and suggestions for accommodations, learning to socialize, and self-advocacy that would be helpful to adolescents and their teachers.

Sweeney, D. P., Forness, S. R., Kavale, K. A., & Levitt, J. G. (1997). An update on psychopharmacologic medication: What teachers, clinicians, and parents need to know. *Intervention in School and Clinic, 33*(1), 4–21, 25.

    This is a long, complex, and thorough review of the four major classes of medications commonly used to treat children with learning or behavioural disorders: stimulant medications, antidepressants or mood stabilizers, antipsychotics, and anticonvulsants. This information can help teachers to participate as informed members of teams for students with attention deficit disorders.

Wong, B. Y. L. (1996). *The ABCs of learning disabilities.* Toronto, ON: Academic Press.

    Because many individuals with ADD also have learning disabilities, this volume would be useful to anyone seeking to understand this condition. In particular, Chapter 5, Social Aspects of Learning Disabilities, contains a thorough but readable review of the literature and suggests the sorts of actions that teachers and schools can take in dealing with the social aspects of learning disabilities and ADD.

WEBLINKS

http://www.campkodiak.com/
Camp Kodiak: An example of the specialized camps in Canada that offer integrated, non-competitive programs—for children and adolescents with learning disabilities, with ADD/ADHD, and without disabilities—designed to enhance confidence.

http://www.add.org/
Attention Deficit Disorder Association: An American organization that advocates for persons with ADD; wide range of helpful information available on everything from family issues to school and legal issues.

http://www.schoolpsychology.net/
School psychology resources for psychologists, parents, and educators on ADD and many other exceptionalities, with links to many helpful sites.

case 22

She Doesn't Know Herself

Cheryl Bird was talking with Ben Thomas, the head of guidance at Sterling Collegiate. "I have been working hard with my Grade 12 homeroom students—oops, my Teacher Advisory Group, my TAG—to help them make realistic choices for their post-secondary applications. Having a Grade 12 homeroom is a lot of work, as you know. I try to give them individual time because they all have important decisions to make about the directions their lives will take." Cheryl and Ben were reviewing how each student who wishes to pursue post-secondary education has to choose institutions for which they want additional information and application forms. Then, for the students, there were information sessions to attend, calendars to read, and countless forms to fill in. Cheryl helped those who were applying to university to book appointments with guidance counsellors who knew much more about the individual universities than Cheryl.

This year, however, Cheryl had a particular problem. "Every year, there are students who overestimate their own abilities and shoot too high in the application process. But I have never had an experience like Donna Hill. And I hope I never will again. Don't get me wrong, I like her; well, more I admire her. She has guts!" Cheryl continued, "You know this reading I have been doing. I've read that Donna's situation is becoming more common every year. Donna doesn't know herself."

Ben asked, "What do you mean, she doesn't know herself?"

"Donna knows a young woman who can dance lightly and beautifully and who never grows tired," replied Cheryl. "Donna knows a woman who can write the entire essay the night before it is due and play field hockey all day the next day. Donna knows a woman who loves to party and have a wild old time. However, the only Donna that I have known cannot carry her own books from her locker to her homeroom without becoming exhausted. She can't remember which day it is or which class she has next. This Donna is overwhelmed when two people talk at once, and she can't figure out which one to listen to. I know the Donna who exists now, but all she knows is the Donna she was before her accident."

Two years ago, on a hot summer night, Donna, the wild and light-footed dancer, was pulled from an automobile accident with massive injuries. Donna had been a passenger in a car full of adolescents, all of whom had been dancing, and drinking, at a festival in the small town where she grew up. Two of the four passengers were killed, one escaped almost uninjured, and Donna suffered traumatic brain injury that left her in a coma for days following the accident, in hospital for four months, and in rehabilitation for eight months.

Prior to the accident, Donna had moved out of her parents' home to live with her boyfriend, the driver of the car. He had been killed in the accident. When Donna was hospitalized in Sterling for an indefinite future, her parents, who had recently retired, sold their house in their hometown and moved to the city. They knew Donna would need support to keep going in the long process of recovery. When she left the residential rehabilitation program, Donna moved into a suite in the basement of her parents' new house. She told Cheryl that she cooked her own meals and managed her own money. However, Donna's mother had met recently with Cheryl and told her that Donna only cooked when her parents were out at mealtime and was constantly borrowing money because she had no idea what she had done with her monthly disability income.

Donna had enrolled in the smallest of the high schools in Sterling on the advice of her case manager. Finishing high school, attending community college, and working as a computer operator were major goals in Donna's rehabilitation plan. Ben Thomas had asked Cheryl to work with Donna in her homeroom and her TAG group. Because Cheryl was of Aboriginal heritage and one of Donna's parents was from the same First Nation, Ben and Donna's case manager thought Donna might trust Cheryl more quickly than other teachers in the school. Cheryl had agreed last summer that their common backgrounds might be helpful, but Cheryl had found it difficult to be patient with Donna day after day.

Being a parent of two teenagers herself, Cheryl couldn't help but think about how she would feel if Donna were her child. She knew that her frustrations were nothing compared to those experienced by Donna's parents. Cheryl's reading about traumatic brain injury had told her that parents can grieve repeatedly for the child they have lost while trying to adapt to the child who takes her place. Cheryl had seen firsthand what was meant by the line in Donna's report, "Recovery is not a continuous and reliable process." One day Donna would remember her agenda book (containing her list of assignments) and bring her career portfolio to homeroom. The next day, she would not remember that she had an agenda book, or more likely would arrive at school long after homeroom was finished, expecting Cheryl to meet with her about her plans for the future.

Cheryl had been warned by both Donna's case manager and Ben that she would become embroiled in conflicts with Donna, from time to time. But Cheryl was not prepared for the daily wrangles. Ben and the resource teacher at Sterling High had extensive experience with adolescents with learning disabilities. Because many aspects of the cognitive functioning of youth with traumatic brain injury are similar to those of young people with learning disabilities, they had focused their interventions on teaching Donna learning strategies. But they had not been prepared for her wide swings in attention, memory, and self-monitoring. Some days, for reasons that were not obvious, Donna could not focus, while other days she was able to concentrate fairly well. Often, she forgot one day what had been clear to her the day before. Donna didn't necessarily recognize when she was having a bad day for focusing or remembering.

Cheryl thought that not knowing who she was now and remembering only the self who had lived for 18 years before the accident was Donna's greatest handicap. Cheryl tried to remind Donna gently that she could no longer do some of the things she had once done. And this was a source of constant friction. Donna still had her heart set on becoming a dancer. As a child, she had taken every kind of dancing lesson imaginable. She remembered those happy, long-ago experiences clearly, although she could forget which direction to walk to get to the guidance office in the school. Donna would describe dance recitals she had been in—jazz and modern dance, tap dancing, ballet, Scottish dancing. Donna had tried everything and excelled in all types of dance. "I love to dance. I've always known I was going to be a dancer," she said frequently.

Cheryl reminded Ben, "What a difference between the Donna she remembers and the Donna sitting in front of me. The goal Donna was supposed to be working toward this year was accumulating enough credits, including math and computer studies, to enrol in the community college program in computer applications. And it's me who has to say, 'Donna, what career goals are we working toward? Do you see dancing on this goals form? What do you see listed here?' It hasn't helped that I think the career goals are unrealistic and wrongheaded. The rehabilitation counsellor knew that Donna was not recovering well in areas such as 'patience with others,' and 'relating to her supervisors,' so the rehabilitation counsellor suggested computer operations as a career goal. I guess she thought this would eliminate the need to relate to people, but it would also take focus and stamina, neither of which Donna has. I think it is more important, at this stage of her recovery, for her to learn about herself and learn about careers, not to be aiming for a specific job."

Ben was surprised by the intensity of Cheryl's anger. "But don't you agree she needs a goal—a career goal? Without something to aim for, do you think she would keep dragging herself in here and struggling through the days?"

"Let me tell you what I think—this is not her goal! This is someone else's goal for her. Listen to the kind of thing she says to me when I say, 'What goals are we working toward?' She says, 'But that is not me. I like to do...do...do things.' You know how she searches for the words, '...to dance, to do...not sit...sit around.' She tells me, 'I don't want you...you, anymore, all you do is tell me what I can't...can't do. You know, you, you, you...put me down. You kill...my dreams!' By this time, she is usually shouting at me."

"I didn't realize you were having such a difficult time with her," said Ben.

"I'm not having a difficult time with her," replied Cheryl. "Well, yes, I am. But mostly she's having a difficult time. I know that it is pointless to argue when Donna gets this angry. But it is so difficult to strike the right note: to be encouraging and realistic at the same time; to help Donna keep going, but not to enter her make-believe world in which she can become a dancer. In this world, Donna told me, 'If you want something, really want...enough, you can get it. But only if...people want...you, want you to get it. You don't want me to. To dance. You hold me...me back. You should be helping me!'"

After Cheryl had recounted this last in a long series of disagreements with Donna to Ben, she asked, "Do you think we are doing her any favours by keeping her at Sterling? She uses so much energy to move around the building and gets so frustrated when she is tired by 11:00 AM. We have her on a shorter school day, with understanding teachers, in courses where we think she has the greatest chance of success, but is it working? What other options does she have?"

Ben countered, "Well, remember that recovery continues for a long time, with many setbacks. We could suggest she enrol in correspondence courses, but her mother says coming to school is what gets her out of bed in the morning. So I think correspondence courses would be even less successful. I guess we have to see ourselves as part of her treatment program. And remember that the brain heals slowly. And they tell us that hers is still recovering. She will function better than this, if she keeps using her cognitive, social, and motor functions. And what better place to do that than at school? Something we should keep in mind is that consistency is very important. Remember, the treatment team has told us it would be best for Donna to have the same team of teachers, including the same TAG advisor, for as long as possible."

"But Ben, see my side, too. I'm a teacher, not a therapist. I am the one who has to tell her she can't be a dancer. I'm the one who gets chewed out when I burst her balloon. And I have two adolescents of my own—who drive cars, take rides in cars with their friends, and probably drink when they think they won't get caught. Working with Donna is giving me nightmares about my own kids. Maybe you could work with her one-on-one during TAG time. Or someone else could, so I could get on with advising the rest of my Grade 12 class. They have deadlines, and they only get one fall term in Grade 12 to make all these applications to university and community college. We both know Donna will not be going to college next year. If anything, she will be back here. Can we set some priorities for the next two months? And get me some help in how to be realistic and encouraging at the same time? Let's think about whether she needs career development more than career goals. I don't think she is ready for goals, yet. And will you consider that maybe I'm not the best person to be her TAG teacher? Thanks, Ben, I guess I really needed to let off steam. Get back to me soon, OK?"

QUESTIONS FOR REFLECTION AND DISCUSSION

1. What are the facts of the case?
2. What do we know about the teacher, Cheryl Bird? What do we know about the student, Donna?
3. Describe the major problem(s) or dilemma(s) of the case.
4. How else can the problem(s) be framed? Look at the problem(s) from the guidance counsellor's perspective. How might he frame the problem(s)?
5. What actions should Cheryl Bird take to resolve the major dilemma(s)?
6. What will the consequences be of the actions you suggest for Donna, Donna's parents, other students in Cheryl Bird's homeroom, Cheryl Bird?
7. What questions arise about taken-for-granted assumptions and beliefs we may have recognized while we worked on this case?

EXHIBIT 22.1	Educational Interventions for Students with Traumatic Brain Injury (TBI)

In the past, students who have experienced brain injury were not recognized as requiring adapted programs in school. Students with TBI vary widely in the nature and extent of their disabilities. Recovery continues much longer than previously thought. Many who look like they have recovered may make inappropriate responses to routine tasks as a function of the injury. However, teachers may interpret this as intentional misbehaving. Students with TBI require SOS—Structure, Organization, Strategies—in order to succeed at school.

Structure

- Create consistency and stability because the individual tends to have a low tolerance for change, especially early in recovery.
- Make a partnership between home and school.
- Develop a transition plan and consider work experience.
- Maintain the same team of teachers over a number of years, if possible.
- Keep stimulation and confusion to a minimum.
- Consider lack of stamina and endurance.
- Listen to and validate feelings.

Organization

- Planning is often impaired. Reacquaint the student with how to learn and plan.
- Organize assignments; be prepared to modify assignments and assessments.
- Provide life skills and career development curricula.

Strategies

- Teach strategies explicitly; be prepared to review them frequently.
- Strategies for memory enhancement may be necessary.
- Some skills may never be relearned and compensatory approaches may be necessary.
- Teach social skills. Use teachers and peers as role models.

Relevant sources:
D'Amato, R. C. & Rothlisberg, B. A. (1996). How education should respond to students with traumatic brain injury. *Journal of learning disabilities, 29,* 670-683.
Siantz Tyler, J., & Mira, M. P. (1999). *Traumatic brain injury in children and adolescents: A sourcebook for teachers and other school personnel* (2nd ed.). Austin, TX: PRO-ED, Inc.

EXHIBIT 22.2	Key Points to Include in Family Education and Counselling for TBI

1. Anger, frustration, and sorrow are natural reactions of family members when a relative experiences a brain injury.

2. Caretakers should preserve their own emotional health, physical well-being, and sanity in order to be of benefit to the child with a head injury.

3. Families should be informed and helped to process details surrounding the child's injury and organic limitations to recovery.

4. Recovery is not a continuous and reliable process. A child may show rapid recovery in some areas and during some phases of rehabilitation; in other cases, recovery may be slow or absent. These realities can help families resist blaming treatment staff, medical facilities or school personnel when recovery is halted.

5. Conflicts and disagreements with the individual with a head injury are inevitable. Caretakers must rely on their own judgment in making decisions regarding care.

6. The family role changes that are concomitant to a member sustaining a brain injury can be stressful to all.

7. Real limits exist pertaining to what family members can do to change the head-injured individual's behaviors and personality. Feelings of guilt or ineptitude are normal but not realistic.

8. The family ultimately may be faced with decisions about alternate living or care arrangements for the member with a head injury.

9. The family should review legal documents and financial arrangements concerning the care of the individual with a head injury.

[From Lezak (1978, 1986).]
Source: From "Pediatric Traumatic Brain Injury: Challenges and Interventions for Families" by J. C. Conoley and S. M. Sheridan, 1996, *Journal of Learning Disabilities*, 29, 662-669. Copyright © 1996 by PRO-ED, Inc. Reprinted with permission.

EXHIBIT 22.3	Meaningful Career Development Programs for Young People with Disabilities

After conducting nine focus groups with youth with disabilities, Mary Morningstar of University of Kansas suggested that some programs focus too much on preparing individuals for particular jobs and limit their sights by defining success as employment upon graduation. She suggests that the more important experiences may be those that help high school students with disabilities to develop skills they can use to continue their career development after leaving high school. Youth with disabilities may need even more time than their peers to attain career maturity, especially if they mature slowly because of their disability or the protected life they lead due to their disability. However, because they are frequently guided into employment upon graduation or into short post-secondary programs, they may have even less time than their peers without disabilities before they are expected to attain career maturity.

Morningstar, who has worked with youth with medical disabilities, recommends that the focus shift from employment preparation to career development. She makes five recommendations:

1. Focus on the developmental nature of career preparation across the life span; give youth skills that will lead to ongoing and lifelong career development.
2. Focus on career maturity through developmental experiences:
   a. Understand self (values, needs, interests, abilities, etc.); acknowledge challenges associated with disability;
   b. Understand the world of work (expectations, specific careers) and relevant influences (family, society); be persistent and proactive;
   c. Understand the process of making decisions; ensure goodness of fit between abilities and career choices;
   d. Implement educational and career decisions in unison;
   e. Adjust and adapt to the world of school and work; build and use support systems.
3. Provide purposeful work experiences that promote reflection, self-knowledge and career maturity, and do not simply provide work experience.
4. Encourage and acknowledge participation of families in career development.
5. Encourage student agency, initiative, and self-determination. Don't allow students to permit others to tell them what careers they should aspire to. Work with students' dreams, rather than dismissing them.

The Co-operative Education and Workplace Learning (CEWL) research team at Queen's University has developed case studies of many adolescents in co-operative education, including youths with learning disabilities, who were participating in a workplace daily for four months. They make the following recommendations for ensuring meaningful workplace experiences for youth with disabilities:

1. Teach adolescents to *ask questions* effectively of their co-workers and supervisors to obtain the knowledge they need to contribute in the workplace.

2. Teach adolescents the significance of *showing and taking initiative*. Show them how to take initiative.

3. Help workplace supervisors to understand that there is an element of *coaching* (which is not the same as classroom teaching) in their role.

4. Help workplace supervisors to explain the function of, and the reasons for, the *routines* that the co-op student will be expected to follow in the workplace.

5. Use the *IEP as a guide* to making adaptations in the workplace.

Relevant Sources:
Morningstar, M. E. (1997). Critical issues in career development and employment preparation for adolescents with disabilities. *Remedial and special education, 18,* 307–320.
Versnel, J., Hutchinson, N. L., Munby, H., Chin, P., & Chapman, C. (2002). *Learning in garages: Co-operative education experiences of two adolescents.* Paper presented at the annual meeting of the Canadian Society for the Study of Education, Toronto, ON.

SUGGESTIONS FOR FURTHER READING

D'Amato, R. C., & Rothlisberg, B. A. (1996). How education should respond to students with traumatic brain injury. *Journal of Learning Disabilities, 29,* 670–683.

These authors grapple with the educational implications of traumatic brain injury. They point out that, although no two students are alike, these students usually require adjustments in assessment, expectations, and teaching based on current functioning in order to succeed in educational settings.

Hutchinson, N. L., & Freeman, J. G. (1994). *Pathways: Knowing about yourself, knowing about careers.* Scarborough, ON: ITP Nelson (Canada).

In this Canadian career development program, adolescents engage in collaborative activities in which they are stimulated to think about their interests, strengths, and preferences. This module is one of five that enable youth with disabilities to learn about all aspects of themselves and their career aspirations, and to learn to solve problems and handle criticism and frustration.

Hutchinson, N. L., Chin, P., Munby, H., Mills de Espana, W., Young, J., & Edwards, K. L. (1998). How inclusive is co-operative education in Canada? Getting the story and the numbers. *Exceptionality Education Canada, 8*(3), 15-43.

This brief paper describes cooperative education and other forms of workplace learning across Canada, and considers the extent to which these programs include students with disabilities and other members of minorities.

Morningstar, M. E. (1997). Critical issues in career development and employment preparation for adolescents with disabilities. *Remedial and Special Education, 18,* 307–320.

This report of focus groups involving youth with disabilities raises important questions about the overly pragmatic approaches often used in career education in North America, which may sometimes be more about job placement than about education and development of career maturity.

Ontario Ministry of Education. (2002). *Transition planning: A resource guide*. Toronto, ON: Queen's Printer for Ontario.

Suggests how to help exceptional students make the transition from high school to further education, employment, and living in the community.

Siantz Tyler, J., & Mira, M. P. (1999). *Traumatic brain injury in children and adolescents: A sourcebook for teachers and other school personnel* (2nd ed.). Austin, TX: PRO-ED, Inc.

An excellent guide for schools that includes information about IEP planning, daily scheduling, responses to behavioural problems, planning transitions, and many other relevant issues.

WEBLINKS

http://educ.queensu.ca/~cewl/
Web page of the Co-operative Education and Workplace Learning research team at Queen's University; includes brief descriptions of Canadian research papers on cooperative education and links to other sites. Includes research on co-operative education for adolescents with disabilities.

http://www.bced.gov.bc.ca/irp/capp/capptoc.htm
British Columbia Ministry of Education Career and Personal Planning Curriculum, grades 8 to 12. Contains the integrated resource packages for all these curricula; worth exploring.

http://www.nbia.nf.ca/
Newfoundland Brain Injury Association: This site contains links to brain injury associations in other provinces and information for individuals with brain injury and those who work with them.

How You Can Learn About Your Teaching Practice by Writing Cases

INTRODUCTION

You have been engaged in discussion of cases and you may want to turn your attention to your own practice, those dilemmas that arise in your classroom. This chapter focuses on how you can use the approaches and knowledge gained through studying cases to learn about your own teaching practice by writing cases about what you have experienced.

RATIONALE FOR LEARNING FROM WRITING CASES: LEARNING TO ENGAGE IN CRITICAL REFLECTION

Teaching takes place in real time, that is, in the press of the classroom where the hands on the clock keep moving, students expect answers to their questions, and challenging situations can easily spiral out of control when we do not act. On the other hand, when we do act, it is easy to leap to conclusions, make assumptions, and respond to the surface features of complex situations. When we have the opportunity to stand back and take stock, we often find an initially challenging situation to be different than it first appeared. It may be part of a pattern rather than an isolated incident. Perhaps it is a dilemma with many routes to solution, but none free from disadvantages, rather than merely a vignette or critical incident. Often we say that what we need is time to make sense of what happened, time to reflect on our experience, and time to learn about our own practice *from* our own practice. Writing cases based on experience forces us to take the time we say we need.

Teachers who take the time to understand the problems that arise in their practice engage in critical reflection. They begin to consider how various participants view the same situation. They may find themselves reconstructing a student's comments, thinking about the meaning behind the words of a note from a parent, or wondering how the editor of the local newspaper would represent an incident to her readership. Taking others' perspectives enables teachers to see that there are many sides to a discussion. And many of these other points of view may be in conflict with the interpretation made by teachers. Once teachers open themselves to other perspectives, it is a short distance to considering the impact of any course of action for all those who might have a perspective. Actions are no longer taken in haste but are thought through for the consequences to many who might be affected. Finally, when teachers ask how they can do something better, or to obtain better consequences all around, they have usually come to the point of asking what they must have been taking for granted before. This kind of wholehearted questioning of assumptions is at the core of critical reflection as described by John Dewey.

One way to take the time we need to become reflective practitioners is to write cases that help us learn from our experience. Writing cases forces us to take perspectives, consider consequences, and question taken-for-granted assumptions, and especially so when we represent our experiences as dilemmas. We see the experience in a new way. We learn about ourselves as teachers and we learn about our teaching. One of the most frequent comments I receive from teacher candidates who write cases is that the experience allows them to work out something that happened to them which has been bothering them. After working it out, most realize that the experience didn't happen *to* them; they played an active role in it. And most often, case writers come to understand that they could have played a different role. In fact, many student-authored cases end with a statement of intent to play a very different role the next time they have such an experience. Case writing, thus, prompts catharsis, self-knowledge, and resolve to become better teachers.

Another reason for writing experience-based cases lies in the nature of the knowledge we construct about teaching. At one time we thought that to know about teaching meant to know general rules. We have recently come to question this idea, because even if general rules are guides to teaching, "the question is still how exactly they (general rules) should be handled in a reasonable and practical way that is appropriate to the specific situation." This insightful perspective was written by Jos Kessels and Fred Korthagen, two European researchers in teacher education. In understanding a case of teaching, it is *necessary* to know the concrete details in the situation and *helpful* to know general rules. These authors argue that one develops an "eye" for paradigmatic or type cases by teaching and reflecting on teaching.

Some teacher candidates do not see themselves as writers and proclaim that they would find it difficult to write a case based in experience. However, when I ask whether they talk with colleagues and friends about the puzzles of practice they encounter in teaching, I have never had a teacher candidate say *no*. Many say that writing a case based in experience is much like telling a friend about an experience, except that it forces you to organize your thinking. This organization usually brings a discipline to our thinking, as well. For those who find it difficult to write, I suggest talking with a friend or colleague and recording the whole thing on a tape recorder. After listening to it, my experience and that of my students is that the act of writing the case seems less daunting and many of the words just need to be put down on paper as they were said "with a bit more organization."

ETHICAL ISSUES ASSOCIATED WITH WRITING CASES

If you are a classroom teacher learning from experience by writing a case, you will have to take care to mention no students or colleagues by name in your case. You must honour confidentiality and anonymity. Provide no identifying information that would allow people to recognize themselves or others in what you write. Your case must also show respect for the dignity of the individual. If you are writing a case in the context of an assignment for a university course, you will have to do everything described above as well as adhere to the specific university's policies for the participation of "human subjects in research." Be sure to check with your professor about the ethical review procedures used in your university before you begin writing your case.

CHOOSING AN EXPERIENCE TO WRITE ABOUT

There is a lot happening in a classroom whether you are a secondary or an elementary teacher. Matthew cannot follow oral directions, Mara spills paint, cooperative groups fail to cooperate, students socialize at the expense of their academic learning. Sometimes it seems difficult to choose an incident. The question to ask is this: Which would teach you the most about yourself as a teacher, and about teaching? I recommend three steps to choosing a case to write.

1. First: Choose a situation that occurred while you were teaching. That is, choose an experience that occurred *in your practice*.

2. Second: Select a situation that you found troubling, puzzling, or that aroused your emotions. Select a situation that posed a *dilemma* about which you were uncertain. You may still feel unsure or unsatisfied about the way you handled the situation. Choose a situation with moral or ethical implications.

3. Third: Engage in self-study with the *goal of becoming a better teacher* and attaining a deeper understanding of the experience by writing a case about it.

ELEMENTS OF THE CASE

These elements can be written in an order that makes sense for the dilemma you are describing. But all of these elements should be included.

Part I

- What is the *context* in which the case occurred? Describe the set or set the scene. Describe the relevant details of the classroom—relevant physical factors and relevant social factors. What was happening when the incident first caught your attention, or when you first realized this was a situation that had to be dealt with? The curriculum, the school, the community, and other social groups may also be important parts of the context.

- Who are the *actors* in this case? The teacher (usually the protagonist) will be you, so write in the first person. Describe the student or students who are at the heart of the dilemma. As you have seen in this book of cases, sometimes a whole class is central to a case. Others who have perspectives on, and may be influenced by, the consequences of the case may also be actors in the case.

- What was the *critical event* and how did you deal with it? Describe the sequence of events, and the inherent conflicts that made this a *dilemma* for you. Describe your *actions,* feelings, choices (or failures to choose), and the aspects of the event that still trouble you.

- What were the *effects* of the actions you took, or of your failure to act? Examine the impact on aspects of the context, on other actors, and on the key actors in the case. Consider the extent to which the dilemma was resolved and how you fared in an assessment of yourself; by this, I mean were you empowered, did you enhance your respect for yourself as a professional, did you learn.

- *"Sleep on it!"* In her book about writing cases, Selma Wasserman urges case writers to put their writing away at this point, after the narrative is complete. I say, "Sleep on it."

Part II

- What *perspectives* and *consequences* have you represented? When you pick the case up a day or two later, you will be revisiting, clarifying what you have already written, and then moving into analysis and reflection. Look back at the opening chapter of this book to refresh your memory about critical reflection. Then write about how you see the case differently now than when you wrote it. Think about your role, what it was, and what it could have been. Whose perspective is the case written from? What are the other perspectives to consider in this case? For whom have you considered consequences; have you faced the moral and ethical consequences of the actions taken or not taken?

- What *assumptions* have you made? Focus on hunting the assumptions you made in writing the case—assumptions about people, places, teaching approaches, the purposes of education, other relevant issues. What did you take for granted? How valid were these assumptions? What changes do you have to make? Have you attributed words, feelings, motives, etc., to others in your writing of the case, as if they were factual truths? Look for your beliefs, your value judgments, and the ways in which you might have oversimplified or polarized the issues in the case.

- What is the *meaning* of this case? What can we learn from it? What have you learned from experiencing, writing, and reflecting critically on this case? Hard questions are in order here. You are but one interpreter of your case. I encourage my students to ask two peers for written feedback—in the form of critical reflections and hard questions—on their cases. I also encourage students to pen a brief, pointed self-assessment. If there are weaknesses in the case, I would prefer the student to tell me about them, rather than having to point them out in my written feedback about the case. This final process is clearly one of interpretation. This means that if you stay close to the data, acknowledge limitations, engage in critical reflection, and embrace dilemmas, you will be setting a pattern for learning from your experience as you move into the challenges of a teaching career.

TAKE CONTROL!

Teaching is a challenging and rewarding profession, and including exceptional learners gives rise to many dilemmas of practice. Writing cases and engaging in critical reflection is a form of self-study or action research that empowers teachers to give meaning to their dilemmas, and to take control of their professional development. You can engage in this process, formally, by bringing your case notes to conferences of in-school teams about exceptional students. And you can engage in this process, informally, by talking with your colleagues and learning together about the meaning of your teaching dilemmas. Take control and enjoy!

SUGGESTIONS FOR FURTHER READING

Dewey, J. (1933). *How we think: A restatement of the relation of reflective thinking to the educative process.* Boston, MA: D. C. Heath and Co.

Three of the most important aspects of critical reflection, as developed by Dewey, are open-mindedness (recognizing and acknowledging the validity in other perspectives), responsibility (considering the consequences, including moral and ethical consequences, of choices), and wholeheartedness (identifying and addressing limitations in one's assumptions).

Hutchinson, N. L. (1998). Reflecting critically on teaching to encourage critical reflection. In M. L. Hamilton (Ed.), *Reconceptualizing teaching practice: Self-study in teacher education* (pp. 124–139). London, UK: Falmer Press.

This chapter describes a self-study in which the author engaged in critical reflection with teacher candidates about the process of teaching and learning with cases in a teacher education course on teaching exceptional learners.

Hutchinson, N. L., & Martin, A. K. (1999). The challenges of creating inclusive classrooms: Experiences of teacher candidates in a field-based program. *Teacher education quarterly, 26*(2), 51-70.

We describe the experiences of five teacher candidates who taught in one school for a four-month practicum and discussed their dilemmas of practice frequently. We analyzed the case studies they wrote to demonstrate the high levels of critical reflection that they attained through case discussion and writing cases based in experience.

Kessels, J. P. A. M., & Korthagen, F. A. J. (1996). The relationship between theory and practice: Back to the classics. *Educational researcher, 25*(3), 17–22.

This is a challenging paper that provides a thoughtful conceptual base for learning from experience.

Wasserman, S. (1998). *Getting down to cases: Learning to teach with case studies.* New York, NY: Teachers College Press.

Wasserman does not focus on learning to teach exceptional learners, but she does provide challenging cases for discussion and guidelines for writing cases from experience, similar to the guidelines found in this chapter.

WEBLINKS

http://publish.uwo.ca/~shobson/Guidelines.htm
Guidelines for the Ethical Use of Real Cases in Teaching and Learning: Sandra Hobson of the School of Occupational Therapy at University of Western Ontario has posted this site, which is relevant for education as well as the health sciences.

http://www.inov8.psu.edu/toolbox/instructionaldesigntools.asp
Click on "Guidelines for Case Writing" to find information that could be used by faculty members or teacher candidates writing cases based in experience.

http://www.nserc.ca/programs/ethics/english/policy.htm
Tri-Council Policy Statement: Ethical Conduct for Research Involving Humans contains the policy developed by the three Canadian research councils which must be adhered to by all members of the university research community in Canada conducting research with humans.

① What are expect'ns for Donna
+ how are they helping or hindering D's schooling.

② How did these expect'ns form +
how might they be reformulated

4, 8, 20, 5, 18-

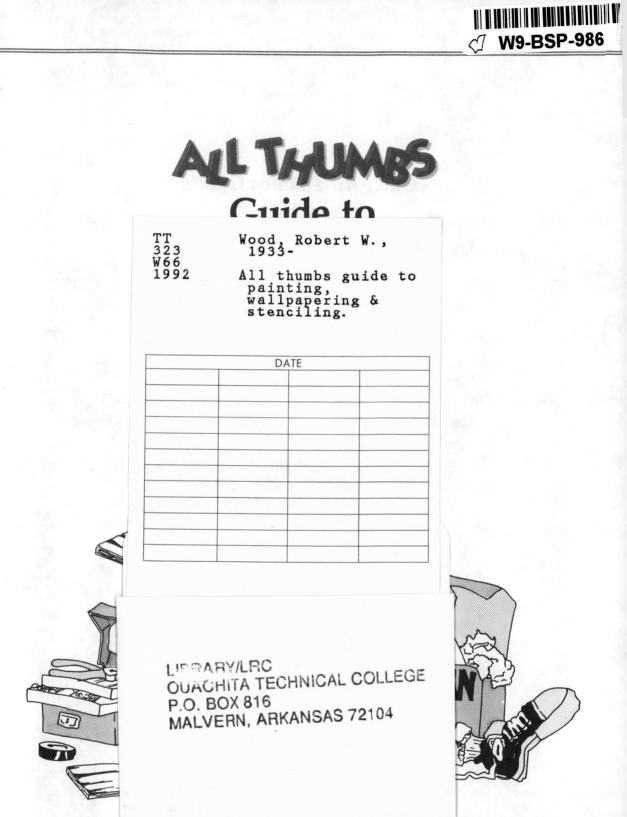

ALL THUMBS

Guide to

DATE			

Other All Thumbs Guides
Home Wiring
Home Plumbing
Repairing Major Home Appliances

ALL THUMBS

Guide to Painting, Wallpapering & Stenciling

Robert W. Wood
Illustrations by Steve Hoeft

TAB BOOKS
Blue Ridge Summit, PA

FIRST EDITION
SECOND PRINTING

© 1992 by **TAB Books**.
TAB Books is a division of McGraw-Hill, Inc.

Library of Congress Cataloging-in-Publication Data

Wood, Robert W., 1933-
   Painting, wallpapering, and stenciling / by Robert W. Wood.
     p. cm.
   Includes index.
   ISBN 0-8306-2548-8 (h) ISBN 0-8306-2547-X (p)
   1. House painting. 2. Paperhanging. 3. Stencil work. I. Title.
TT323.W66 1992   92-2667
698'.14—dc20   CIP

Acquisitions Editor: Kimberly Tabor
Designer: Jaclyn J. Boone
Editorial Team: Susan D. Wahlman, Editor
            Joanne Slike
Production Team: Katherine G. Brown, Director of Production
              Janice Ridenour, Layout
              Jana L. Fisher, Typesetting
Cover Design: Lori E. Schlosser
Cover Illustration: Denny Bond, East Petersburg, PA
Cartoon Caricature: Michael Malle, Pittsburgh, PA   ATS

The All Thumbs Guarantee

TAB Books/McGraw-Hill guarantees that you will be able to follow every step of each project in this book, from beginning to end, or you will receive your money back. If you are unable to follow the All Thumbs steps, return this book, your store receipt, and a brief explanation to:

All Thumbs
P.O. Box 581
Blue Ridge Summit, PA 17214-9998

About the Binding

This and every All Thumbs book has a special lay-flat binding. To take full advantage of this binding, open the book to any page and run your finger along the spine, pressing down as you do so; the book will stay open at the page you've selected.

The lay-flat binding is designed to withstand constant use. Unlike regular book bindings, the spine will not weaken or crack when you press down on the spine to keep the book open.

Contents

Contents

Preface

A collection of books about do-it-yourself home repair and improvement, the All Thumbs series was created not for the skilled jack-of-all-trades, but for the average homeowner. If your familiarity with the various systems in the home is minimal, or your budget doesn't keep pace with today's climbing costs, this series is tailor-made for you.

Several different types of professional contractors are required to construct even the smallest home. Carpenters build the framework, plumbers install the pipes, and electricians complete the wiring. Few people can do it all. The necessary skills often require years to master. The professional works quickly and efficiently and depends on a large volume of work to survive. Because service calls are time-consuming, often requiring more travel time than actual labor, they can be expensive. The All Thumbs series saves you time and money by showing you how to make most common repairs yourself.

The guides cover topics such as home wiring; plumbing; painting, stenciling, and wallpapering; and repairing major appliances, to name a few. Copiously illustrated, each book details the procedures in an easy-to-follow, step-by-step format, making many repairs and home improvements well within the ability of nearly any homeowner.

Introduction

A fresh coat of paint or new wallpaper can brighten almost any room, and few home improvements increase the value of your property more for the money spent. Exterior painting not only preserves your home, it is also the biggest factor in increasing curb appeal. Most people don't realize that painting and wallpapering can be done easily, once the basics are understood. The purpose of this book is to help you keep your costs and efforts to a minimum and to guide you through each project to the desired results. Doing it right means that you don't have to do it often. Knowing the tricks of the painting and wallpapering trades makes the work easier and faster and saves time, money, and aggravation.

I begin by explaining the tools used for painting inside the home. Then I show you how to prepare the surface, choose the right paint, apply the paint, and clean up. Chapter 5 explains the simple techniques of stenciling.

Next, the book introduces the tools and types of equipment used for painting the outside of your house and provides step-by-step instructions for using ladders, preparing the surface, and applying the paint.

The last part of the book is devoted to wallpapering. Different types of wallcoverings are introduced, followed by step-by-step procedures for removing old wallpaper and installing new.

You'll learn how easy it is to be your own decorator: to estimate the amount of material you'll need; to produce a lustrous, easy-clean finish for kitchens and baths with enamel paint; and to paint the exterior of your house without dreading the chore.

To make any project easier:

- Wear comfortable, old clothes that allow you to move around freely. Wear safety goggles when working on a ceiling and a dust mask when doing dusty work such as sanding.

- Be sure that you have all the tools and sufficient materials to complete the job.

- Read all labels carefully.

- Be extra careful when working around electricity and ladders.

- Always keep your work area well ventilated.

CHAPTER ONE

Preparing Interior Surfaces for Painting

A hammer and screwdriver are probably the only basic tools you'll need to prepare for painting. Other tools used in painting are more specialized. Because of the splattering and dripping that goes with painting, clear the area as much as possible, and then protect furniture and floors with drop cloths. You can buy disposable paper drop cloths, or you can use a light ($1/2$ to 2 mil) plastic drop cloth for furniture and a heavier one (about 4 mils) for floors. Professionals use lightweight canvas drop cloths because they are reusable and long-lasting.

A 4- or 6-foot stepladder is handy for higher work. To keep paint from getting on window glass, you can use masking tape or a paint shield. A window scraper is simply a razor blade in a holder, used to scrape dry paint from window glass.

PAINT SHIELD

WINDOW SCRAPER

STEPLADDER

PUTTY KNIFE

MASKING TAPE

If wallboard is damaged, you'll need a putty knife, a 6-inch taping knife, a 10-inch smoothing knife, a can opener, joint cement, and sandpaper. A caulking gun and caulking compound are used for patching and filling cracks.

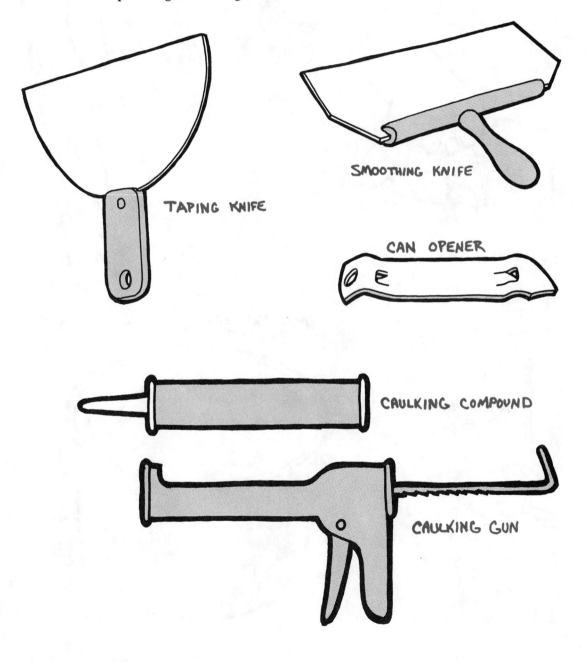

TAPING KNIFE

SMOOTHING KNIFE

CAN OPENER

CAULKING COMPOUND

CAULKING GUN

To mix the paint, you'll need an extra bucket and small wooden mixing paddles or a power mixer that fits into an electric drill.

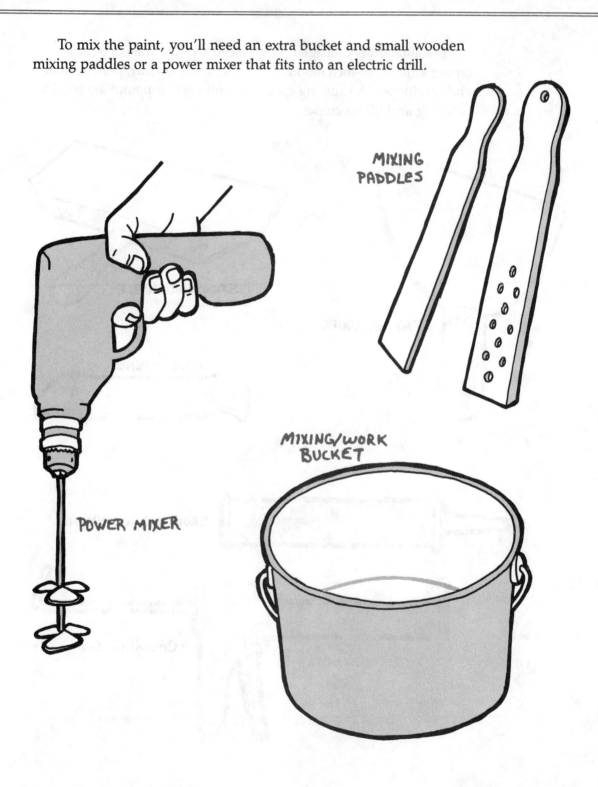

MIXING
PADDLES

MIXING/WORK
BUCKET

POWER MIXER

To apply the paint, you'll need a 2-inch sash brush, 2-inch trim brush and maybe a 3- or 4-inch flat brush, depending on the job. Use a brush with polyester or nylon bristles for latex paints and one with natural bristles for oil-based paints. Rollers make the work go quickly, but they usually give less coverage for each gallon of paint. The type of roller you need to use depends on the kind of paint and the type of surface. A 9-inch roller is best for large areas, and a 3-inch trim roller, a corner roller, and an extension pole might come in handy. You'll need a roller tray with a grid, or grating, to remove excess paint from the roller. For larger painting jobs, use a 5-gallon bucket with a grid to save trips to refill the tray with paint.

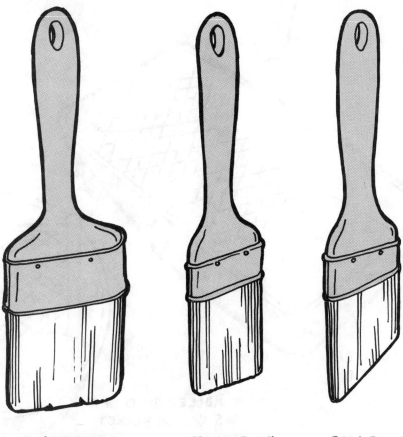

FLAT BRUSH   TRIM BRUSH   SASH BRUSH

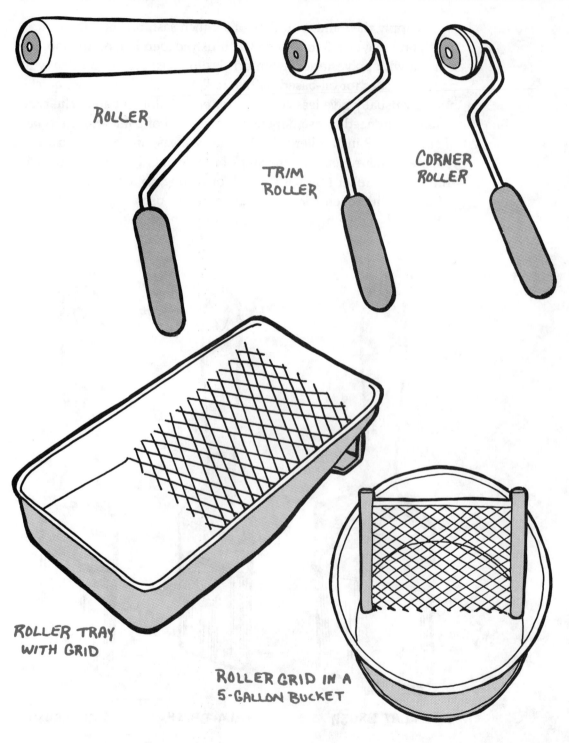

ROLLER

TRIM
ROLLER

CORNER
ROLLER

ROLLER TRAY
WITH GRID

ROLLER GRID IN A
5-GALLON BUCKET

The most important part of painting begins before the paint is mixed. No matter how good the paint, it can't hide blemishes or stick to a dirty or greasy surface. Even in the best-kept homes, dust and grease accumulate on walls and ceilings, particularly in kitchens and baths. Dust settles on *baseboards*, around windows, and on the tops of doors. Often a good cleaning with a heavy-duty detergent is enough. Glossy surfaces should be dulled, or roughed, with sandpaper or a commercial deglosser to let the new paint adhere properly.

Tools & Materials

- ☐ Putty knife
- ☐ Sandpaper and sanding block
- ☐ Spackle paste
- ☐ Paint stripper
- ☐ Goggles
- ☐ Rubber gloves
- ☐ Small paint brush
- ☐ Hammer
- ☐ Nail set
- ☐ Caulking gun and caulking compound

Step 1-1. Removing old paint.
Use a putty knife to remove loose paint. Insert the knife under the edge of the old paint and push off any paint that separates from the old finish.
Try not to gouge the surface.

Step 1-2. Sanding rough edges.
After the loose paint has been removed,
sand rough edges with sandpaper.
Deep depressions should be filled with
Spackle paste. Use a putty knife to fill
small depressions and a 6-inch
taping knife to fill larger ones.

Step 1-3. Using a sanding block.
After the repair has dried, sand it level and
smooth with a sanding block and fine sandpaper.

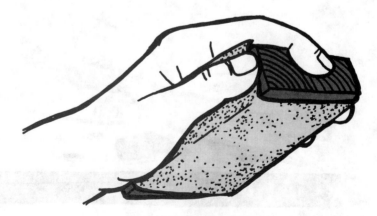

Step 1-4. Applying paint stripper.

To strip off old paint with chemical paint stripper, follow the instructions on the label. Be sure that your work area is well ventilated. Protect the surrounding area with a few layers of old newspapers. Wear goggles and rubber gloves. Apply the paint stripper with a small, inexpensive paint brush. Brush in one direction and work on small areas at a time.

Step 1-5. Removing old paint.

When the paint bubbles and wrinkles, scrape it off with a stiff putty knife or a taping knife. Clean the knife frequently with old newspapers. After the surface has dried, sand it lightly with fine sandpaper.

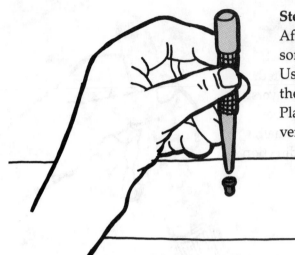

Step 1-6. Using a nail set.

After a period of time, nail heads sometimes pop out from wood trim. Use a hammer and nail set to countersink these finishing nails back into the wood. Place the nail set on the head of the nail, vertically aligned with the nail.

Step 1-7. Setting the nail.

Tap the set sharply and sink the head slightly below the surface.

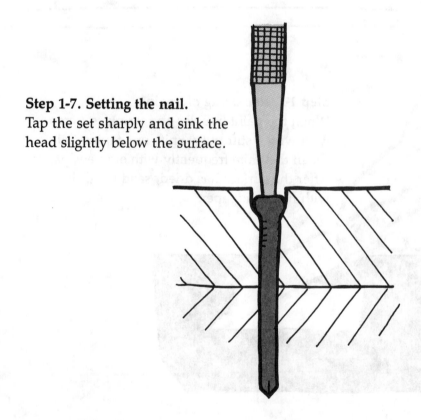

Step 1-8. Filling the hole.
Fill the hole with a small amount of Spackle paste or *putty*.
Press it in with your fingers and brush away any excess.

Step 1-9. Caulking cracks.
Check the joints of wood trim around doors, windows, and
baseboards. Use a caulking gun and caulking to fill any cracks. You
can use your finger to wipe off any excess caulking, but it's a little
rough on fingertips. A clean cloth might be better. After the caulking
has dried, wipe off any rough edges with fine sandpaper.

The following are a few general rules for preparing surfaces for painting:

1. If the surface is glossy, sand or roughen it to promote adhesion.

2. Fill in and smooth any cracks, gouges, and holes.

3. Make sure the surface is free of dust and grease.

4. Fill nail holes and caulk all cracks around windows, doors, and baseboards.

CHAPTER TWO

Patching
Cracks & Holes

Today most homes have walls and ceilings covered with gypsum wallboard, sometimes called *drywall* or Sheetrock plasterboard. It comes in 4-×-8- and 4-×-12-foot panels that are nailed or screwed to the ceiling joists and wall studs. Homes that are 40 years old or older might have walls and ceilings covered with plaster, usually applied to a wood lath. Drywall originally was introduced to reduce costs. It is cheaper and faster to install than plaster. Both surfaces, however, can be repaired easily by the homeowner.

Tools & Materials

☐ Hammer
☐ 6-inch taping knife
☐ Joint cement
☐ Sandpaper and sanding block
☐ Utility knife
☐ Wire mesh
☐ String
☐ Pencil

☐ 2-inch putty knife
☐ Patching plaster
☐ Can opener
☐ Old newspaper
☐ Small paint brush
☐ Spray bottle
☐ Spackle paste

Step 2-1. Resetting a nail.
First reset or replace any nails that have
popped out of the wallboard. Reset the
nail by tapping sharply with a hammer.
Don't hit it too hard—just enough to
make a dimple in the wallboard and drive
the head into the small depression without
breaking the surface. If the nail pops out again,
it might have missed the stud. Remove it and
drive in a new one a few inches away.
Make sure you hit the stud.

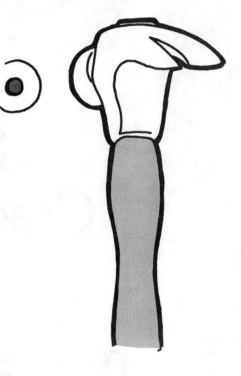

← JOINT CEMENT

Step 2-2. Filling the depression.
Use a 6-inch taping knife to apply a thin layer
of joint cement over the depression. Try to keep
it smooth to save sanding later. Let it dry and
apply a second coat, and probably a third, until
the surface is flat and level with the wall.

Step 2-3. Smoothing the surface.
After the joint cement is completely dry, use fine-grit sandpaper and a sanding block to level the surface and taper, or feather, the edges. Use a block of wood about 3 inches wide and 4$\frac{1}{2}$ inches long. Fold the sandpaper in half and tear it along the fold. Wrap one piece around the block and sand the area in a circular pattern. Work from the center out, and feather the edges to the level of the surrounding area. Tap the block sharply to shake built-up residue from the sandpaper. Wipe the dust from the repair with a dry cloth.

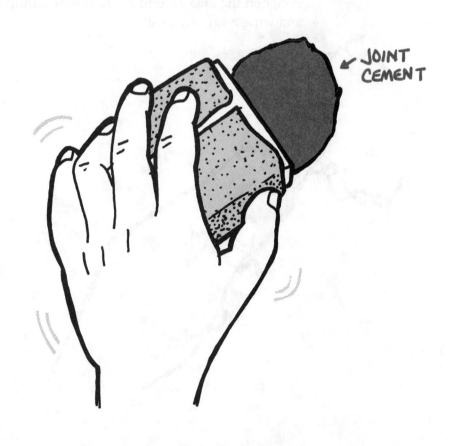

JOINT CEMENT

Next you should repair any holes in the wallboard. Nail holes can
be covered with joint cement. Fill small holes, up to an inch or so in
diameter, with a wad of newspaper, then cover with patching *plaster*.
Let dry; then cover with a layer or two of joint cement. For larger
holes, up to about 6 inches in diameter, you can use patching plaster
and joint cement. Patching plaster dries faster than joint cement, but
joint cement is easier to sand.

Step 2-4. Preparing the hole.
Use a utility knife to trim the edges of the hole,
removing any loose or broken pieces of drywall.
Roughen the area around the hole with sandpaper
and wipe away any dust.

Step 2-5. Cutting the backing.
Cut wire mesh (heavy window screen)
into a piece about 2 inches larger than
the hole. Thread a string through the
center of the screen.

Step 2-6. Installing the backing.
Hold the string with one hand and roll the
screen with the other. Work the screen into the
hole. With a small paint brush dipped in water,
moisten the edges of the hole and the back of
the wallboard. Use a putty knife or your fingers
to apply a heavy layer of plaster to the back of
the wallboard and around the edges of the
hole. Pull the string to draw the screen flat
against the back of the hole and into the
fresh plaster. Take the slack out of the
string and tie it around a pencil.

Step 2-7. Filling the hole.

Use a flexible 2-inch putty knife to push plaster into the mesh of the screen and to cover the edges of the hole. Don't cover the pencil or try to fill the hole—apply just enough material to cover the screen. Now twist the pencil a few times to pull the screen firmly in place. Let the plaster set about 30 minutes.

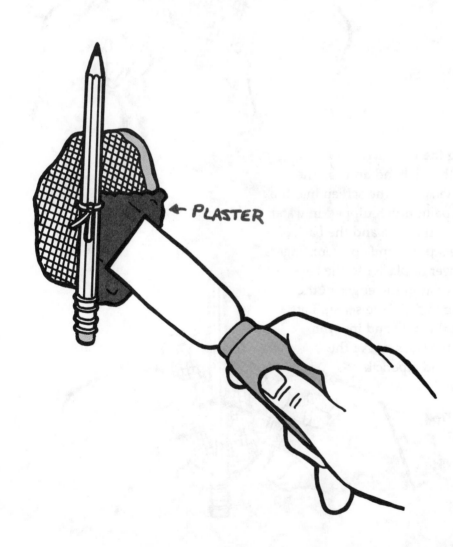

PLASTER

Step 2-8. Completing the repair.
Cut the string as close to the screen as you can. Using a spray bottle or a small paint brush, moisten the area with water. Apply another layer of plaster. This time, fill the hole until the plaster is nearly level with the surface. Let it set and apply a layer of joint cement. Use a 6-inch taping knife to spread a thin, smooth layer just past the edges of the repair. Be sure to feather the edges of the joint cement. Allow the patch to dry overnight. If the patch is still not level with the surface, apply another layer of joint cement, let dry, then sand smooth with fine sandpaper.

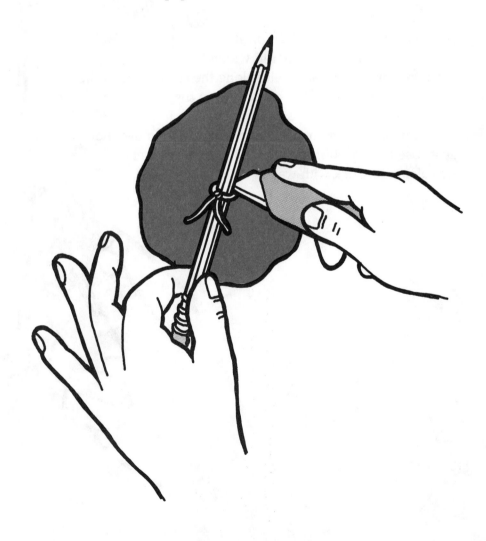

Older homes often have plaster walls and ceilings that were applied over metal or wood laths. Major damage usually means that the repair should be left to a professional, but you can fix minor cracks and holes yourself.

Step 2-9. Preparing a crack in plaster.
Use the point of a can opener to widen the crack slightly and to remove any loose plaster along the crack. Extend the groove past the ends of the crack to keep the crack from growing and to help the patching material grip the plaster. Use a dry paint brush or a vacuum cleaner to remove the dust. Use a spray bottle or small paint brush to wet the area along the crack with water.

Step 2-10. Covering the crack.
Use a flexible putty knife to press joint cement or Spackle paste firmly into the crack. Apply a thin, smooth layer the width of the crack and past each end. Scrape off any excess joint cement and let the patch dry overnight. Joint cement tends to shrink a little, so you might have to apply another coat. After the patch has dried completely, use a sanding block and fine sandpaper to smooth and level the surface.

Step 2-11. Preparing a hole.
Use the point of a can opener to remove any loose plaster around the edge of the hole. After you have established a firm edge, continue using the tip of the opener to cut a V-shaped groove into the inside edge of the hole. This groove helps the new material bond to the edge of the old plaster. Brush out the dust and bits of plaster; then wet the edge of the plaster with water.

Step 2-12. Applying the first layer.
Use a 6-inch taping knife to apply a layer of patching plaster
inside the hole. Don't fill the hole completely—you want to apply
the plaster in a couple of layers. While the first layer is still soft, use
the corner of the taping knife to cut small, crosshatched grooves in
the surface. The grooves help the second layer bond to the first.
Allow the plaster to set for about a half hour.

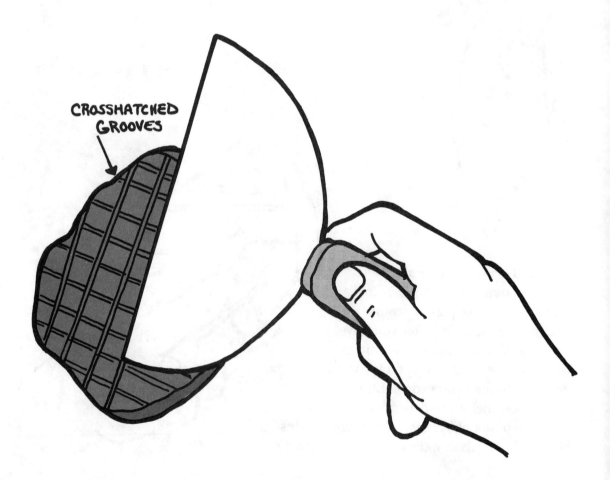

CROSSHATCHED
GROOVES

Step 2-13. Applying the second layer.

Use the spray bottle to moisten the patch and the area around the hole. Now apply the second layer of patching plaster, nearly filling the hole level with the surface of the wall. Scrape off any excess plaster with the taping knife. Let the plaster set up.

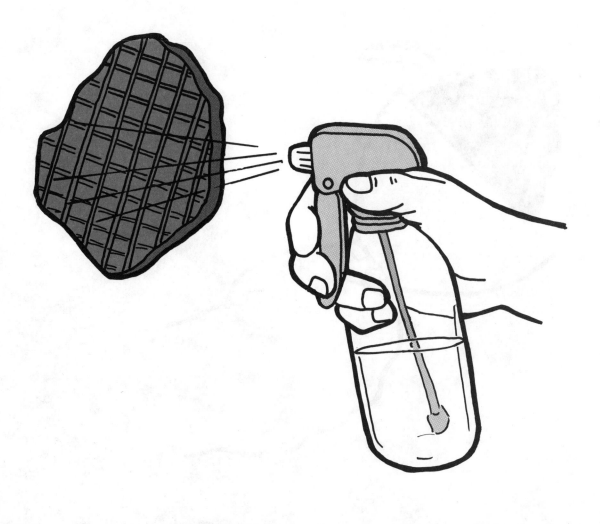

Step 2-14. Completing the repair.

Use the 6-inch taping knife to apply a smooth, thin layer of joint cement or Spackle paste. Work from the center out, spreading the joint cement a few inches past the edges of the patching plaster. Try to make a smooth, flat surface; be sure to feather the edges. Let the joint cement dry for a day or so; then sand the patch level with a sanding block and fine sandpaper.

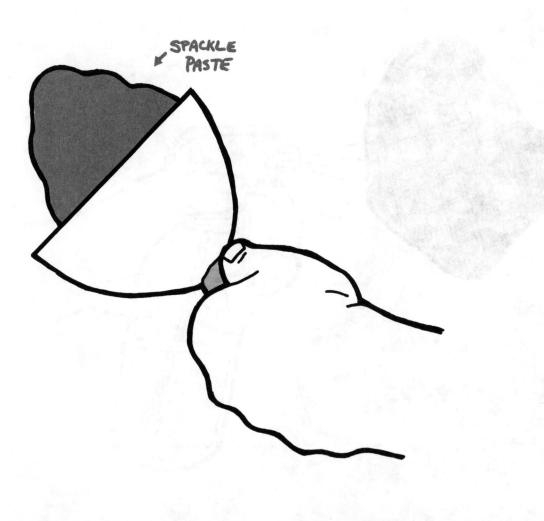

SPACKLE PASTE

CHAPTER THREE

Estimating & Selecting Interior Paint

Before you go to the paint store, know about how much paint you'll need. With most paints, one gallon covers about 400 square feet. Rollers use a little more paint than brushes, since they tend to soak up the paint. Primers might go a little farther than expected; finish coats might not go as far. One gallon for each 400 square feet should be considered just a close estimate.

For the walls, measure the length of each wall, including small offsets or recesses. Round off the numbers to the nearest foot. Add these numbers together and multiply the total by the floor-to-ceiling height. The result is the wall area in square feet. You can deduct about 20 square feet for each door, 15 square feet for each window.

Multiply the length of the room by the width to get the area of the ceiling. If the same paint is to be used on the walls and ceiling, add the two figures to find the total area to be covered.

Divide the total square footage by the spreading rate of the paint shown on the label (approximately 400 square feet per gallon) to find about how much paint you'll need.

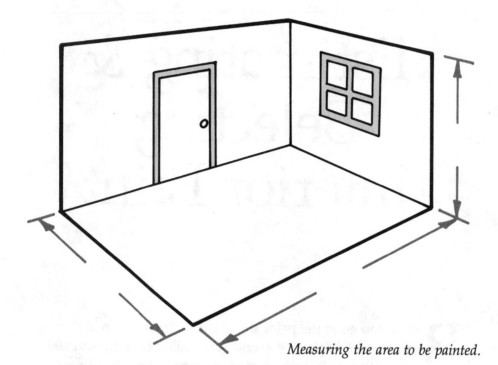

Measuring the area to be painted.

Generally, one gallon is enough paint to cover an average room—
12×15 feet with 8-foot walls. The ceiling for the same room takes
about 2 quarts. You will probably find that 2 quarts cost almost as much
as a gallon. Buy a gallon and save any leftover paint for touch-up.

One coat might be enough unless you're changing colors. In that
case, you'll probably need a second coat. It is usually safe to buy
only enough paint for one coat. But be sure you keep the number or
formula of the paint, so that you can match the color if you need a
second coat. If you think you are running out of paint, finish the wall
you are working on and stop painting at the corner. Start off from the
corner with a new batch of matching paint and you shouldn't notice
any difference. Any time you stop in the middle of a wall or ceiling to
buy more paint, you'll probably have a noticeable overlap.

One person can probably paint a little over 100 square feet in an hour, a 12-×-15-foot room in 4 or 5 hours. But the best way to estimate time is to figure 2 people painting a 12-×-15-foot living room with a single coat over a weekend. Moving furniture usually requires 2 people, and 2 people can normally do more than twice as much work as 1 person working alone. Estimating a weekend, or 2 days, allows you enough time for covering the furniture, cleaning the walls and woodwork, *caulking* and patching as necessary, and applying the paint. Purchase your paint and equipment the previous weekend.

A confusing variety of paints are on the market, but to paint a room in your home you'll probably need only two kinds: paint for the walls and ceiling, and paint for the doors and trim. You can use oil-based paint or water-based latex paint. *Latex* is the most common paint used on walls and ceilings. It dries fast (in a couple of hours), is easy to clean up with soap and water, and has very little odor. Oil paint might take a day to dry, needs paint thinner to clean up, and has a very strong odor. Manufacturers have made so many improvements in water-based paints that some painters believe that a good-quality latex paint is as good as an oil-based paint.

Most paint manufacturers advertise that one-coat coverage is adequate, which is often true. Generally, however, you'll get the best results if you make the first coat a latex *primer*. The primer used for *flat paint* for walls and ceilings is often called primer/sealer, while the primer used for enamel paint for woodwork might be referred to as *undercoater*. The primer serves as a bridge between any incompatible paint and the finish coat, and provides a surface bond for the finish coat. The primer coat should dry in a couple of hours. You can check it by scratching the primed surface with your fingernail. If the primer comes off, let it dry a little longer. When the primer is dry, the wall is ready for the finish coat.

The finish coat for the walls and ceilings should be a flat latex, while the finish coat for the doors and other woodwork should be latex enamel, either semigloss or satin finish. You can apply a finish coat over another finish coat of wall paint, but applying enamel over enamel is not usually recommended, particularly if the original enamel is *glossy*. The new paint won't bond well and probably will chip off. Instead, you should clean the surface and apply an undercoater.

The main things to remember: Two coats, primer and finish, are better than one. Avoid using wall paint on woodwork. Use a primer or undercoater, and always buy a good-quality, name-brand paint. Latex enamel is better for kitchens and baths because it resists moisture and is easier to clean. Flat latex is normally used for the rest of the home. Dark colors tend to make rooms look smaller while light colors make them look larger.

CHAPTER FOUR

Applying & Cleaning Up Interior Paint

Y ou'll need as much working space as possible when you are painting. You should be able to walk around to get to the walls and ceiling easily. If possible, empty the room of furniture. At least move heavy pieces to the center of the room. Cover the areas to be protected with drop cloths and old newspapers. Turn off the circuit breaker to the room. Then remove switch and receptacle plates. Remove the screws holding the mounting plates to ceiling fixtures. Lower the plate from the ceiling and remove any glass shades. If you need the lights for illumination, turn the breaker back on; otherwise, leave it off. Protect the windows from ceiling splatter by covering them with a few old newspapers.

Tools & Materials

- ☐ Stepladder
- ☐ Drop cloths
- ☐ Old newspapers
- ☐ Work paint bucket
- ☐ Mixing paddle or drill with mixing attachment
- ☐ Rubber cement
- ☐ Plastic-coated paper plate
- ☐ Hammer and nail
- ☐ Small paint brush (about 2-inch)
- ☐ Roller with extension handle
- ☐ Roller tray with grating
- ☐ Paint shield or masking tape
- ☐ Water or paint thinner

OUACHITA TECHNICAL COLLEGE

Step 4-1. Mixing the paint.

The paint probably was mixed by machine at the paint store. If you use it in the next day or two, all you'll need to do is stir it a few times with a mixing paddle. If not, the paint must be stirred. Before removing the lid, shake the can vigorously. Open the can and pour about a third of the paint into a separate bucket. Don't try to work from a full can. Use a separate pail or bucket as a work bucket. Use a wooden paddle to stir the paint in the can to a smooth consistency. Then add small amounts of the paint from the bucket to the can, stirring as you go, until all the paint is back in the can. Now pour the paint back and forth from the can to the bucket a few times for a final mixing. You can use a variable-speed drill with a mixer to mix paint. Have the drill off, lower the mixer into the paint, and turn the drill to a low speed to stir the paint. Then turn the drill off and remove the mixer from the paint.

Step 4-2. Preventing drips.
To keep paint from dripping from a gallon can, use rubber cement to glue a plastic-coated paper plate to the bottom of the can. Punch several holes in the lip of the can with a hammer and a nail to allow paint to run back into the can. Latex paint dries quickly and clogs the holes, so keep the nail handy to reopen them.

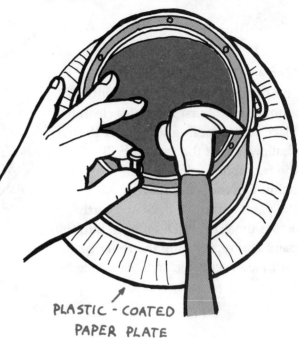

PLASTIC - COATED
PAPER PLATE

Step 4-3. Loading the brush.
To load the brush with paint, dip the tip of the brush about an inch into the paint. If you dip it too far, the paint will run down the handle when you are working. Lift the brush from the paint and, keeping the brush inside the can, abruptly shake the bristles sideways to remove excess paint. Apply very little pressure as you paint. Make each brush stroke about twice the length of the bristles of the brush. Make the strokes slowly and evenly to avoid drips and splattering.

Step 4-4. Loading the roller.
You might want to line the tray with
aluminum foil first for easier cleanup.
Place a wire-mesh grating over the
shallow end of the tray and fill
the tray about half full of
paint. Dip the roller into
the paint and roll it back and forth
across the grating. Dip it back into the
paint and repeat until the roller is
saturated evenly, but not overloaded.

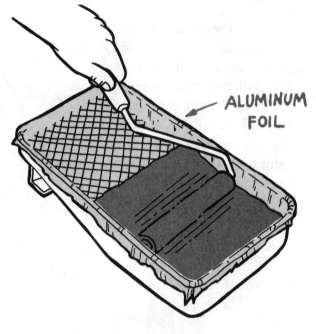

ALUMINUM
FOIL

Step 4-5. Using a roller.
Make the first stroke, or roll,
away from you on ceilings, and
upward on walls. Work the
roller back and forth in a W
or M pattern about 3 feet
square, then fill it in. Work
slowly—rolling too fast
causes splatters—and avoid
lifting the roller from the
surface. Spread the paint
evenly and completely to
cover the section. Load
the roller again, move
to an unpainted area,
and repeat the process.

Step 4-6. Painting the ceiling.
Paint the ceiling first. Use the brush to *cut in* (paint to the edge) the
ceiling just to the wall, but not on the wall. You'll cut in the wall to
the ceiling when you paint the walls. Paint a 2- or 3-inch-wide strip
where the ceiling meets the wall. The roller can't paint in corners.
Paint a strip about 2 or 3 feet long,
then use the roller on the ceiling
while the corner paint is still
wet. Working with two people
eliminates switching from brush
to roller to brush. One person cuts
in the corners while the other rolls
on the ceiling. If you paint the
corners of the entire room at one
time, the paint will dry before the
rest of the room is painted, and
you'll have a *lap* around the edges.
Start at one end of the ceiling and
work in 2- or 3-foot sections down
the length. Don't try to spread the
paint too far; if you do, when the
paint dries, you'll have skips
and need another coat.

Step 4-7. Painting the walls.

Next, paint the walls. Start at the ceiling and cut in with the brush.
You need to cut in corners, around windows, doors, and baseboards,
but remember to work in sections, just like you did on the ceiling.
Start in an upper corner and work across the wall. Work carefully
around any exposed switches or receptacles. The paint could conduct
electricity and give you a shock.

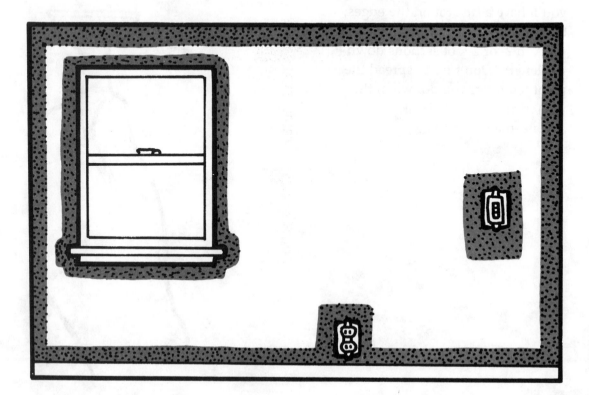

The next thing you need to paint is the window trim. Many homes have aluminum windows that are left unpainted, but some have wooden, double-hung windows. These standard two-part windows slide up and down. They are, like everything else, painted from the top down.

Step 4-8. Painting the upper halves of window trim.
First remove the handles and locks. Lower the top window about 3 inches and raise the bottom window about 3 inches. Paint the top edge of the upper window. Paint the top edge of the lower window. Paint across the top and halfway down the sides of the upper window. Paint the *mullions* in the top part of the upper window. Mullions are the pieces of *molding* that hold the glass in place. You can use a paint shield or masking tape to keep paint off the glass. Paint across the top and down the sides of the lower window. Paint the mullions in the lower window.

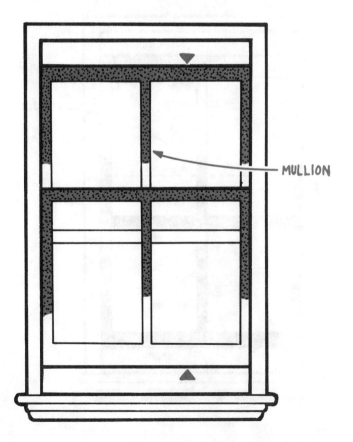

MULLION

Step 4-9. Painting the lower halves.

Now raise the bottom window almost all the way up and lower the top window to about 3 inches from the window sill. The bottom window is now at the top. Paint the lower edge of the bottom window. Paint the remaining part of the bottom window. Paint the bottom edge of the top window. Paint the bottom and remaining sides of the top window. Paint the remaining mullions in the top window. Paint the *trim* around the window. Paint the window sill. Leave the windows open slightly to prevent sticking. When the paint is dry, work the windows up and down a few times before closing them completely. If you used masking tape, remove it just after the paint has set slightly to ensure a clean separation between the tape and the paint. If the paint has dried, use a razor blade and carefully cut the paint along the edge of the tape. Then remove the tape.

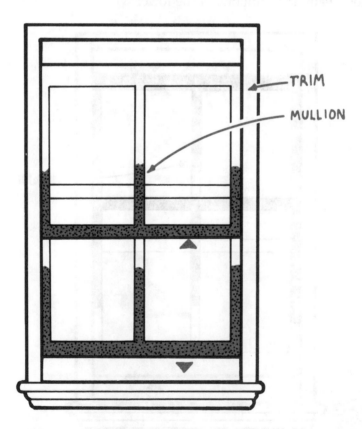

Step 4-10. Preparing to paint the doors.

Next, paint the doors. Remove the doorknob or cover it with a plastic bag. Place newspapers under the door to catch any drips. You can use a roller to paint a flat door quickly, but a brush does a better job.

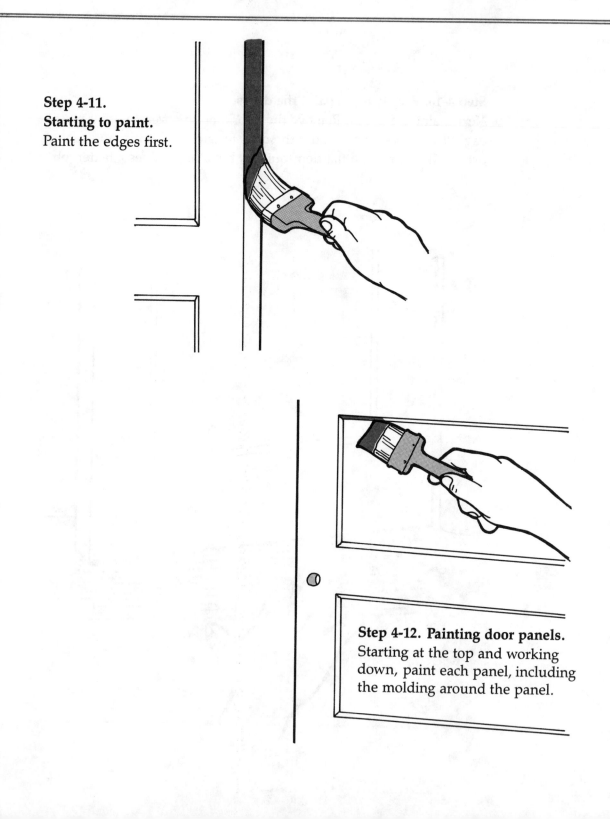

**Step 4-11.
Starting to paint.**
Paint the edges first.

Step 4-12. Painting door panels.
Starting at the top and working down, paint each panel, including the molding around the panel.

Step 4-13. Painting horizontal and vertical sections.

Paint the cross pieces, then the vertical pieces. Now go back and check for *runs*. The molding in paneled doors tends to hold excess paint and is the source of most runs.

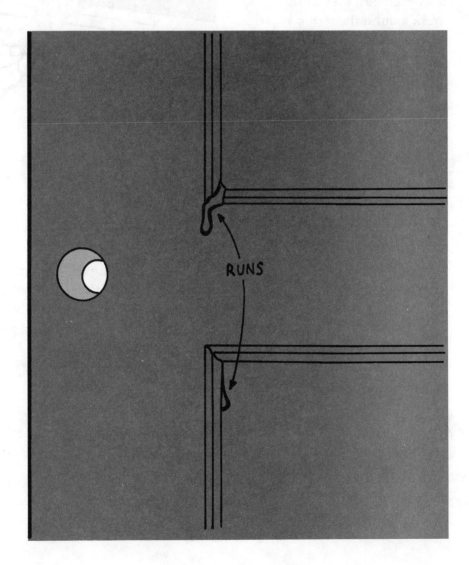

RUNS

Step 4-14.
Painting the top half of baseboards.
Paint the baseboards last. Use a straightedge, or paint shield, to protect walls and floors. Place the long edge of the shield on top of the baseboard and paint the top half of the baseboard. Hold the shield with one hand and paint with the other. Make smooth, even strokes. Work around the room, wiping off the shield after each move.

PAINT SHIELD

Step 4-15. Painting the bottom of baseboards.
Press the edge of the shield between the floor and the baseboard. Paint the bottom half of the baseboard. Wipe accumulated paint from the shield frequently.

After you have painted everything you wanted to paint, clean up your equipment and work area right away.

Step 4-16. Storing unused paint.

Pour any unused paint from your work bucket or paint tray back into the original can. Place the lid on top of the can, lay a cloth over the lid to avoid splatters, and tap the lid in place with a hammer. Clean the work bucket for future use, using water for latex paint or thinner for oil-based paint. Many painters discard inexpensive rollers after the painting is completed.

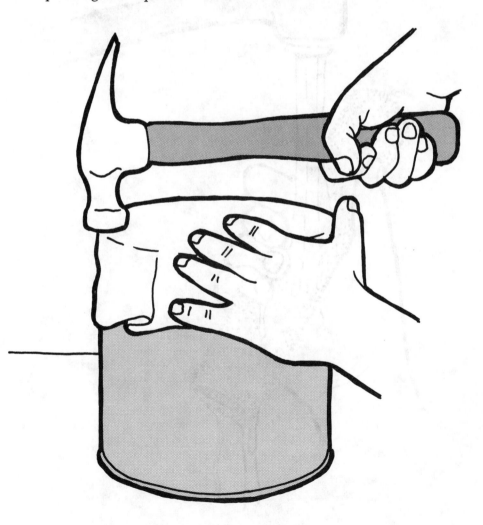

Step 4-17. Cleaning latex paint from brushes and rollers.
To clean latex paint from brushes and rollers, rinse them with warm
running water. Knead the bristles or nap until all traces of paint are
gone. Then add a few drops of dishwashing detergent to the bristles
or roller cover and rinse for a final cleaning. Shake or spin off excess
water. Wrap brushes in heavy brown paper or newspaper and fasten
with a string or a rubber band. Lay flat to store.

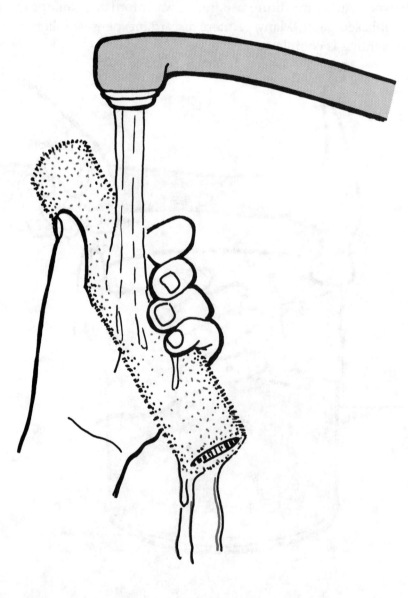

Step 4-18. Cleaning oil-based paint from brushes and rollers.
Clean up oil-based paint in a well-ventilated area. Get a clean can, like a coffee can, and pour a little thinner or *mineral spirits* into the can. Push the bristles up and down against the bottom of the can to work out the paint. When the thinner becomes cloudy, pour it into another can and add fresh thinner to the first can. Repeat the steps, adding fresh thinner about four times. Shake the brush dry and wrap it in brown paper or newspaper and lay flat. Rinse the roller in thinner and knead the nap to remove the paint. Shake or spin off excess thinner.

CHAPTER FIVE

Decorating with Stencils

Stencils can be used to brighten a kitchen, customize a bathroom, or enrich a living room. You can create your own designs and cut the stencils from materials purchased from art-supply stores. A simpler way is to buy a wall-stencil kit. These kits have about everything you need to stencil a wall, including precut stencils (one for each color), a stencil brush, fast-drying paint, and tape.

If you use an oil-based paint, you'll need to buy a little paint thinner or mineral spirits for cleanup. Water-soluble paints are available, and the cleanup requires only soap and water. Premixed paints usually come in 1- or 2-ounce jars. The key is to use fast-drying paint, and very little of it. Otherwise, you'll have to wait until the paint dries before going to a different color or the paint will smear and run behind the stencil.

Stencil brushes are round, stiff-bristled, and cut flat across the end. Use a separate brush for each color so that you don't have to clean the brush when you switch to a different color. However, the paint dries quickly on the brushes, so place used brushes in the appropriate thinner until you can clean them.

Stencils are usually thin plastic sheets with a design cut in a repeating pattern. Each stencil also has alignment and centering lines for proper alignment. A separate stencil is used for each color in the design. The stencils are numbered 1, 2, 3, or lettered A, B, C, etc. For example, if the pattern has red flowers with green stems, flanked with blue ribbon, the first stencil might have the ribbon, the second might have the stems, and the third, the flowers.

Before you begin on a wall, make a paper proof or test sample on a piece of white paper. This test gives you an idea of how the pattern will look on the wall and also can be useful as a measuring tool later as you go around corners.

Tools & Materials

- ☐ Stepladder
- ☐ Stencils
- ☐ Stencil brushes
- ☐ Masking tape
- ☐ Paint
- ☐ Tape measure or yardstick
- ☐ Pencil
- ☐ Paper towels
- ☐ Rags
- ☐ Water or mineral spirits

Begin at the most prominent corner in the room—the corner you see when you first enter the room. Stencil down one side of the room; then go back to the starting point and stencil down the other side. End the stenciling at the opposite corner, usually the corner next to the door, so that any mismatch won't be too noticeable.

Step 5-1. Placing the stencil.

Tape the first stencil (#1 or A) to the wall, applying tape to
both the top and bottom edges of the stencil, or to each end.

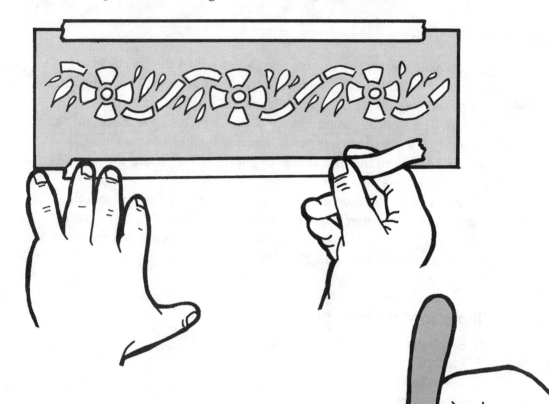

Step 5-2. Loading the brush.

Lower just the tip of the bristles into the paint,
then blot them on a paper towel to remove
excess paint. You want to have very little paint
on a nearly dry brush. Problems occur when
you have too much paint, not too little.

Step 5-3. Applying the paint.

Hold the brush perpendicular to the wall (straight out from the stencil) and apply the paint in very light strokes, using a circular motion.

To shade, simply start applying the paint to the area you want darker and work toward the lighter area, usually from the edge of the pattern toward the center. Paint should not build up on the cut edge of the stencil. If it does, you might be using too much paint, too much pressure, or a noncircular motion.

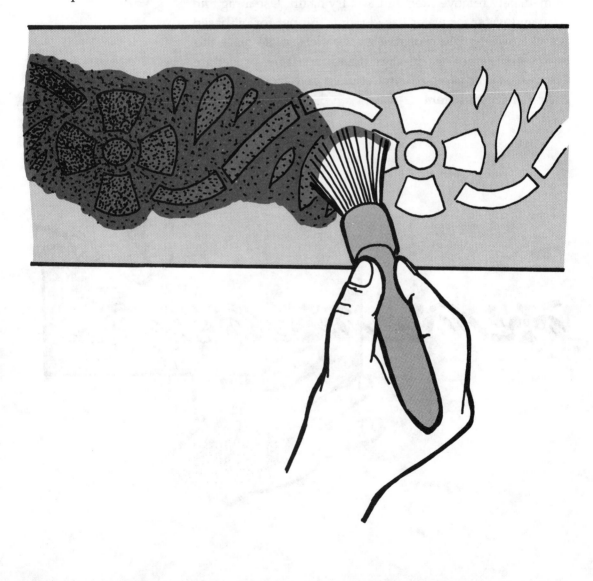

Step 5-4. Moving the stencil.
After completing the first stencil, remove it by lifting it
straight out from the wall. If you don't like the results,
immediately remove the paint and try again. Use a rag and
soap and water for water-based paint, thinner for oil-based
paint. However, you probably will be pleased, so place the
stencil to the right or left, align it and repeat the procedure.
Try to apply the same amount of paint and shading to make
each pattern consistent.

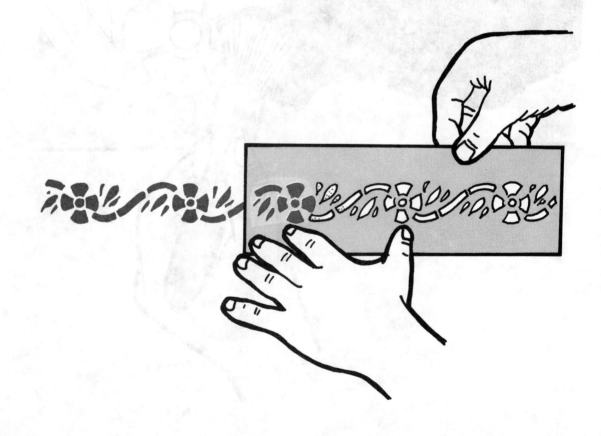

Step 5-5. Fitting the wall.

Stencil about two-thirds of the wall;
then use the test stencil to see how the pattern
will fit into the corner. If the flower or main part
of the pattern hits directly in the corner, you can
add or reduce 1/4-inch to 1/2-inch space between
applications to move the flower out of the corner.
When you come to the corner, bend the stencil into
the corner. Don't crease the stencil to form the corner.

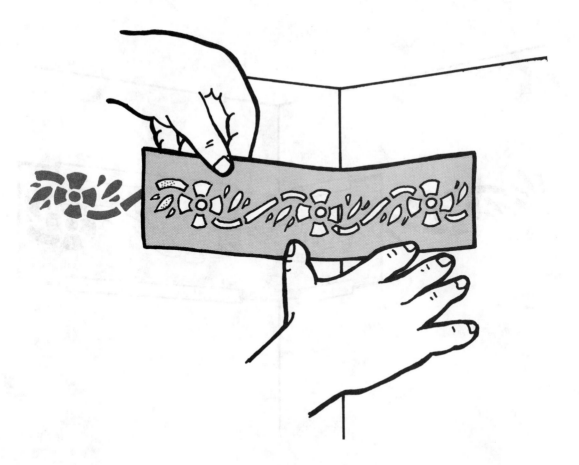

Step 5-6. Stenciling corners.
Tape the stencil to the wall and apply the paint in light, feathering
strokes. Paint as much as you can reach. Don't dab paint in the
corner. Go to a light shade as the design approaches the corner.
Then shade back as you pick up the design on the other wall.

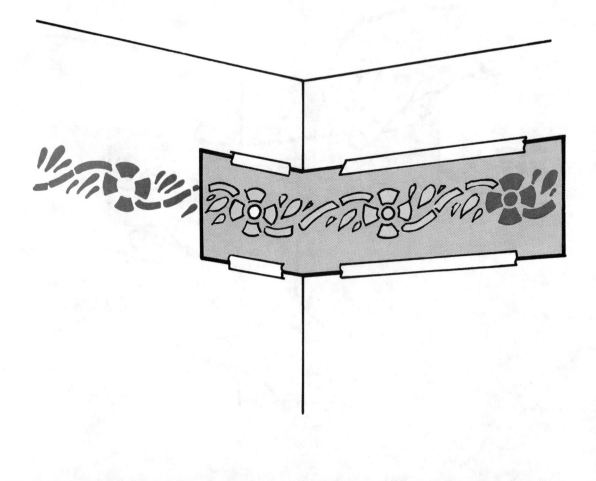

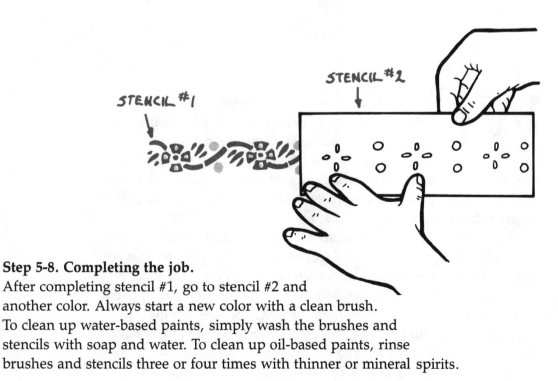

Step 5-7. Fitting short walls.
On very short walls, you can start
your stencil in the center of the
wall. Find the center of the wall
and mark it lightly with a pencil.
Locate the center point of the test
stencil and place it over the center
mark on the wall. Now space the
test stencil to each corner to see if
any adjustments need to be made
to fit the wall. Begin painting at the
center of the wall and work toward
the corners.

STENCIL #1

STENCIL #2

Step 5-8. Completing the job.
After completing stencil #1, go to stencil #2 and
another color. Always start a new color with a clean brush.
To clean up water-based paints, simply wash the brushes and
stencils with soap and water. To clean up oil-based paints, rinse
brushes and stencils three or four times with thinner or mineral spirits.

CHAPTER SIX

Preparing Exterior Surfaces for Painting

While the thought of painting the exterior of your home can be overwhelming, it needn't be. Just relax and try to make it a pleasant experience. Don't be in a hurry. Pace yourself. Don't apply any paint when the temperature is below 50 degrees F. Try to work on the shady side of the house and move with the shadows. Make sure the surface is properly prepared, and use the paint designed for your specific needs.

Good ladders are expensive, so you might consider renting. You will need a 6-foot stepladder and (depending on the job) an extension ladder. Working heights for ladders can be misleading. You should never stand on the top or second-from-top step of a stepladder. Use a stepladder at least 2 feet longer than the height where you need to stand to reach the highest point on the wall. Extension ladders have an overlap between the base and the extended upper part, so figure a working reach of about 17 feet for a 20-foot extension ladder.

Some of the tools you need include a paint *scraper* to remove peeling paint from wood surfaces; a putty knife and putty for filling holes; a caulking gun and caulking compound to fill cracks; coarse-grade sandpaper for sanding small areas; and an orbital, not rotary, power sander to remove large areas of damaged paint. You also need

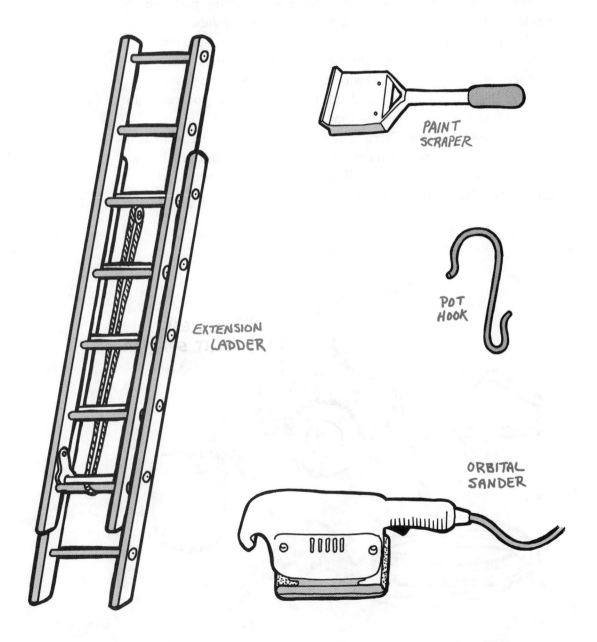

PAINT
SCRAPER

POT
HOOK

EXTENSION
LADDER

ORBITAL
SANDER

a metal pot hook to hang the paint bucket from a ladder rung; a trim brush and a 4- or 6-inch paint brush; a roller with an extension pole; a roller tray or 5-gallon bucket with a roller grid; mixing paddles; and rags for cleaning hands, spilled paint, and brush handles.

An option you might consider is renting an airless sprayer. They are fast, and they apply the equivalent of two coats at once. Consequently, they use up to twice as much paint as a brush or roller. After masking and normal surface preparations, you can paint a typical two-story home in less than a day.

Dull glossy surfaces with a little sanding, and prime any areas of bare wood. Use a wire brush on any chalky surfaces and brush the dust away. Scrape off any loose, bubbled, or peeling paint, and feather the edges with sandpaper.

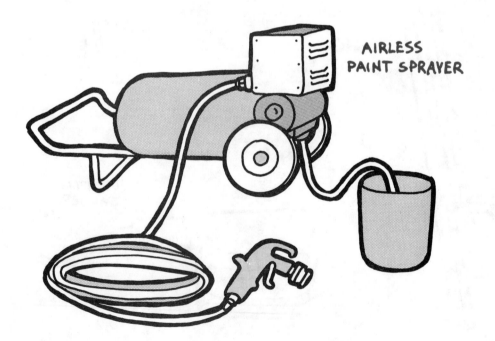

AIRLESS
PAINT SPRAYER

Remove *mildew* with a solution of 1 gallon of warm water, 2/3 cup of chlorine bleach, and 1/3 cup of detergent. Wash the area with the solution, allowing it to set until the discoloration bleaches out. Then rinse with fresh water and let dry completely.

Countersink exposed nail heads and fill the holes with caulking. Remove any cracked putty around window panes and replace with *glazing compound*. Caulking and glazing compound should be dry before you begin painting.

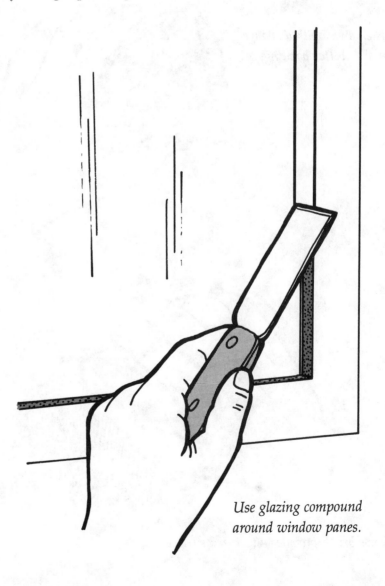

Use glazing compound around window panes.

Repair cracks and holes in *stucco* walls with stucco patching material. Dampen the damaged area with a sponge and clean water to provide better bonding. To achieve a textured surface on a smooth patch, use a coarse bristle brush like a scrub brush. Rub it over the partially set patching in a circular motion until you have a matching pattern.

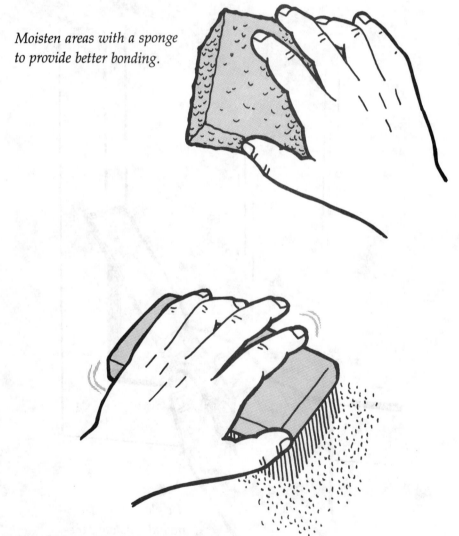

Moisten areas with a sponge to provide better bonding.

A coarse brush provides a textured surface.

CHAPTER SEVEN

Estimating & Selecting Exterior Paint

E stimating the amount of paint needed for the outside of a house is done much the same way as for a room. You need to divide the area to be painted by the spreading rate of the paint. To get the area, add the lengths of all the sides, then multiply the total by the height of the walls. For example, if you have 2 sides at 40 feet, and 2 ends at 20 feet, the perimeter is 120 feet. If the wall is 12 feet high, multiply 120 by 12 to get 1,440 square feet.

If you have a *gable*, multiply 1/2 the length of its base by the height. For example, if half the length of the gable is 10 feet and the height is 8 feet, the area of the gable is 80 square feet. If you have 2 gables, you have 160 square feet of gable area. Add the 1,440 square feet of the sides to the 160 square feet of the gables for a total area of 1,600 square feet to be painted. If 1 gallon of paint covers 400 square feet, you need about 4 gallons for each coat. Keep in mind that the spreading rate on the paint labels can be optimistic. Latex paint doesn't go as far as oil-based paint.

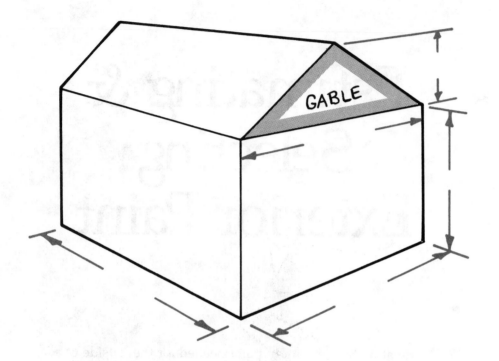

Measuring the area to be painted.

Always read the labels to make sure that you are selecting the right paint for your particular job. Primers are special coatings that provide a bond for the finish coat. They also provide metal, masonry, and bare wood with protection against moisture. Block filler is a masonry sealer and is used as an undercoater for paint. This thick white coating seals rough, porous masonry surfaces. It is an excellent base for latex or oil-based paints and can be applied with a roller or stiff brush. Exterior flat latex is often used because it cleans up with soap and water and is almost odor-free. Latex gloss contains more resin than flat paint. Resin makes the paint more resistant to wear and weathering. Latex gloss is used for windows, doors, and shutters. Select the new paint according to the type of surface you are covering.

Apply block sealer to masonry surfaces with a roller before painting.

CHAPTER EIGHT

Applying & Cleaning Up Exterior Paint

P aint the outside of your house in the same sequence as the inside: top to bottom. After the surface has been properly prepared, make sure you have a clear working area. Trim any shrubs or tie them back with ropes and stakes so that you can paint behind them. Protect shrubs from splatters with paper or canvas drop cloths. Read and follow the instructions on paint labels. Thin paint only with the recommended thinner. Stir paint thoroughly before starting and occasionally while you are working. Since you start at the top and work down, you'll probably be using a ladder. When setting up a stepladder, always open it all the way and lock the spreader braces in place. Place all four legs on firm, level ground. Never use a rock or similar object to level the feet. Never stand on the next-to-top step, the top step, or the bucket shelf.

When using an extension ladder, place it securely against the side of the house. When the ladder is extended, the upper section should overlap the lower part by at least 3 feet. Angle the ladder so that the distance between the feet and the wall is about one-fourth the height of the ladder. The bottom of a 20-foot ladder should be about 5 feet from the wall. Never step from one ladder to another, and don't try to reach too far. If you have to climb onto the roof to paint a dormer, extend the ladder at least 3 feet above the edge of the roof so that you can step safely from the ladder to the roof.

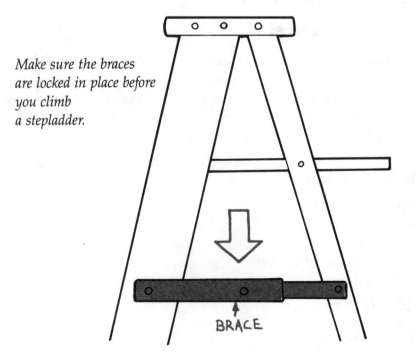

*Make sure the braces
are locked in place before
you climb
a stepladder.*

BRACE

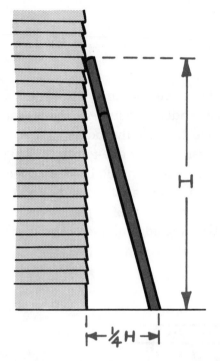

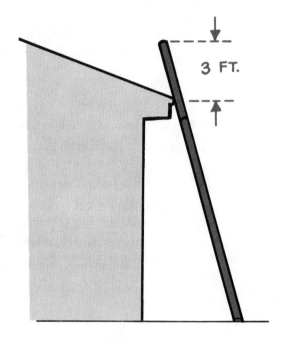

Place the ladder securely against the house. For stability, make sure the distance between its feet and the wall is one-fourth its height.

If you need to climb onto the roof, extend the ladder at least 3 feet above the edge of the roof.

Tools & Materials

☐ Stepladder
☐ Extension ladder
☐ Drop cloths
☐ Brushes, rollers, or sprayer
☐ Mixing paddles
☐ Paint strainers
☐ Rags
☐ Water or paint thinner

Step 8-1. Painting the side.
Paint the house in two stages: first the sides, then the trim.
Begin with any dormers, then go to the side of the house.
When you've finished painting one section, climb down
and move the ladder to the next section. Paint down to
about the same level and move the ladder again. Work
your way across the side of the house until you reach
the end of that wall.

Step 8-2. Moving back.
Lower the ladder and work your
way back. Gutters and downspouts
are usually painted the same color
as the *siding* so that they blend in.

Step 8-3. Painting the trim.

If you are painting the trim the same color as the siding, just go to a trim brush when you get to the windows and continue painting. You will save time when working from a ladder. If the trim is a different color, finish painting the siding, then go back and do the trim.

Paint the windows, shutters, and doors.

Step 8-4. Painting porches and railings.

Paint porch railings and steps next. If the steps must be used before the paint dries, paint all the risers, but only every other tread. When these treads dry, paint the remaining ones. The porch floor and steps should be painted with *deck paint*. Deck paint usually has a high gloss and can be slippery when just a little wet. You can add a fine, sandy powder, called anti-slip powder, to the paint. Just stir it in when you mix the paint.

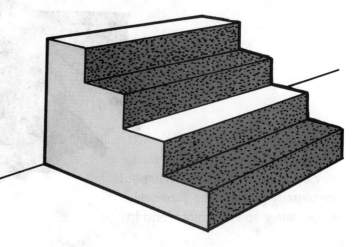

Airless sprayers are easy to use, but you should take some safety precautions. The paint comes out the tip at up to 3,000 pounds per square inch and up to 200 miles per hour. This pressure is enough to force paint right into your finger if it gets too close to the nozzle. Get thorough instructions when you rent the sprayer. Be sure to get the proper tip for the type of paint you'll be using. Latex paint requires a larger tip than thinner liquids like stains.

Step 8-5. Straining paint.
Always *strain* the paint through paint strainers or two or three layers of cheesecloth before you put it in the sprayer.

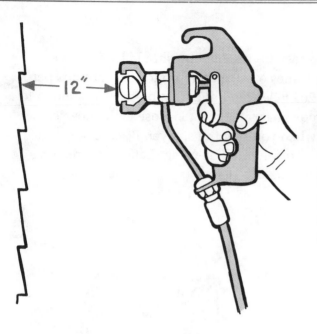

← 12" →

Step 8-6. Holding the gun.
Hold the gun about 12 inches from the surface and keep it aimed directly at the wall as you make each pass. Tilting it up and down or swinging it from side to side causes uneven patterns and runs. Let each pass overlap the previous one by about an inch or so.

Step 8-7. Making passes.
To make each pass, start the gun moving before spraying the paint and keep the gun moving after stopping the spray. This method takes a little practice. Just start the pass, squeeze the trigger, release the trigger, stop the pass. Keep the passes a comfortable length, not more than 3 feet long.

Step 8-8. Cleaning up.

After you finish, clean all tools with warm, soapy water or paint thinner. Check the paint label for specific cleaning instructions. To clean a sprayer, pump out any remaining paint, then flush the hoses and gun with the proper thinner.

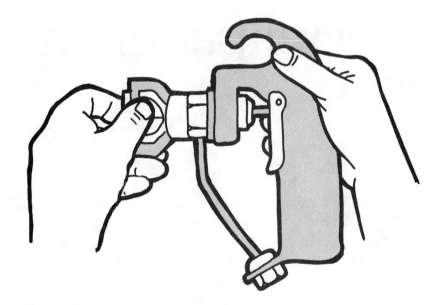

Caution: Do not disassemble any part of the sprayer to clean a nozzle or filter, without first disconnecting the plug and squeezing the trigger to release any pressure.

CHAPTER NINE

Preparing Surfaces for Wallpapering

Because the materials now include vinyls and fabrics, or a combination, wallpaper is now called wallcovering. Of course, you can still call it wallpaper; the people at the store will know what you want. Present-day wallcoverings are an attractive alternative to paint, and they are easy to apply.

Tools for hanging wallpaper include a stepladder and a 36-inch metal *straightedge* for measuring and guiding cuts along edges. You'll also need scissors; a utility knife with extra razor blades; a *plumb bob* for making vertical lines; and a paste bucket and paste brush for mixing and applying the paste. You also can use a roller tray and a short nap roller to apply the paste; an extra bucket of clean water and a sponge to remove excess paste after hanging each strip; a smoothing brush to smooth the paper flat against the wall; and a seam roller to make sure that the wallpaper seams are smoothed flat against the wall.

If you're using prepasted wallpaper, you won't need the paste bucket or brush, but you will need a water box for wetting the paper. A sponge can be used in place of the smoothing brush and seam roller.

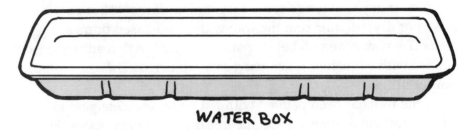

WATER BOX

A proper work table is important. You need something about 3 feet wide and 6 or 8 feet long at a height of about 30 to 35 inches. A flat door with the knob removed, set on a dinette table, makes a good work table. You can use a couple of sawhorses and a sheet of plywood covered with a piece of plastic, but sawhorses are lower than most tables, and you'll have to do more bending. Try to get something about waist-high.

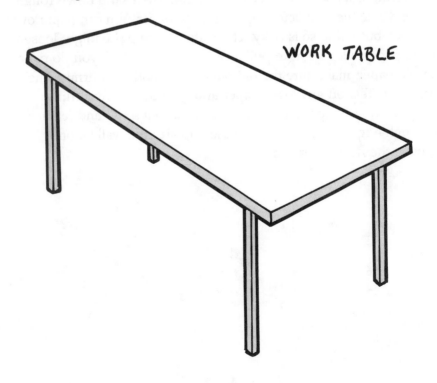

WORK TABLE

Almost any wall needs some preparation. If the wall is bare plaster or drywall, first coat the wall with an oil-based primer or sealer. Then size the wall before papering. *Size* is a thin adhesive, applied with a brush or roller, used as an undercoater for wallcoverings.

If the wall has been painted with flat paint, use detergent to remove any dirt and grease. Scrape or sand any rough places. Fill cracks and holes with Spackle paste, and then sand smooth (see chapter 2). Size the wall before applying the wallpaper.

If the wall has been painted with a glossy paint, use detergent to remove dirt and grease. Repair cracks with Spackle paste. Then remove the gloss by sanding lightly with sandpaper. Brush off all the dust; then size the wall before applying the wallpaper.

If the wall is covered with wallcovering, removing the old wallcovering is a good idea (see chapter 10). Then sand down rough areas and size the wall before applying the paper. You can paper over old paper, but doing so is risky. The water in the paste might loosen the old paper, allowing it to pull away from the wall. If you do paper over old paper, make sure the old paper is smooth and firmly stuck to the wall. Tear off any loose paper and glue down any curling corners with wallpaper paste. Sand down *lapped seams* and feather any rough edges. Wash off any grease and size the wall before applying the new paper.

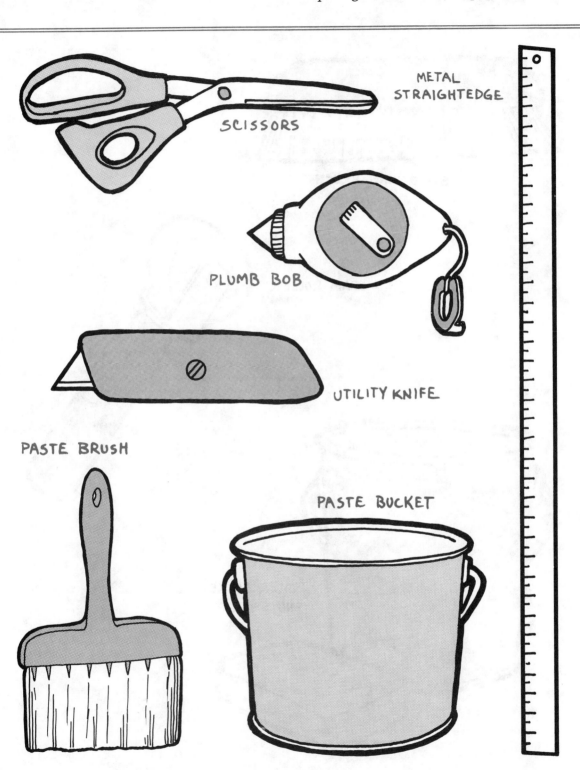

SCISSORS

METAL STRAIGHTEDGE

PLUMB BOB

UTILITY KNIFE

PASTE BRUSH

PASTE BUCKET

SMOOTHING BRUSH

SEAM ROLLER

WATER BUCKET
AND SPONGE

CHAPTER TEN

Removing Old Wallpaper

Removing old wallcoverings can be done in three different ways. The first, and easiest, is to *strip* it off the walls dry. Newer wallcoverings are made so that you can simply pull them off the walls without wetting the walls with water or chemicals. Steaming is another way to remove old paper; however, I don't recommend it because of the danger of burns from the steam and hot water. It is also a slower process because you wind up trying to do two things at once: steaming and scraping. You have to spend extra time and effort cleaning up the equipment, as well as extra money to rent the *steamer*. Wetting and scraping is the third way to remove wallpaper; it might be the best way, next to dry stripping.

First try lifting a corner of the wallcovering with a scraper or putty knife. Try an inconspicuous corner behind a door. If the wall had been sealed or painted, you might be able to peel the old paper right off. However, if someone took a shortcut and applied the wallpaper directly to bare wallboard, removing it can be a problem.

The paper coating on the wallboard might come off when you remove the wallpaper, exposing the chalky inside of the board. In this case, just remove any loose paper and prepare the wall to apply the new paper over the old paper.

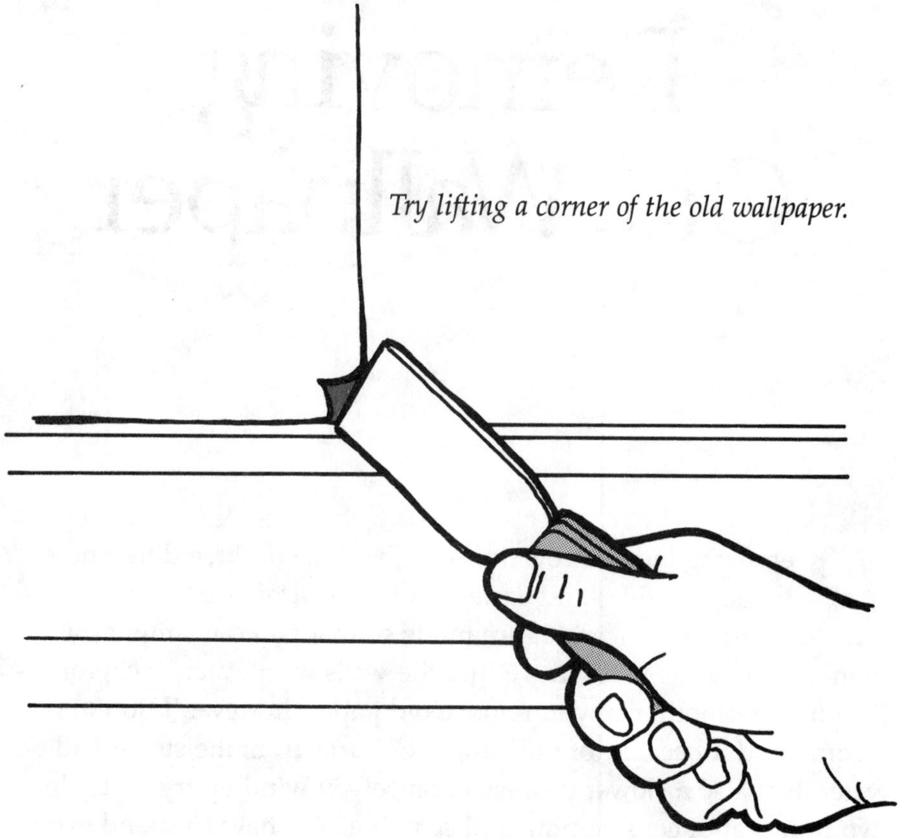

Try lifting a corner of the old wallpaper.

Tools & Materials

- [ ] Stepladder
- [ ] Garden sprayer
- [ ] Sandpaper (if necessary)
- [ ] Scraper
- [ ] Paint brush

- [ ] Bucket
- [ ] Warm water
- [ ] Newspapers
- [ ] Garbage bags
- [ ] Drop cloths

Step 10-1. Preparing the old wallpaper.
If the old wallpaper won't peel off, you must thoroughly wet it with water. Because you will be working with water, do not remove any electrical switch or receptacle plates. To be safer, turn off the circuit breaker to that room.

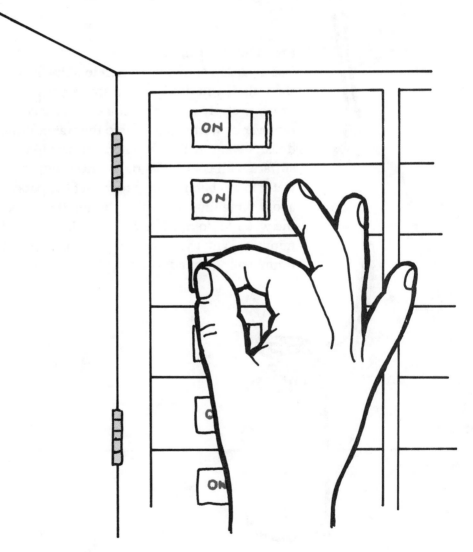

Step 10-2. Wetting the paper.

Use a garden sprayer adjusted to a fine mist to wet down the wall. If you don't have a sprayer, use a bucket and brush to apply the water. You can mix a chemical wallpaper remover or wetting agent into the water. If the old paper doesn't want to absorb water, you will have to scratch the surface with coarse (50- or 60-grit) sandpaper to allow the water to get behind the paper. Wet the paper with water about three times—the more water, the better. You want the water to do most of the work. Let it soak for about 30 minutes. When you can scrape some paper off with your thumbnail, it's ready.

Step 10-3. Scraping the paper.

Use a $2^1/_2$- or 3-inch scraper or flexible putty knife. Hold the knife in one hand at about a 30-degree angle from the wall. Press the blade under the paper and push from the bottom up. The paper should wrinkle and peel away from the wall.

Step 10-4. Completing the job.

Hold the loosened strip of paper with your other hand and pull steadily upward. The paper should peel away easily in long strips. If it doesn't, rewet the paper and try again. Discard the old paper in a plastic garbage bag as you remove it.

CHAPTER ELEVEN

Estimating & Selecting Wallcovering

Wallpapering can be considered decorating since thousands of different designs and color combinations of wallcoverings are available. Most wallcoverings now are prepasted and require soaking to activate the adhesive. Some wallcoverings, such as grass cloth, burlap, and cork, are not prepasted. The most popular wallcovering consists of vinyl laminated to a paper or cloth backing. Lightweight vinyl-coated paper and solid vinyl wallcovering are available prepasted, while some heavier paper-backed and cloth-backed vinyls might require premixed adhesives. Prepasted vinyl wallcovering is the easiest type to use.

The type of wallcovering you choose will depend a lot on where it will be used. Paper wallcovering is normally very sensitive to water and doesn't stand up well under rough treatment. High-traffic areas, such as hallways, kitchens, baths, and kids' bedrooms, need a wallcovering made of vinyl or one with a good vinyl coating—something that resists grease and water and is washable.

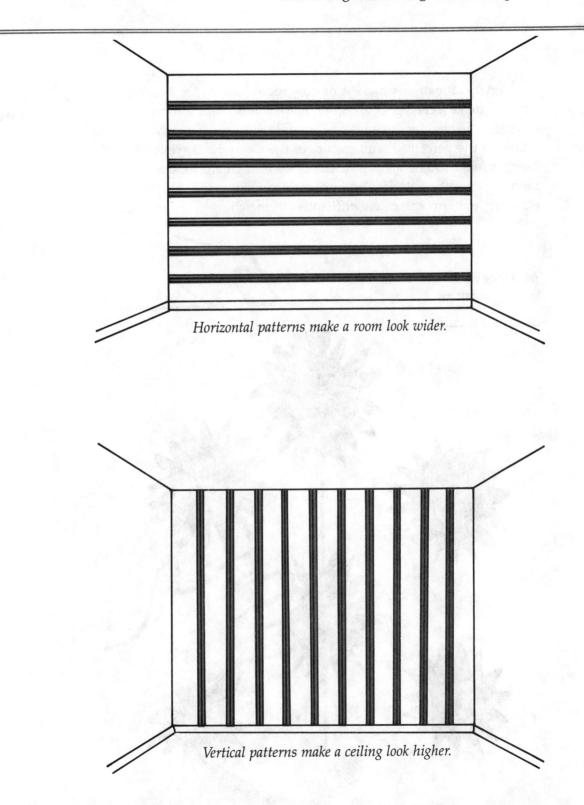

Horizontal patterns make a room look wider.

Vertical patterns make a ceiling look higher.

Horizontal patterns make a narrow room look wider. Vertical patterns make a ceiling look higher. Dark colors make a room look smaller, while lighter ones make a room look larger. Colors also influence the perceived temperature of the room. Reds, yellows, and oranges make rooms seem warmer; blues and greens tend to cool rooms. The pattern itself is an important consideration. Large, elaborate patterns can cause difficulties in matching at the seams.

Matching seams can be difficult on a large pattern.

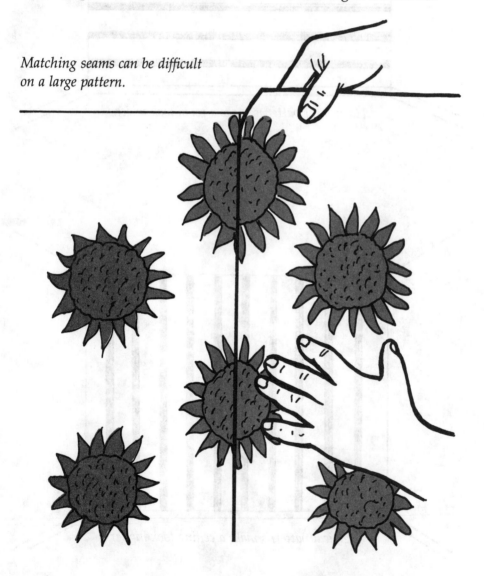

Straight match patterns repeat horizontally.

Drop match patterns repeat diagonally.

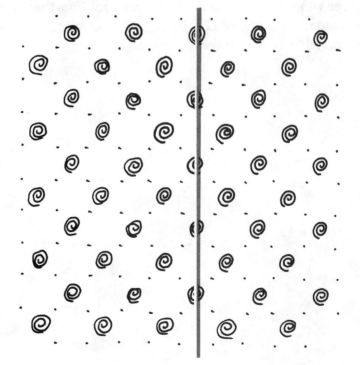

Most patterns fall into two categories: straight match and drop match. A typical straight pattern repeats horizontally across each sheet. A typical drop pattern repeats diagonally across each sheet.

The easiest way to determine how much wallpaper you need is to let the salesperson at the store figure it out. They have charts that give the number of rolls needed for a particular size room. But you can get a close estimate by measuring the distance around the room and multiplying by the height of the ceiling to get the square feet of the room. Divide this number by 30 to get the number of rolls of paper. Each roll has 36 square feet, but by using 30, you allow for matching patterns and waste. Now deduct 1 roll for every 2 windows or doors.

For example: If the room is 12 × 14 feet with an 8-foot ceiling, the distance around the room is 52 feet. Multiplying this number by the 8 feet for the height of the ceiling gives you 416 square feet. Divide 416 square feet by 30 square feet to get 14 rolls. Suppose the room has three windows and one door. Deduct 2 rolls for these openings. You should need a total of 12 rolls to paper the room. Consider buying an extra roll or two to correct for any mistakes.

CHAPTER TWELVE

Applying Wallcovering

Before you start, make sure that the walls are properly prepared and sized, that you have all the necessary tools and plenty of room to work, that the power to the room has been turned off, and that the switch plates and wall plates have been removed. Carefully read the instructions that came with the wallcovering. Replace blades in the trim knife frequently; razor blades lose their edge quickly, and dull blades will tear the wallpaper. Change water in the water box every four or five strips to keep the front of the paper from becoming coated with paste. Use a separate bucket and clean water to rinse sponges. Save leftover paper to make future repairs.

Tools & Materials

- Stepladder
- Plumb bob
- Sponge
- Bucket
- Water box
- Smoothing brush
- Metal trim edge or straightedge
- Trim knife and extra razor blades
- Scissors
- Tape measure
- Newspapers
- Table with plastic cover
- Paste brush and bucket

Where you start is also where you will make your final seam. Sometimes the last seam does not line up exactly, so try to begin in an inconspicuous corner, one close to a door or window. This way, the final seam will be hidden as much as possible.

Step 12-1. Measuring the wall for the first strip.
Because few homes have true vertical corners, you have to start with a straight plumb line. First measure the width of the wallcovering. Now measure out from the corner you chose to a point an inch or so less than the width of the wallcovering. The extra inch will wrap around the corner of the other wall. Measure near the ceiling and to the right of the corner. Mark this point with a pencil.

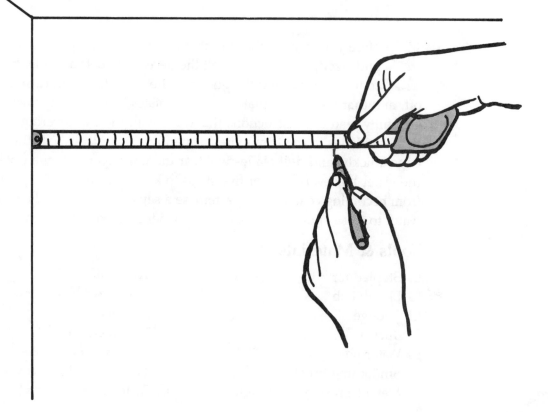

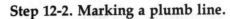

Step 12-2. Marking a plumb line.
Now place a plumb line or a carpenter's level at the pencil mark to mark a straight line from the ceiling to the top of the baseboard.

Step 12-3. Measuring the first strip.

Measure the height of the line; then add an extra 4 to 6 inches to allow for matching patterns and for tight fits against the ceiling and baseboards. For example, if the overall height of the wall is 96 inches, you'll want to cut each strip (after matching the pattern of the previous strip) at least 100 inches long. Now cut the first strip of wallcovering to your measurement.

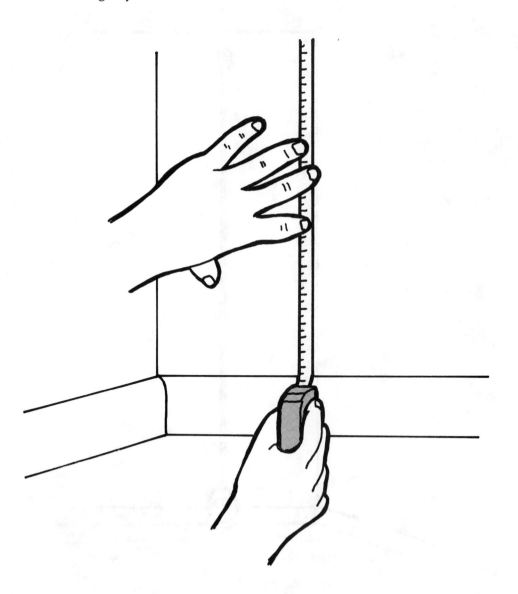

Most of today's wallcoverings are prepasted; however, if the one you have selected is not, you will have to do the pasting. Follow the manufacturer's instructions for the type of paste to use. If you are using a prepasted wallcovering, you can skip to Step 12-11.

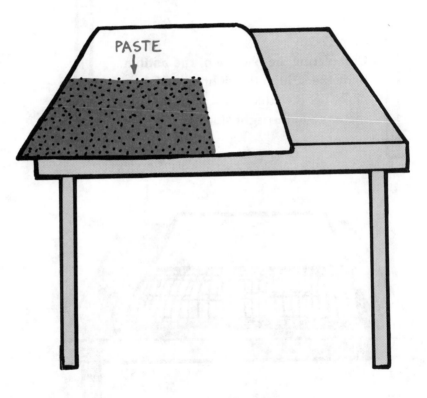

Step 12-4. Pasting the bottom.
Place the bottom of the strip on the table with the back side up. Allow the bottom and left side of the strip to hang over the edge of the table about 1/2 inch. Apply the paste to the lower left part and about halfway up the strip.

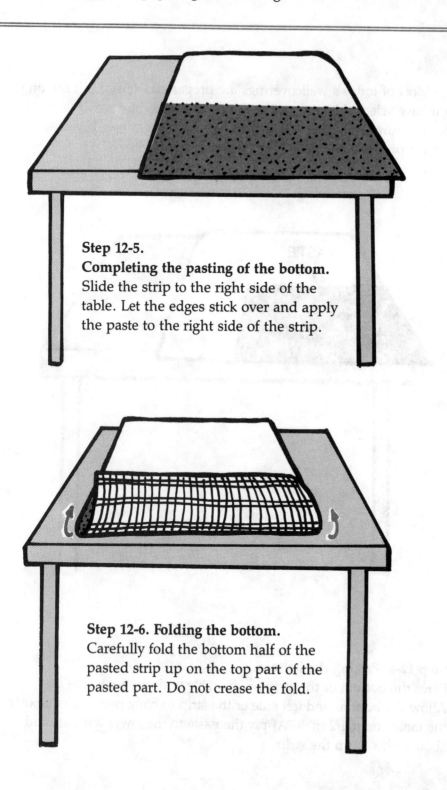

Step 12-5.
Completing the pasting of the bottom.
Slide the strip to the right side of the
table. Let the edges stick over and apply
the paste to the right side of the strip.

Step 12-6. Folding the bottom.
Carefully fold the bottom half of the
pasted strip up on the top part of the
pasted part. Do not crease the fold.

Step 12-7. Finishing the pasting.

Now slide the pasted section off the end of the table.
Position the strip so that the top edge and left side stick
over the edge of the table about 1/2 inch. Apply the paste to
the left half of the strip. Now slide the strip to the right side
of the table. With the edges hanging over the table, apply
the paste to the remaining part of the strip.

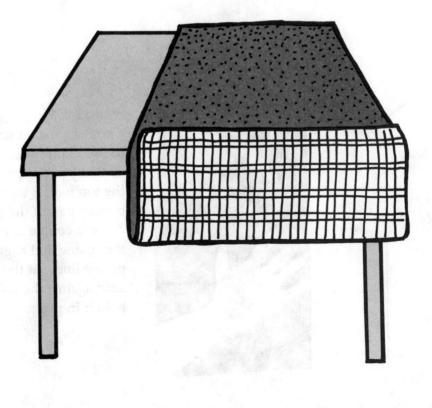

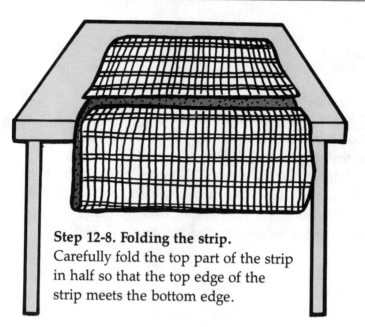

Step 12-8. Folding the strip.
Carefully fold the top part of the strip
in half so that the top edge of the
strip meets the bottom edge.

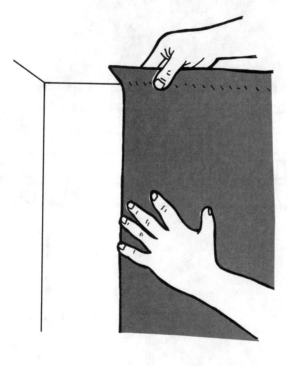

Step 12-9. Hanging the strip.
Carry the folded strip to the wall next
to the plumb line. Climb the ladder
so that you can position and unfold
the top part of the strip. Let the folded
bottom part of the strip hang free.
Allow a couple of inches to overlap
the ceiling and align the strip with the
plumb line. Pat the upper part of the
strip against the wall—just enough to
hold it in place.

Step 12-10. Smoothing the strip.

Move back to check the alignment. If you need to adjust the strip, use the palms of your hands to slide the strip where you want it. If you get a wrinkle, carefully pull the lower part of the strip away from the wall until it reaches the wrinkle, then pat the strip back smooth. Use a smoothing brush to press the upper part of the strip against the wall. Unfold the bottom of the strip and smooth it against the wall. Work from the middle out toward the edges and from top to bottom. Follow the same procedures as with prepasted wallcoverings (skip to Step 12-15).

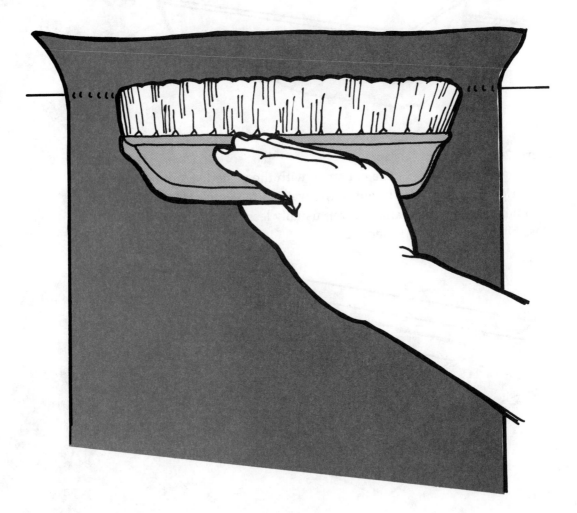

When you hang prepasted wallpaper, you use a special plastic container called a water box. The box is long enough to accommodate the width of a strip of wallpaper.

Step 12-11. Using the water box.

Fill the box about two-thirds full of clean, cold water and place it on a few layers of newspaper near the baseboard where you'll be working. Place the stepladder sideways in front of the water box.

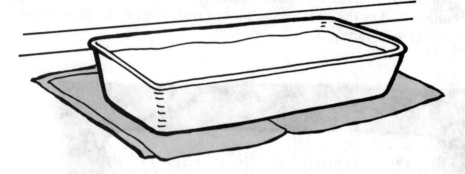

Step 12-12. Wetting the paper.

Starting at the bottom of the cut strip, with the pasted side out, roll the strip in a loose roll. Place it in the water box to soak for the time recommended by the manufacturer, usually less than a minute and possibly no more than 10 seconds.

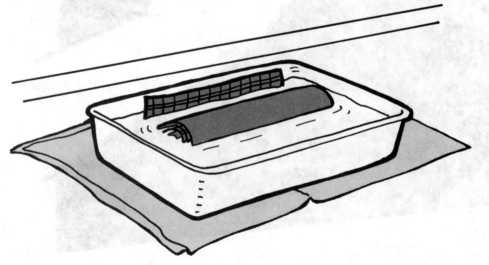

Step 12-13. Hanging the first strip.

Take the top of the strip, with the pattern facing you, and slowly unroll it as you move up the ladder. Allow a couple of inches to overlap the ceiling and align the edge of the strip with the plumb line. Pat the top part against the wall with your hand, just enough to make it stay up. Move back to check the alignment. If you need to adjust the strip, use the palms of your hands to slide the strip where you want it. If you get a wrinkle, carefully pull the lower part of the strip away from the wall until it reaches the wrinkle, then pat the strip back smooth.

Step 12-14. Smoothing the strip.
Use the smoothing brush to sweep the strip down the wall. Work
from the middle of the strip out toward the edges and corners.

Step 12-15. Fitting into a corner.
For a snug fit, slit the top and bottom of the
strip in the corner where it overlaps the other
wall. Use the smoothing brush to press the
strip firmly into the corner. The overlap will
curl around to the other wall. Smooth the
overlap on the other wall. Be sure to remove
all air bubbles.

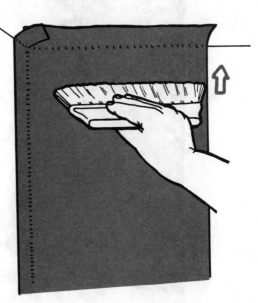

Step 12-16. Fitting up to the ceiling.
Now make short, upward strokes with
the brush to smooth the top of the strip
and press it up to, but not on, the ceiling.

Step 12-17. Trimming.

Use a metal guide, such as a wide-blade putty knife or a trim guide (sold in paint stores), to press the strip firmly into the corner next to the ceiling. Hold the guide with one hand and the trim knife with the other. Make a cut through the strip across the full width of the guide. Now move the guide over and make another cut like the first. Continue moving and cutting until the top of the strip and the top of the overlap on the other wall are cut. Peel the excess from the ceiling, and wash any paste off the ceiling. Repeat the same procedure to trim along the top of the baseboard. Use a wet sponge to remove any paste from the surface of the wallpaper.

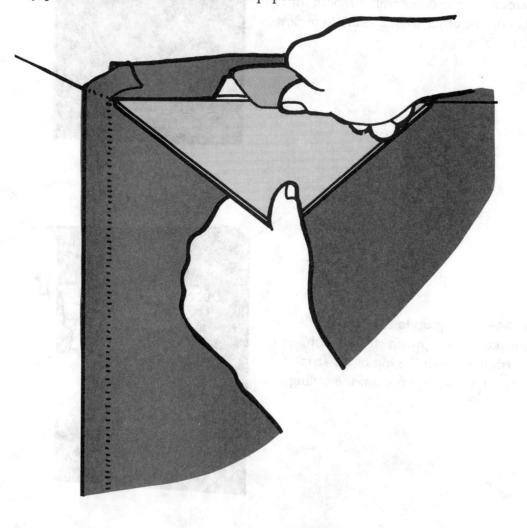

Step 12-18. Hanging the second strip.

Before you cut the second strip, hold the cut end of the roll up next to the ceiling and match the pattern. Make sure to allow the extra inches to overlap the baseboard and ceiling; then make the cut. Wet the paper and repeat the same steps to hang the second strip. Make sure to match the patterns exactly and butt the second strip tightly against the first. Smooth each strip with the smoothing brush. Work from the middle toward the edges and from top to bottom.

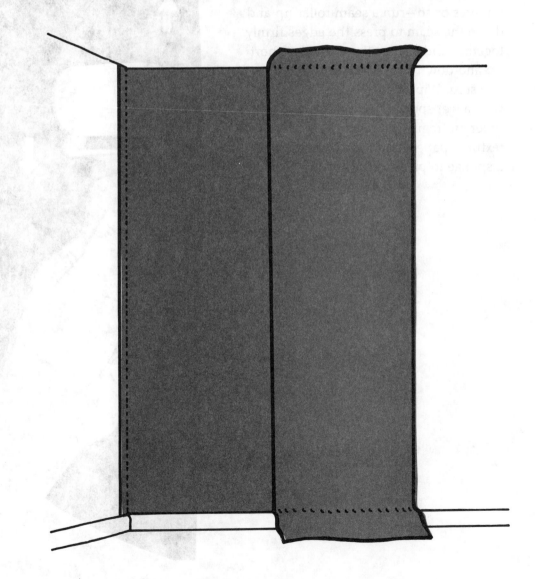

Step 12-19. Rolling seams.
After the paste has begun to dry—allow 10 minutes or so—run a seam roller up and down the seam to press the edges firmly together and against the wall. Use short up-and-down strokes without much pressure. Wipe off any excess paste with a wet sponge. Do not use a seam roller on fragile wallcoverings such as textured papers and foils. Instead, use a sponge to press the seams together.

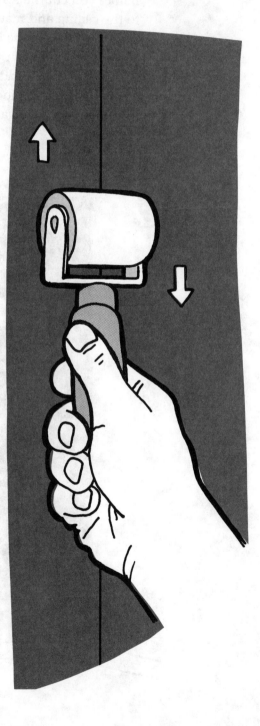

Corners require special treatment. You'll need to cut a strip lengthwise. Try to keep this cut as straight as possible.

Step 12-20. Hanging the first corner strip.

When you come to a corner, don't use a full-width strip. Measure the distance from the edge of the last strip to the corner. Add an inch or so to overlap the corner. Cut the strip lengthwise to this measurement. Hang this strip, allowing the cut edge to overlap the corner. Trim it at the top and bottom and smooth it around the corner.

Step 12-21. Marking a plumb line.

Now measure the remaining part of the strip (unless it is too narrow to use) and mark a new plumb line on the other wall.

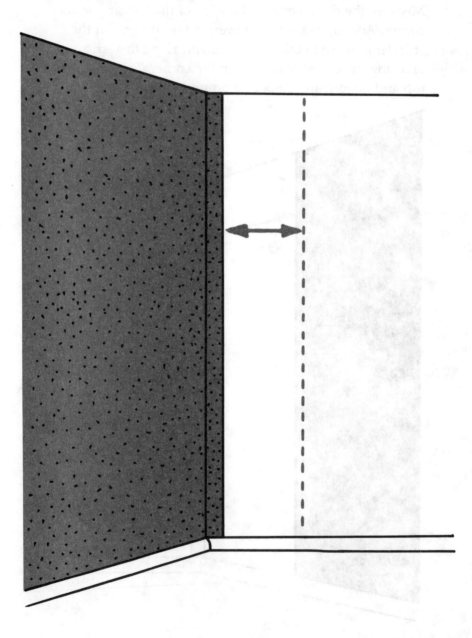

Step 12-22. Hanging the next strip.

Allow the remaining part of the strip (or the new strip) to overlap
the previous strip slightly. You might have a slight mismatch,
but it shouldn't be noticeable. Some vinyls require a special glue
to overlap vinyl to vinyl. Check with the salespeople
when you buy the material.

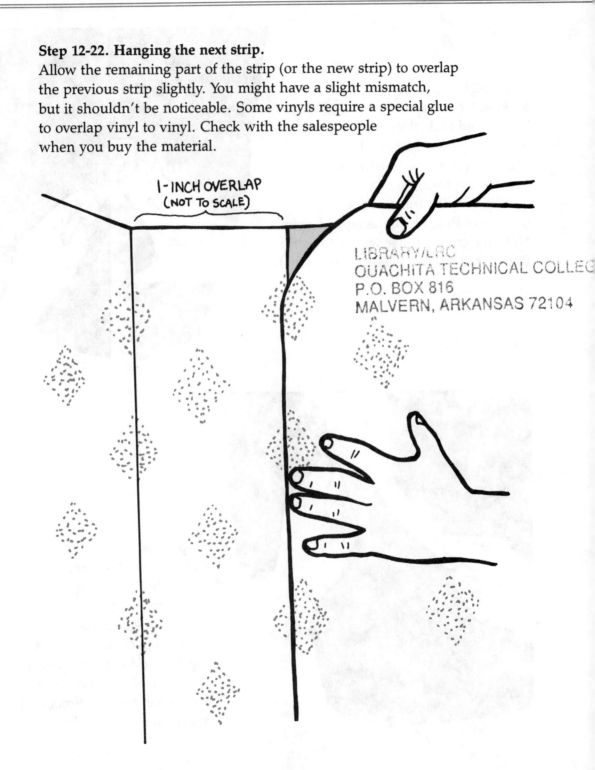

1-INCH OVERLAP
(NOT TO SCALE)

Step 12-23.
Making a double-cut.
If you need to double-cut the
wallcovering where it overlaps,
place the edge of a straightedge
over the approximate middle of the
overlap. Use the trim knife to slice
through both layers of the lapped seam.
Make the cut the full length of the strip.
Peel off the top excess edge you just cut.

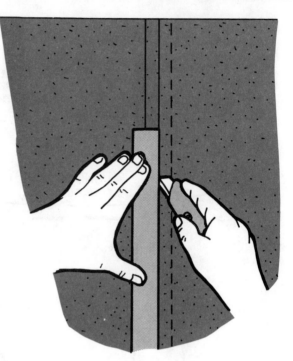

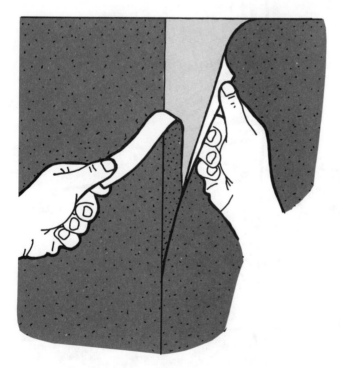

Step 12-24.
Completing the seam.
Carefully lift the edge of the strip
of wallcovering and peel the
excess edge underneath. Press
both edges of the cut strips
together to form a smooth seam
and wipe off any surface paste
with a wet sponge. Smooth the
seam with a seam roller.

Some rooms have outside corners as well as inside corners. Treat outside corners just like inside corners. Remember to make your lengthwise cut as straight as possible.

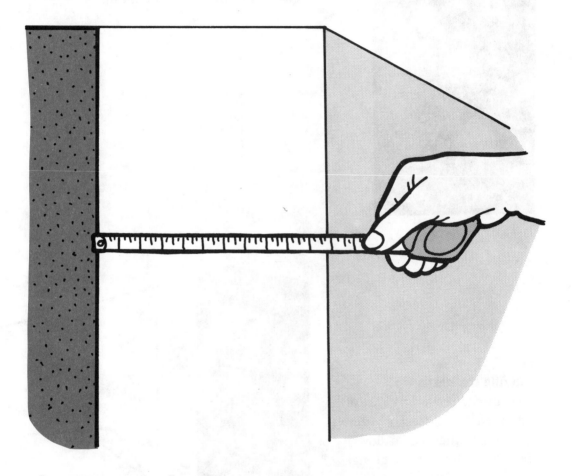

Step 12-25. Hanging the first corner strip.
Measure the distance from the edge of the last strip to the corner and then add an inch or so to go around the corner. Cut a strip to this width. Hang this strip and smooth it on the wall up to the corner.

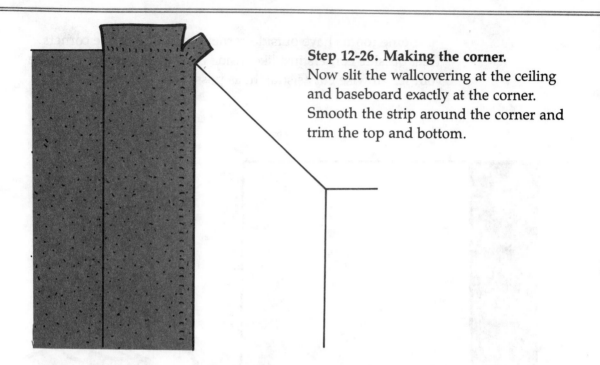

Step 12-26. Making the corner.
Now slit the wallcovering at the ceiling and baseboard exactly at the corner. Smooth the strip around the corner and trim the top and bottom.

Step 12-27.
Hanging the next strip.
Measure the remaining part of the cut strip and mark a plumb line on the other wall. Allow about an inch for overlapping the previous strip. Hang this strip and glue or double-cut the overlap if the covering is vinyl.

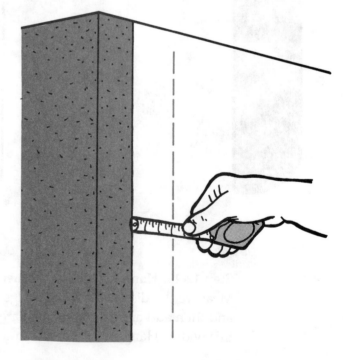

Wallpapering around switches and outlets is easy if you know how. Remember, whenever you are working around electricity, you should turn off the appropriate circuit breaker to avoid the possibility of electric shock.

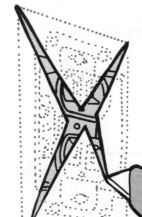

Step 12-28. Making the cut.
When you come to a switch or wall outlet (with the electricity off and the plate removed), hang the strip on the wall, covering the electrical box. Use the trim knife to cut an X over the outlet to each corner of the box.

Step 12-29. Trimming.
Trim off the excess paper using the inside of the box as a guide. Smooth the area around the box and replace the plate.

Windows can be framed or unframed. If you have framed windows, you need to follow the instructions beginning with Step 12-30. If you have unframed windows, skip to Step 12-38.

Step 12-30. Hanging the first strip.
When you come to a framed window or door, hang the strip as you normally would, overlapping the windows. Smooth the strip up to the side edge of the molding, but not at the top or bottom of the window.

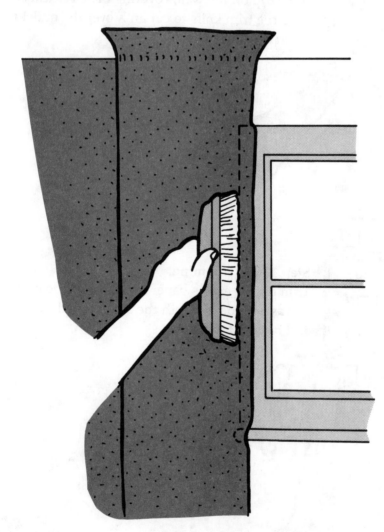

Step 12-31. Cutting off excess.

Use scissors to trim off the part of the strip covering the window. Leave a couple of extra inches for final trimming.

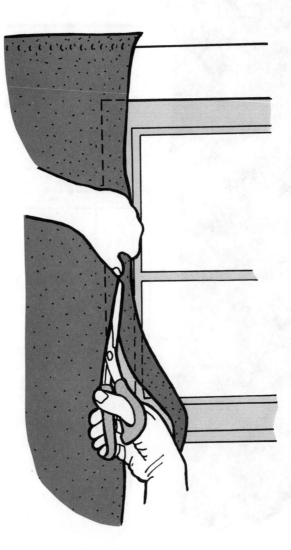

Step 12-32. Cutting into corners.

Use the scissors to make a diagonal cut to the top and bottom
corners of the molding. End the cuts where the wall meets
the corner of the molding.

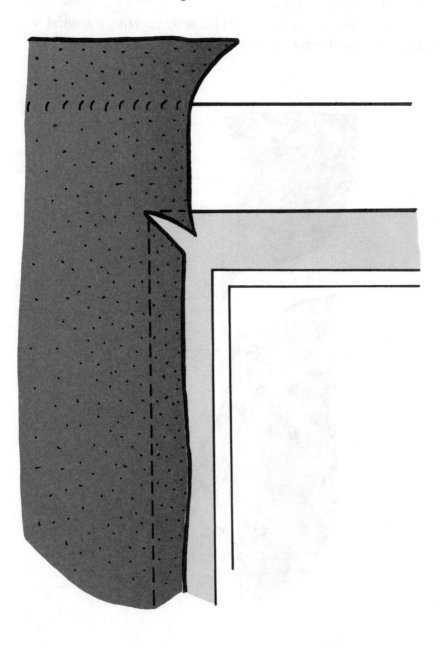

Step 12-33. Trimming off excess.
Smooth the paper to the wall and up to the top and bottom molding.
Use a trim guide and knife to trim off the excess paper from the
ceiling, baseboard, and window molding.

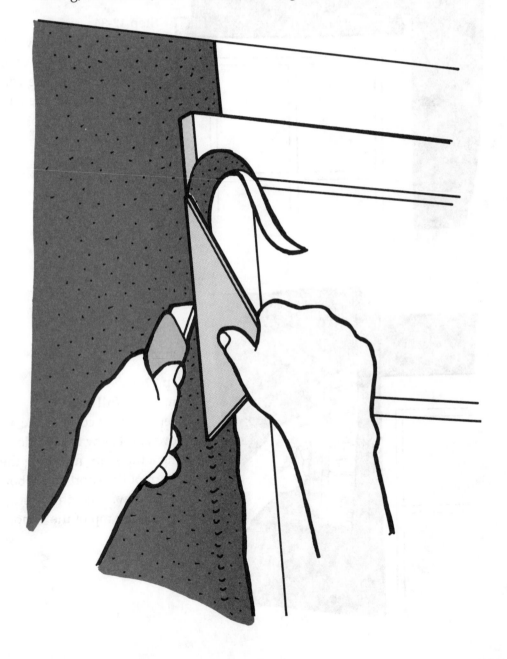

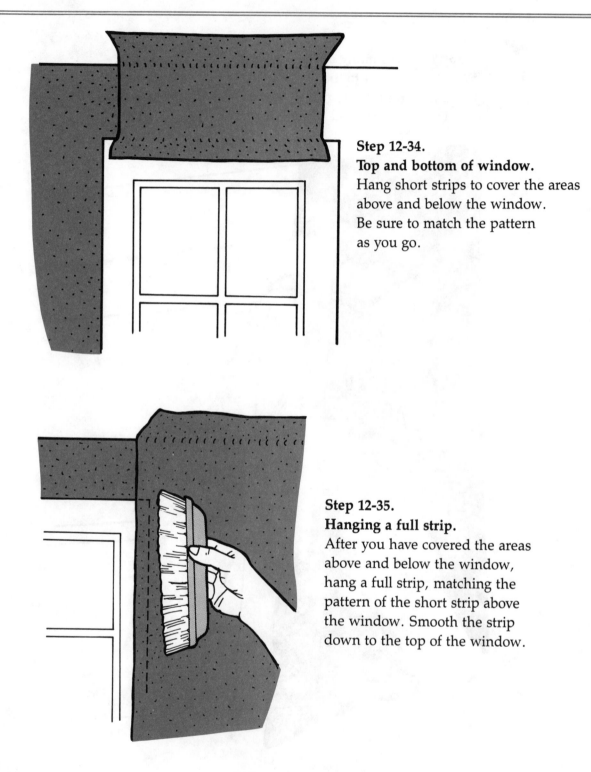

Step 12-34.
Top and bottom of window.
Hang short strips to cover the areas above and below the window. Be sure to match the pattern as you go.

Step 12-35.
Hanging a full strip.
After you have covered the areas above and below the window, hang a full strip, matching the pattern of the short strip above the window. Smooth the strip down to the top of the window.

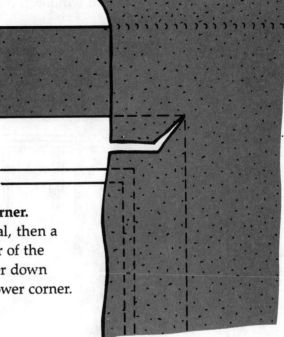

Step 12-36. Fitting the upper corner.
Use scissors to make a horizontal, then a
diagonal cut to the upper corner of the
molding. Now smooth the paper down
the side of the window to the lower corner.

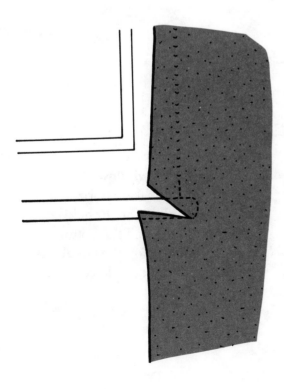

Step 12-37. Fitting the lower corner.
Cut off the excess paper and make a
diagonal cut to the lower corner of the
window. Now match the lower edge of
the strip with the short strip below the
window. Smooth the strip against the
wall and up to the molding. Using the
guide and trim knife, trim off the excess
around the window, the ceiling, and
the baseboard.

To wallpaper around unframed windows, follow Steps 12-38 through 12-42.

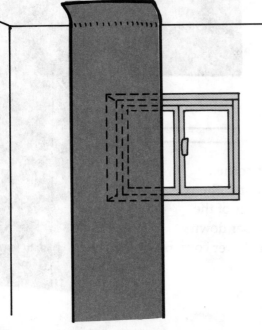

Step 12-38.
Hanging the first strip.
Unframed windows have both inside and outside corners. When you come to the window, hang a full strip in the usual way, allowing the paper to overlap the window. Smooth the strip against the wall and trim off the excess at the ceiling and baseboard.

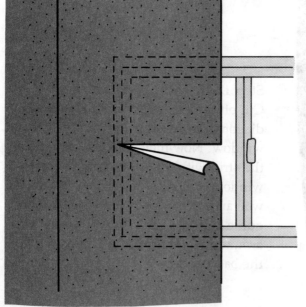

Step 12-39.
Cutting into the window.
Use scissors to make a horizontal cut across the strip about halfway between the top and the bottom of the window. Stop the cut about an inch from the outside corner of the window.

Step 12-40. Cutting into corners.

Now cut along the edge of the window up to a point near the upper corner. Make a diagonal cut into the corner. Repeat the procedure to make the cuts to the lower corner of the window.

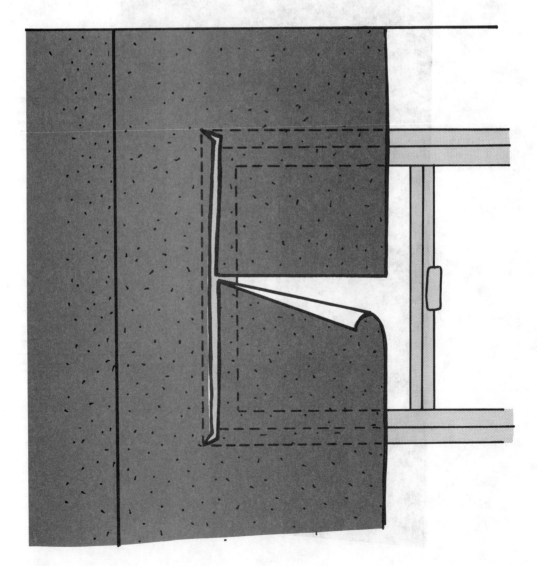

Step 12-41. Wrapping the inside.
Wrap the cut flaps of the strip around the upper and lower corners and along the edge of the window. Smooth the strips into place and trim off the excess.

Step 12-42. Completing the job.
Measure the uncovered side of the window and cut a strip to fit. Allow a little extra room so that the piece overlaps the inside corners at the top and bottom of the window. Hang any short strips above and below the window as necessary. Complete the other side of the window like the previous side.

Murals are an option you might consider when wallpapering a room. They are available in most of the popular wallpapering materials. For the best results, hang the mural on a very smooth wall. You might need to first hang a layer of blank stock, sometimes called lining paper. Blank stock is inexpensive and easier to hang than regular paper because it has no patterns and requires no trimming or butted seams.

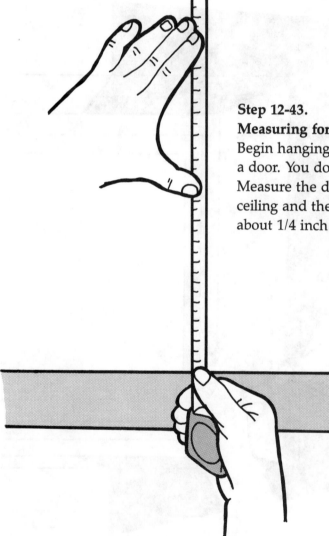

Step 12-43.
Measuring for blank stock.
Begin hanging at a corner or alongside a door. You don't need a plumb line. Measure the distance between the ceiling and the baseboard. Deduct about 1/4 inch from this measurement.

Step 12-44.
Hanging the first strip of blank stock.
Cut the strip to this length and hang it so that it is about 1/8 inch from the corner or door frame, the ceiling, and the baseboard.

1/8"

Step 12-45. Completing the hanging of blank stock.
Hang the next strip the same way. Leave a gap of approximately 1/8 inch between it and the previous strip. You can hang narrow strips horizontally above doors, and above and below windows. Just leave the 1/8-inch space between each strip and between the strips and the ceiling, baseboard, and any moldings.

Step 12-46. Positioning the design.

Hanging a mural is easier with 2 people. The mural is precut into strips 10 to 12 feet long, instead of coming on a roll. One person should hold the strip that has the tallest section of the design against the wall while the other determines the proper height of the design between the ceiling and the baseboard.

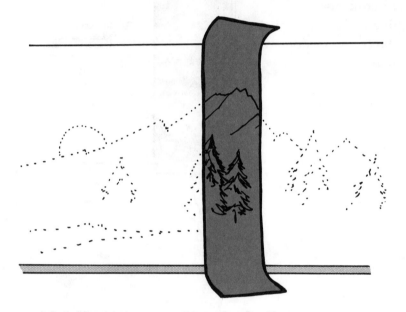

Step 12-47. Marking the strip.

When the pattern is positioned satisfactorily, make light pencil marks on each edge of the strip at the ceiling and the baseboard.

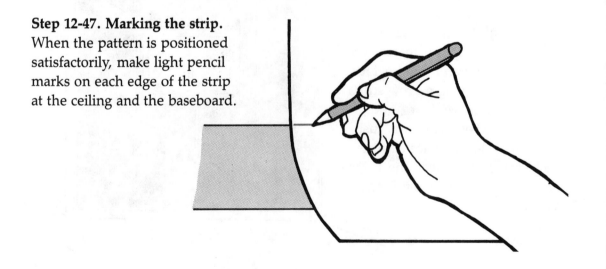

Step 12-48. Cutting the strips.

Lay out the strip on a flat surface. Place the next strip alongside the first. Match up the patterns and make light pencil marks on the second strip matching those on the first strip. Repeat laying out strips, matching patterns, and making pencil marks until all of the strips have been marked. Allow about 2 inches extra at each end for trimming; cut off any excess beyond that. The instructions that come with the mural probably have numbers showing which strip to hang first, second, third, and so on. Murals usually have one or more strips that can be eliminated to fit narrower walls.

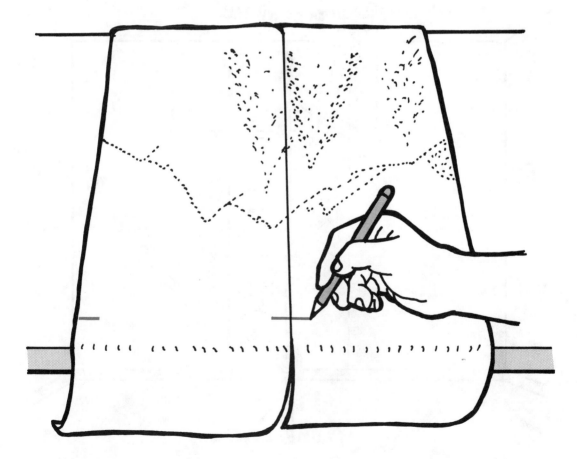

Step 12-49. Hanging an even number of strips.
If you have an even number of strips, locate the point on the wall where the center of the mural will go. Mark a plumb line on this mark and hang the two center strips on either side of the line.

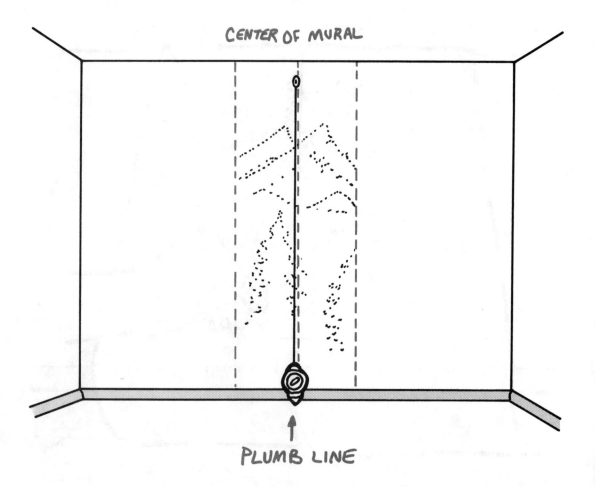

CENTER OF MURAL

PLUMB LINE

Step 12-50. Odd number of strips.

If you have an odd number of strips, mark the location of the center of the mural on the wall. Measure to the left of this mark one half the width of the strip and make a mark. Draw the plumb line on this mark and hang the first strip to the right of the plumb line.

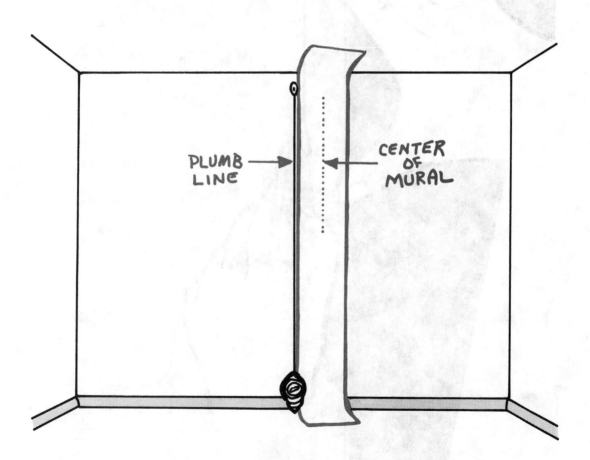

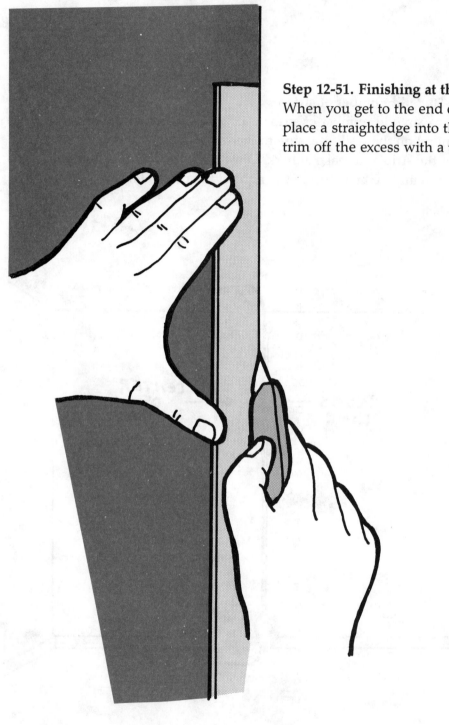

Step 12-51. Finishing at the corner. When you get to the end of the wall, place a straightedge into the corner and trim off the excess with a trim knife.

Glossary

baseboard A wooden *molding* covering the space between the bottom of the wall and the floor.

butted seam The joint where the edge of one strip of wallcovering touches the edge of the previous strip.

caulking A waterproof compound used to seal cracks.

cutting in Using a small brush to paint areas, such as where the wall and ceiling come together, that a larger brush or roller can't reach.

deck paint An enamel paint, highly resistant to wear, used on floors.

drywall Wallboard or plasterboard that comes in 4-×-8- and 4-×-12-foot panels, commonly used to cover interior walls.

flat paint A paint that dries to a dull finish. Flat paint has a high percentage of pigment.

gable The triangular portion of an end wall of a building enclosed by the sloping ends of the roof.

glazing compound A waterproof compound used to seal window panes and hold the pane in place in the window frame.

gloss paint   A paint that dries to a shiny finish. Gloss paint has a small percentage of pigment.

lap   The place where one coat of paint overlaps the edge of a previous coat.

lapped seam   The seam where the edge of one strip of wallcovering overlaps the edge of another strip.

latex   A water-based paint.

mildew   A fungus caused by moisture that appears as a black stain on the surface of paint.

mineral spirits   A liquid thinner used to dilute oil-based paints.

molding   A shaped strip of wood used for decorative purposes on walls and doors.

mullion   The slender bar dividing the panes of glass in a window or door.

plaster   A pasty mixture of fast-drying powder used to cover walls and ceilings and as a patching material.

plumb bob   A weight hung at the end of a line used to determine a true vertical direction.

primer   A preliminary coat of paint or sizing used to prepare the surface for the finish coat.

putty   A soft flexible material used for sealing glass panes and filling small holes and cracks.

run   Excess paint forming a small stream down the surface.

scraper   A tool with a stiff blade used to remove unwanted material such as paint or wallcovering.

siding   The outer covering of an exterior wall of a building.

size   A thin adhesive applied with a brush or roller used as a glaze or filler on porous materials such as plaster, paper, or cloth.

Spackle   A brand name for a powder that, when mixed with water, makes a paste that dries very hard and is used to fill small cracks and holes.

Spackle knife   A tool similar to a putty knife, but with a 3- or 4-inch flexible blade.

steamer   A device that heats water to steam, used for loosening wallpaper.

straightedge   A strip of wood or metal that has a perfectly straight side used for drawing or cutting a straight line.

strain   To remove unmixed material by pouring paint through a screening material such as cheesecloth.

stripping   Removing paint or wallcovering to get to the bare wall.

stucco   Plaster or cement, either fine or coarse, used as a surface material for exterior and sometimes interior walls.

thinning   To dilute paint by adding turpentine or mineral spirits to oil-based paint or water to latex paint.

trim   The decorative *molding* or borders around doors and windows.

turpentine   A colorless, volatile oil used as a paint thinner.

undercoating   The first coat used to prepare the surface for the finished coat, usually on enamel; often used in reference to interior painting.

Index